INDENTURED!

A LABOURER'S JOURNEY

Indentured!

A Labourer's Journey

Vicki Bismilla

TAMARIND TREE
Toronto

Library and Archives Canada Cataloguing in Publication

Bismilla, Vicki H., author
Indentured! : a labourer's journey / Vicki Bismilla.

ISBN 978-0-9950538-2-3 (paperback)

I. Title.

PS8553.I87I64 2016   C813'.54   C2016-903593-X

This book is manufactured under Sustainable Forestry Initiative® (SFI®) Certified Sourcing.

"For my grandparents and parents whose journeys, strength and dedication have been precious."

Foreword

When I received Vicki Bismilla's manuscript I couldn't resist taking a peek at the first page. It grabbed me immediately. I loved the description of the ship, the ropes, the bay and Amir Sing's thoughts. I knew right away that this book is going to be a winner!

As I finished reading the engrossing tale of these larger than life heroes I was in tears. However, the book is not mired in pathos. Rather, it is a testament to the resilience and nobility of the human spirit, as the indentured migrants forever change the host country into something rich and exceptional, bringing about a "sea change". It is a book that one cannot put down, with its universal theme of suffering and of rising "like a Phoenix from the ashes".

It is about the conundrum that is a globally stirring story of migrants all over the world and throughout history - those forced to leave familiar territory, the country that was the home they loved, to flee to oftentimes inhospitable climes. The underlying circumstances may be different - war, oppression, persecution, pogroms, unrelenting poverty- but the common factor is the impulse for survival.

The indentured labourers in this story, lured from their villages by the British Raj, to work the cane fields of Natal, South Africa, on vague promises of great opportunity, venture into a new and unknown territory only to be pushed to the limit of human endurance. But bound by contracts and separated from home by the superstitiously feared *kala pani,* the dark waters of a cold and foreboding ocean, they stoically persevere. Shaped by the land, the labourers survive through their strength of character and conviction of purpose. What a testament to the author's grandfather's life! I hope she continues the story of later descendants.

Passionately written and meticulously researched this book takes us into the ebb and flow of the lives of indentured labourers. The narrative is a profound description of proud and upright indentured labourers, who embraced their new country and who really were the stalwarts that made Natal, South Africa what it is today.

The in-depth research and understated writing style of this brilliant author make this story a poignant testament to our ancestors. In her description of the sea-voyage with labourers housed in slave-like quarters, the reader can actually taste the fear, recoil from the roiling waves.

Her description of labourers waiting to hear their fate moved me viscerally, imagining our forefathers' fear, excitement and trepidation in stepping into this strange new land. Such courage and forbearance makes one reflect on their legacy of mind-numbing physical labour, their thrift, their commitment to the new country and family values, all of which laid the foundation for the success of the next generations. Her metaphors throughout the book are masterpieces of fine writing.

Seen from the eyes of new immigrants from India, the bone-punishing sugar cane fields laid out like block patterns on saris would be ironically reminiscent of their lives left behind, especially the voiceless women indentured labourers. With her well executed facts woven in, like the sugar estates, the mill with its water wheel, mosques and temples being built, the veiled women, carriages, the washing of clothes in streams, the fire pits for cooking, the winding river and fledgling shops, she uniquely uses environment as a strong character in the book.

These details take this narrative beyond the ordinary. The contrast between the small kindnesses by the labourers toward their masters' children and the great tragedies in their own lives is touching. Her writing pierces the heart. The women in this story deserve their own book; they are powerful portraits of our female ancestors! The subplots, especially the comparative lives of the colonizers are engaging.

This book must have been close to the author's heart and it is of such historical value for all of us in this country. I salute her.

Rashida Mulla,
Lawyer, Durban, South Africa

Part 1
1883 - The Voyage

Chapter 1

Setting Out

Amir Sing fixed his eyes on the frothy waves in the wake of the ship as it cut through the ocean. Ropes crisscrossed above his head securing sails that thudded in the wind. Absent-mindedly he raised his arms, muscles rippling, to grasp the rope nearest him, the thick, rough fibres grating against his palms. Not another ship in sight, just dusk and its haunting mists. The ship was in the Bay of Bengal, three days south of Calcutta.

His thoughts were fixed on his parents back in Muzaffarnagar.

*"Bapuji, Mathaji, mujhe maaf kar do…*Mother, Father, forgive me," Amir's face contorted with tears. Like the turbulent waters below, his anguished thoughts whirled in his mind as he struggled with his decision to leave his parents and seek the opportunities promised by the British Raj recruiter.

His parents were aging. Hard work, long hours and worry about losing their land to larger estates were taking their toll. Young Gulab would help them with the sugarcane crops for the next five years while Amir worked out his indenture contract in Natal, South Africa. At fifteen, his brother was already a strong man, but their plot of land, like that of many poor villagers, was vulnerable to the land grabbing landlords or *zamindars*. The neigbouring *zamindars'* estates were growing rapidly as they forcibly took over smaller plots.

"Amir… Amir? Lost in thought *yaar*, friend?"

Amir looked back into the tired and drawn face of Purat, slightly shorter, but as fit and strapping as Amir. They both had tin discs on a string around their necks, which had identification numbers. Both had scattered smallpox scars on their cheeks and forehead, but not as marked as some of the other men on board. Both men were around the same age and had been recruited at the same government centre in the nearby city of Meerut. Their recruiter was Eurasian, a smiling, healthy-looking, middle-aged man, with neatly oiled and combed-back hair, who dressed in dapper western suits. He had promised that Natal had excellent opportunities for young and experienced sugarcane hands.

"Amir, don't be discouraged. Our blisters will heal."

"*Nayh... nayh...* no, no... I am not worried about our feet. I am thinking about my parents and young brother left to fend for themselves. Did we do the right thing, Purat?" Amir twisted his long moustache between his gnarled fingers. At twenty-two, he was a strapping six-foot *chatriyah*, a fighter class, and this strained look was unusual for him who never allowed any hardship to defeat him. But heartache about his parents... that was another matter.

"Yes, I worry about my family too. My *Bapu* and *Ma* are younger than yours. My three brothers I know will take care of them. But you must not despair. They have such good support in the village. Despite the problems with the crops and the greedy *zamindars*, the people in the village stick together. Don't worry *Bhayah*, my brother. You are now my brother, Amir. Let's stay positive about this chance we are taking. What happened at the depot I am sure will be the worst of what we have to endure."

Amir looked at him with tired eyes. The depot at the port in Calcutta was a wood and corrugated iron shack, a hovel teeming with hundreds of recruits crammed into a space meant to hold half their number. Cots were jammed together and the musty odour of unwashed bodies and beds was overpowering at times.

"*Bhayah*, that depot! How will we ever wash that stink from our nostrils? *Bhayah*, washing in that putrid water? Our own river back home was clean!"

The stench had grown over the month-long wait for the ship to arrive. Ships headed for the West Indies and Fiji arrived and left, but the ship bound for the port of Durban, Natal, on the east coast of southern Africa was yet to arrive.

"And the doctors? Why did they have to touch us in that way? We can bear the physical pain, the hurt as they thrust those metal instruments everywhere. But *Bhayah*...the shame?"

Health checks of the men were conducted by a few doctors and their helpers, who were often rough, snarly and grossly invasive. The young indentured men, who were so meticulous about their hygiene back in their villages, were reduced to washing themselves at the water's edge and relieving themselves discreetly, but not privately enough.

Amir and Purat, together with twenty other men from neighbouring villages had walked for most of the month-long journey from Muzaffarnagar, hitching rides on bullock carts for some stretches. They had been watched over by two of the recruiter's assistants, cruel men dressed in *dhoti*s like themselves. The assistants carried *lahti*s, sticks, in order to dissuade any recruit who might change his mind and back out of his indentureship.

Purat rolled his head in agreement and put his arm on Amir's shoulder.

"I know *Bhayah*. I know...*salo gorawallah*!!! Damn white men!"

"*Nayh*...*nayh*...no...no, let's not get angry, Purat...we have started this journey. Let's keep our minds on the opportunities in Natal...the recruiter said we will get land after our indenture! Maybe we can bring our families once we are landowners there! Did your *Mathaji* pack your trunk, *Bhayah*?"

Amir smiled thinking about how his mother packed his trunk as Purat nodded and remembered too. Each labourer was allowed one small metal trunk. Amir's and Purat's mothers had lovingly packed clothing, other essentials and a memento or two of home. In Amir's case, the memento was a small clay image of *Ganeshji*, a manifestation of God as the remover of obstacles.

"*Bhayah*...my brother Gulab wrote my name so large on my trunk!" Amir burst out laughing, "*Areh*...hey...those *salo gorawallas* will see my name big and bright red! But Gulab had to paint it just as it was spelled on my contract. That *gadha gorawallalah*, donkey white man, in the office, left out the "h" in my surname so now I am 'Sing' instead of the proper *chatriyah* 'Singh.'" Amir sang this last sentence laughing out loud.

They had their names painted on the trunk lids, which were then entrusted to the British Recruiting Office for transportation to the Calcutta depot for loading on to the ship.

"*Areh*…not only the *gorawallah*! What about that *aadhe*…half-white recruiter? Did you see the grease on his head? We should have held him and cooked *unda*…eggs, on his head!"

The tension broken, Purat continued, "Never mind…he did promise us a good wage and land at the end."

The recruiter had arrived in Calcutta mostly by train to recruit more young men along the way. He knew his earnings would be good on this batch of recruits. Train tracks were still being built, but the British Raj paid well and transport was not an issue for well-heeled agents. So while his recruits hobbled on blistered feet, walking most of the thousand kilometres, the recruiter travelled by train where there were tracks and by horse and buggy where there were none.

A commotion below deck distracted Amir and Purat. The John Davie was a steamship, which was still a relatively new concept, but the steerage accommodation had not been much improved from the slave ship days. Propulsion was provided by steam engines turning a single, four-bladed screw propeller, generating horsepower. A two-mast rig provided additional propulsion. Two boilers situated forward of the engines were maintained by a team of Scottish engineers and mechanics as the ship had been built for the Raj in Glasgow, Scotland. These were burly, hardworking men, who had a variety of opinions about Indians being shipped to the many British colonies.

Apart from the Captain's suite, which adjoined the wheel house and bridge, all other cabins were below the top promenade dining deck. The ship had accommodation on the first bedroom deck for sixty first class passengers, mostly the elite of the British Raj or servicemen. Some of them had families returning home to England. The second class deck below accommodated the crew, mechanics, engineers and staff who served first class passengers. The steerage far below was narrow and extended from the front of the ship toward almost the very back and was cut-off from all other cabin decks. This level accommodated the indentured labourers, the 'property' of the colonial empire.

Amir and Purat ran down the four flights of shaky wooden ladders to find the steerage passengers agitated and shouting in various Indian dialects. Two of the Scottish mechanics were surrounded as they tried to explain that they needed men to help them with the rig masts to provide power to the ship while the engineers repaired one of the boilers. Amir and Purat understood English, having attended school for two years together in Muzaffarnagar.

Amir lifted his hands in the air to calm the commotion and asked "What's the problem, Sir?"

"We need four niggers to help us with the rig..."

"Sir, we are not niggers! We have signed contracts with the..."

The other Scotsman held out both his greasy hands in a calming fashion and pushed his colleague aside.

"We mean no disrespect. Can some of your strong men accompany us to the hull? We have to get the sails to work while an engine is being fixed."

Amir turned to the men. Some were clad in clean white *dhotis*, some with white tunics, others bare chested. He spoke quietly and calmly and explained the need. Several young men volunteered and went with the mechanics.

The long, dark, low-ceilinged steerage compartment, completely cut off from the rest of the ship, was divided into three living quarters, each curtained off from one another. One small section was for families on board. Three men had brought their wives and young children. One of them was a young Muslim man, Adam, who intended to set up shop in Durban. The other two men were Hindu *pundits*, priests, who were permitted by agreement through the Colonial British Indian Government Regulations to go to Indian settlements with their families. The cramped middle part of the compartment was for most of the men, thirty-two in all. It contained wooden bunk beds with string coils that held thin grass-filled mattresses.

The last small section, close to the toilet area was for the ten men who were considered lower class *dhalits*. These men washed and cleaned the latrines, which were sectioned off at the far front of steerage. Each of the four latrines was separated by low wooden walls and had a cast iron grill fitted into the floor planks. A large thick rubber tubing drain went from the grill to the roiling sea thirty feet below. With latrines situated at the front of the ship, the waste was washed away by the forward movement of the ship and backward splash of the waves. Another four little latrine-like compartments separated by wooden walls contained buckets of sea water. These were the bath areas for all those in steerage. A sari was draped over the entrance of one latrine and bath area, which was for use by the women and children.

Amir and Purat shared two levels of a bunk. After the mechanics left with the young Indian volunteers, they sat down on Amir's lower bunk.

"Purat, we are all in this together, are we not?'

"Yes we are… no doubt about it."

"Then why do we have a separate area for *dhalits* whom we treat as below our class?"

"Well, they are, aren't they, Amir?"

"But we are now in a country of our own on this ship. We are together. You heard that white man call us all niggers. Do you know what that word means? Yet one of the four young boys who volunteered to help them with their rig is a *dhalit*. All he cared about was that the ship operates safely. For whose safety, Purat? Ours, all of ours!"

"But what can we do? We can't change what they are… who they are."

"Yes we can. We are going into an unknown land to serve a regime that has ruled over us with an iron fist. They call us coolies and worse… we have to stick together, Purat."

The two friends sat silently together. They looked around them at the tired labourers, some of whom were lying on the bunks, others squatting in groups, rubbing their limbs talking quietly. The *dhalits* had resumed sweeping the floors and cleaning the bathrooms and latrines.

Amir rose purposefully, "I am going to talk with the priests."

He walked with head slightly bent to avoid banging against the low ceiling and made his way towards the sectioned off area across from the rows of bunk beds. Purat followed.

The six 'private' rooms were separated by thin wooden walls and each room was furnished with one bunk bed and a wooden stool. There was just enough room to push a steel trunk under the bed. Adam's wife and five-year-old daughter slept on the bottom bunk while he and his eight-year-old son slept on the top bunk.

Each of the two Hindu *Dharma* priests and their families had a similar room. One of the empty rooms was designated by the ship's Surgeon Superintendent as a sick bay. In the past decade the British had tried to improve conditions on indenture ships since several of their ships had been quarantined at ports of call and some had been turned back due to outbreaks of dysentery, cholera and other communicable diseases. The Surgeon Superintendent conducted weekly inspections of all areas including steerage to ensure that sanitary conditions were being maintained.

As Amir entered the private area he was met by Adam and his family who were just leaving their room.

"*Salaam*, Adam. How is your family today?"

"We are well, Amir. You were very good with those greasy mechanics."

Amir laughed with him, "*Areh*, why, Adam we will be on this ship for fifty days. Can't get into their bad books, *nayh?*"

"You are right. Have to get along. I am taking my family up to the deck for some fresh air before dark," Adam said as his wife, veiled in a large shawl, followed him with their children.

"Don't stay out too late. Where are the *pundits?*"

"I think in their rooms, Amir."

Adam smiled and nodded to Purat, making his way past the general area to the plank ladders mid-ship, half way up from the rows of bunks.

Amir found Pundit Sajiv seated on his bunk reading to his family. His wife Parvati was seated on the stool holding their little six-year-old daughter and seated next to him was his son, who was almost twelve years old.

"*Namasthe Punditji. Maaf kijiye*, sorry, to disturb…"

"*Nayh nayh*, it's okay *Bhayah*, my brother."

He stepped out of his room and pulled the curtain across the door.

"*Punditji*, we wanted to talk with you and *Punditji* Rajiv together. Do you know where he is?"

The other *pundit* came out of his room.

"I heard you, Amir. How are you, *Bhayah?*"

"Sorry to disturb, *Punditji*…"

"No not at all. Our little one is sleeping so Namita and I are just talking."

They sat on the floor and politely looked at one another.

"*Bolo Bhayah…* say brother… what's on your mind?"

Amir began hesitantly at first, but decided to just get on with it.

"*Punditji*, we are going to an unknown land. We are all going as a group of friends are we not, a band of brothers?"

Pundit Rajiv, the younger of the two, spoke animatedly, "Yes, yes, of course! Look at how respectful Adam and we are even though we pray differently. Adam reads his Quran right in the next room…"

"I am glad you mentioned that Pundit Rajiv, because that's exactly what we want to talk to you about."

"*Areh…* why… is there a problem reading your prayers…?

"No, no nothing like that…" Purat began. "No, Amir wants to talk about another matter."

"Yes, *Punditji*. We want to talk to you about the *dhalits*."

"You mean the *chamaars*? *Areh* Amir! We must be tolerant *nayh*? Amir, Amir… the *chamaars* or *dhalits* as you call them are God's children too. They serve and have served for many generations…"

Amir cut in, "*Punditji*, we want to talk to you about just the opposite of what you think we want. Why must we just be tolerant? Why can't we welcome them just as we are welcoming Adam and all the other sects of people on this ship?"

"What are you saying?" Sajiv looked from Amir to Purat and then questioningly at Rajiv.

"*Punditji*, I am saying that we should not exclude them and curtain them off from us like they are pariah."

"But they are… but they are unclean… no, I don't mean unclean… I mean… But…"

"*Punditji*, we are on this ship together. The white masters call us niggers and coolies, all of us, Muslim, Hindu, *chatriyah* caste, *brahmin* caste like you, merchant class, everyone! Why must we too treat our own as less than us? You saw one of the *dhalit* boys readily went to help the Scotsmen."

"But *Bhayah* that does not change the basic laws of…"

Just then, Adam and his family returned from their walk and smilingly waved goodnight. "Look, let Rajiv and I think about what you are asking. Let's talk about this again in a few days."

Amir and Purat joined their hands in greeting, bade the priests goodnight and left.

Sitting on his bunk, Amir untied the three yards of soft white cotton cloth that formed his *pugri*, turban, and stretched out on his bunk. Purat climbed into his bed above and lay quietly in thought. Amir's chiseled features and thick, wavy hair was a little different from Purat's softer, more rounded facial lines and straight black short hair. The friends closed their eyes and rested for a few minutes. They would soon need to go up the ladder to supervise the cooking of the evening meal. The Surgeon Superintendent had appointed Amir as lead man of the steerage passengers. He had noticed how Amir had calmed the men at the depot as they embarked the ship, how he had shown everyone where to go and helped with the single metal trunks that each steerage passenger was allowed to bring onboard.

For the past few days the white crew or *lascars* had shown tolerance for Amir and Purat as they helped bring rations down the ladders. Small daily rations of preserved milk and a barrel of drinking water was brought by the crew to the double-bolted iron gates on deck separating the white passengers from steerage. One of the white crewmen, Mr. Landers, was at the recruiting station in Meerut and remembered Amir and Purat.

Their eye contact each morning was pleasant enough. At embarkation, the men had carried sacks of rice, flour, lentils, dried beans, corn kernels and salt through these same heavy gates. The company also included one sack of potatoes, onions, a barrel of vegetable oil and a sack of various Indian spices in pouches for use by the steerage passengers. No meat was provided since meat was scarce on board ship and was stored in the few cold holds in the galley for white passengers. Another reason was that meat would be offensive to the many Hindu vegetarians in steerage. Amir and Purat were not vegetarian, but neither liked nor needed meat. The food along with sacks of coal, a few pots, pans, metal plates and cups, spoons and other utensils were stored in the tight space under the ladder in the steerage compartment.

Amir heard the designated cook for the week rattling the pots and pans under the ladder. He quickly rose, wrapped his turban back on and went to help Bhimnad.

"*Areh* Bhimnad!! You are as noisy as your name suggests!" The two men laughed together as they went up the ladders carrying a bucket of coal, a large bowl each of rice, *dhal* lentils, water, some potatoes and onions, and a small pouch of condiments.

The 'kitchen' on deck was a tin structure about six feet square with a hole in the roof to allow smoke to escape. Along the back wall against the ship's rail the company had securely bolted a single cast iron black coal stove. The steerage men, all of whom had agreed to take turns cooking, were grateful for this arrangement. Cooking was done twice daily. The early morning cooking was mostly rice or oat porridge and the evening meal was rice and *dhal* or other pulses. Each pair cooked a little differently using the spices in their own family's way so the food was tasty and the variety eagerly anticipated by all. The men made sure that the children were served first, had enough to eat, and especially had enough from the short supply of milk. The men sat on the floor to eat, in the aisle between the rows of bunk beds. The women and children sat on the floor of the private quarter.

The next day the ship would dock in Madras and take on more men and supplies. Bhimnad's cooking partner, Narpal, joined them in the kitchen. The men chatted companionably. The deck and kitchen were scrubbed regularly by the cleaners among them and sand was sprinkled to keep the floors dry. The sand was stored with other freight in the lowest hold where the heaviest weight was stowed in order to steady the ship. That hold also held such items as coal, sand, sea water that was collected through evaporation each day, and the rations of fresh water for consumption. The hold could be reached by a ladder below steerage, but the door was always locked and heavily barred. The steerage men had been given two bags of sand and coal on the second day of the voyage. They had waited patiently at that door to be given the rations by crewmen working the storage hold.

***

Amir and Purat stood on deck as the ship eased into the Madras harbour. Twinkling lamps of early risers could be seen in the coastal fishing villages. The steerage cooks on duty were busy in their small deck kitchen. In the light of kerosene lamps, their swift hands kneaded dough for coal stove *chappatis*, flat bread, for breakfast. Steerage passengers were awake especially early anticipating new arrivals on board. Some wandered up on deck. Amir welcomed the children of the priests and Adam.

"Come, come, see the lamps along the coast. You can just start to see the trees… and look on the other side… there… isn't the sunrise very beautiful, *nayh*? They moved away from the iron gates separating them from the ship's privileged passengers.

The front portion of the ship's first class top deck served as a small breakfast area for the few white passengers who ventured out on deck. Sheltered under awnings, this was an ideal space on the open deck since it was upwind and away from the smells of the latrines at the front of the ship, which washed backward as the ship cut across the open seas. The bolted iron gates kept the first class passengers secluded from the steerage labourers. Steerage passengers were able to use the remainder of the top deck around the back of the ship to the other side of the deck, where they could watch the ship pulling into harbour. On that side as well there were heavy, bolted iron gates that separated them from white passengers.

The Indian children stood on tiptoe, wide-eyed, watching as the ship slowly approached the harbour. Wrapped in warm shawls they followed the ship's gentle turns until it berthed several hundred yards from the cement dock. As soon as the ship anchored, loud pumps could be heard pumping sea water into the ship's lowest holds, causing even the adults to stand tiptoed to crane to see over the sides. The *chappatis* ready, the cooks and Amir ushered everyone down the ladders to eat and make ready to welcome new passengers. Amir went back on deck to await instructions from the Surgeon Superintendent or from the captain himself. He might not be allowed off the ship, but he still wanted to help. After a short wait Surgeon Superintendent Wilkie came to the double iron barricaded gate near the first class breakfast area.

"Morning, Amir. Not sure if you speak Tamil, but we could use your help to bring some supplies aboard," he muttered as he unlocked the gate and gestured to Amir and Purat to accompany him. They followed past the first class deck seating area, the silk awnings fluttering gently and the small tables and chairs occupied by a few early risers having tea. In the heat of Madras, Amir and Purat were bare-chested, dressed only in *dhotis*. They moved swiftly down the wooden steps on the side of the ship and on to a gangplank, from which they jumped into a small open air boat that took them to the dock. A small group of ten young South Indian men and two women stood waiting. Amir greeted the men with joined hands and asked in Hindi if they understood him. Tamil was the language in Madras, but a few nodded in understanding.

"*Namasthe*, greetings, I am Anpu – Anpusamy – but call me Anpu. This ship is going to Durban, *nayh?*"

"Yes, yes, Anpu. My name is Amir and this is Purat. We come from near Delhi. Come bring some of the young men. Let's load your trunks and also help the crew to load some supplies."

In Calcutta, Amir and Purat and several other men at the depot had helped load tons of coal into the bottom hold. They had wheeled barrows up gangways for several days in order to store the enormous tonnage of coal required by the steamship for its fifty-day journey. Today it wasn't coal, but other provisions that needed to be loaded on to small boats to be taken to the ship.

While some of the indentured men joined in to carry and load several boats with trunks and supplies, the other new passengers got on a boat headed for the ship. They were met with curious gazes by the now larger group of white passengers on the first-class deck. The new recruits were quickly herded by two crewmen through the iron gates to the steerage side of the deck. They huddled on deck awaiting further instructions, anxiously looking toward the boats carrying their trunks. These were brought on deck by the Indian men and once all the boats were in and all trunks accounted for, the heavy iron gate was once again bolted. Amir and Purat were still with crewmen helping to load supplies into the holds of the ship.

Priests Rajiv and Sajiv gently ushered the group down the ladders to their quarters. The two married couples, one with two children, were shown to two of the private cubicles. The remaining men were shown to the bunk area. With the additional men the bunk area was now filled to capacity. Along with the families in the cubicles, steerage now had fifty-five men, five women and seven children. The ship stayed anchored until the next day when the officials had ensured that all new indentured labourers had undergone medical tests at the depot, been given their indenture identification numbers and all paperwork had met with the captain's approval.

Early the next morning, Surgeon Superintendent Wilkie came through the deck gate with two crew men to inspect steerage.

"How is everyone, Amir?"

"Sir, we are now filled to capacity. All bunks are occupied and trunks stowed underneath."

"Good, good. What about the cubicles?" he spoke as he entered the private area. The five women hurried into their curtained spaces pulling the children with them.

"All full, Sir. Five families and one sick bay."

"Good, good. Sick bay still available. Tight fit in the general bunk area, yes?"

"Yes, Sir. But okay. Thank you for the food supplies. But maybe a little more milk? Children, you know?"

"Hmmm… see what we can do."

"And Sir? More sea water and a few more buckets for the latrines… for washing, you know?"

"Yes, I will send those. Hygiene is very important, Amir. See to it that everyone understands. No rats yet?"

"No Sir. Only few days on ship… no problem yet."

"All right. We are set to sail this evening."

Wilkie turned and nodded to people as he climbed the ladder to the top deck.

Chapter 2

On The Seas

The saloon was quiet in the morning. The ship had set out from Madras the previous evening and now picked up speed. The captain had called a meeting early before the other officers and families started to filter into the dining and leisure areas of first class. Captain Taylor sat at the head of his table, with Surgeon Superintendent Wilkie to his right. Around the gleaming teak table laden with steaming coffee, tea, biscuits, bread, molasses and preserves, were officers of the Raj of various ranks including second-class crewmen, who were instrumental in recruiting the Indian labourers now being transported below.

"Well, gentlemen, so far so good. I think the Protector of Immigrants in Durban, General Williams, will be quite pleased with this lot. What do you think, Superintendent Wilkie?"

"Sir, our lead man Amir is reporting good hygiene and no infestations in steerage. I will make my rounds weekly over the next forty or so days…"

"Wilkie, I have a good record with Durban. My ship has had the good fortune of never being quarantined in harbour and I'd like to keep it that way. So continue sterilizing the water, use vinegar if necessary, and be sure to supply enough sheep-dip to steerage to keep the latrines clean. Do they have enough nutritious food? Their no-meat diet all right?"

"Yes Sir."

The captain looked around the table at the other men.

"Any problems I need to be aware of during recruitment, gentlemen? No conflicts among the men?"

The men reported no significant issues for the recruits other than the exhausting, arduous journey on foot and the over-crowded, unsanitary depots. The captain was sympathetic, but shrugged. Those issues were beyond his control.

"Well, let's be sure that we keep our recruits as healthy as we can. I don't want to have to take any of them back due to sickness or misfortune."

Landers spoke up quietly with averted eyes. "Sir, if I may. I know that it's not your jurisdiction but at some of the recruitment centres the officers are rather forceful. Whipping men into submission and threatening them to cooperate with recruitment agents will bring us embittered passengers..."

"You are right, of course, Landers. I do not have jurisdiction over what happens there!"

Landers remained quiet. There was no use then of mentioning the behaviour and racist slurs of some of the crewmen. Andrew Landers, just twenty-three years old, had three years' experience as a junior officer of the Raj stationed in northern India. He was on his way now to Natal to assume higher responsibilities in a rising empire. He knew when to speak and when to be silent.

The adjoining dining area began to fill up with smartly-dressed officers, some with wives and two couples with young children. Their feet made no sound on the lush, carpeted floors as they took their places at tables laid with white linen, fine glassware, and silver. Three men deep in conversation had wandered into the small adjoining game room and sat on cushioned seats along the outside walls ignoring the small card and game tables set up in the middle of the room.

The meeting adjourned and the officers joined others in the promenade and dining room, while crewmen like Landers rushed away to their duties. While in Meerut, Andrew Landers wore the khaki uniform, long boots and round helmet expected of the officers of the Raj. But on board the ship, the handsome young junior officer with dark hair and a fine clipped moustache, wore a tailored jacket, casual pants and comfortable shoes. Landers walked briskly through the dining room into the interior hallway leading down the short polished stairway that led to the first class cabins. The carpeted hallway muffled footsteps so he did not see the maid until he almost ran into her.

"Oh pardon me… Oh Annie… how are you?"

"I am well, Andrew. Just going in to do the Major's rooms," she said as she unlocked the suite closest to the staircase balancing a stack of linen in her arms.

"I will help you." Andrew Landers' duties were diverse, everything from supervising the cleaning staff to ensuring that the galley was sanitized and that provisions were brought up from the cargo holds.

"Thank you, Andrew. But is it not meat preparation day down below?"

"Yes Annie, but cook is still busy with breakfast preparation. I have about an hour and I would rather be here helping you," and as Annie blushed Andrew gave a cursory glance over his duty folder.

After an hour Andrew would need to go below to oversee the Chinese cook in the galley who supervised the slaughtering of chickens and pigs kept in small pens below the boiler room. The slaughtering was to be done once every ten or so days and Andrew ensured that all clean-up was done thoroughly. The refrigeration equipment provided safe storage of meat and fish for short periods of time. The cook and a small team of Chinese workers had bunks in the boiler room area. They were responsible for cleaning all the latrines and crew rooms and for washing the clothes and linen in the boiler room for all first class passengers and crew. They had been hired in Singapore and southern China. On British trading ships like the John Davie, these Chinese labourers, referred to as "coolies" by the crew, were the silent cogs in the complex operations needed to keep passengers comfortable. The British maids, engineers, mechanics and workers on the ship were divided among three officers and Annie was on Andrew's roster. Annie, just eighteen years old, was one of several maids assigned to clean the first class suites. The maids' quarters were next to the large linen room and discreetly located at the far end of the first class deck to ensure that senior officers and their families could access them readily if needed. There were four small rooms with two beds in each.

Andrew and Annie set about changing sheets in Major and Mrs. Ballantyne's room and the adjoining room, which the two little Ballantyne boys shared. A small water closet held a porcelain jug and dish and, for the use of the children, a small slop pail which maids emptied in the servants' latrines below deck. Andrew offered to empty it for Annie and left to walk briskly to the crew's deck below. The Major and Mrs. Ballantyne used the brightly tiled bathrooms and lavatories reserved for first class passengers at the front end of the first class deck. Annie daily accompanied her lady to the bath area to assist as did other ladies' maids. The baths were fitted with hot and cold water pumps and the hot water pipes ran through all the corridors so that passengers could remain reasonably warm especially at night. With the introduction of pumping technology at ports, sea water was pumped in and stored in the large tanks on the lowest deck and once the ship was out at sea, the used dirty water was pumped out of separate tanks. The water storage also helped to provide the ballast weight to steady the ship.

"Annie..." Startled, she turned from wiping the already shining night table.

Andrew continued, "Sorry, you did not hear me come back. Annie, will you think about what I asked yesterday?"

"Aye, Andrew. But the Major's family is headed back home to England. They will need me..."

"But there are many other girls in London who will gladly welcome the chance to take care of them, Annie. Stay with me in Durban. We can make a life...I can ask the captain to marry us, Annie."

"Aye, Andrew. I would like that... but perhaps at the end of our voyage?"

"You make me so happy, Annie...yes at the end of this voyage."

Andrew had met Annie in Calcutta at the Major's residence. He had been commissioned to help the Major pack some of his belongings for his journey back to England at the end of his tour of duty which, twice renewed, had been nearly ten years long. Mrs. Ballantyne was not happy in India. She did not take to the weather, the language, the customs and longed for her English home.

"I will miss the wee boys, Andrew. I have cared for them for two years now."

"Aye, I know, Annie. But Laura is going on to England too and her master is getting off in Mauritius. She was to be assigned to another family in Durban. I can see that she accompanies the Major's family."

"That will be good, Andrew."

They worked quietly together for the rest of the hour it took to clean the rooms. Andrew then headed off to the galley and Annie to the linen room. The men who laundered the linen and garments quietly brought them up daily and Annie checked to see that they had kept the linen room tidy. She then headed to the top of the first class stairs to await the Ballantyne boys returning for their morning lessons after their family breakfast.

***

Tired from the heavy lifting all day, Amir and Purat stood on deck watching the ship ease out of Madras harbour.

"My Uncle and Aunt are settling into their cubicle with their little boy and girl…"

Amir and Purat turned around and welcomed Anpu. His Hindi mixed with English was easily understood and Amir was grateful since he did not speak Tamil.

"Oh good, I am glad Anpu, you must tell us what we can do to make them comfortable."

Amir explained the shared duties of the steerage passengers.

"Oh yes, yes. We are used to hard work. But the depot was so… so disgusting… so crowded… so dirty…"

"Yes we know," Purat cut in and they shared their grunts of discomfort. "We are hoping that is the worst part and that part is over for us, Anpu."

The men chatted comfortably as the ship picked up speed and the flickering lights from lamps along the coastline slowly disappeared. The men doing the cooking this evening could be heard talking cheerfully and the smells of the spices lured Amir and his friends to the kitchen. The food was carried down to the crowded bunk area for the evening meal. New friends talked mainly with gestures and the mixed tongues of Tamil, Telugu, English and Hindi. A new camaraderie began to develop down in the steerage. After eating, Amir took a few of the *dhalits* aside.

"Bhayah…brothers… I am going to help you clean the latrines tonight… no no… it's okay I want to help."

The young men looked at Amir, confused, as Purat and Anpu joined them and listened. Both Purat and Anpu spoke together.

"We will help too."

Purat continued, "*Bhayah* Amir is right. We are all going to an unknown land together. We are brothers now…"

The *dalit* boys looked with some confusion at these kind strangers. The one who had helped the Scotsmen spoke up. "*Bhayah*…areh… it seems strange calling you that… *Bhayah*, we are grateful to you. I am Bhodraj and this is my friend Himal."

The group fell silent as they headed off to clean the latrines. Amir and Purat brought along the extra buckets of sea water that had been promised by the Surgeon Superintendent and had been handed to them at the storage door. Some of the men from the bunk area came and stood staring in wide-eyed disbelief. But the men just quietly went on with their chores. During the next week, several other men took turns with the *dalits* in the cleaning chores as well. There was some discussion about the change in traditions and attitudes. The *pundits* looked on bewildered, but said nothing.

Life on the ship took on a routine as the days and evenings rolled by. Although the bunk areas were crowded, they were kept clean and camaraderie developed among the men, including the priests. Caste and class, though deeply embedded back home seemed to be fading as the men talked about their lives, their families and the great unknown toward which they were heading. Although not spoken, they each felt a trust building among them.

The steerage passengers rarely saw the crew or first class passengers. Their only contact was with the daily ration providers at the iron gate and every third day or so at the lower deck door for heavier provisions like sand and coal. Sometimes when the Indians walked on the upper deck they saw first class passengers having breakfast at the outdoor tables under the awnings, but they knew better than to stare. The indentured men and the few women and children found pleasure in the food they cooked and the fresh air walks on the upper deck.

On the fourteenth day of crossing the wide open Indian Ocean, strong winds started to whip stingingly cold and unfriendly. The ship had evaded severe weather for the first ten days as it steered close to the Indian coastline, but now several days of being out in the open sea they could feel the chill, especially in the nights. This evening the winds were strong, lashing against the tin kitchen, rattling the entire structure. Amir and Bhimnad were cooking.

"*Areh…* hold the pots… hold the pots Amir!" Bhimnad shouted as the boiling rice water spilled over the sides of the huge pots.

"*Aachah...aachah...*okay...okay... let's take the food down. This wind is not slowing down."

Amir shouted down the ladder for other men to come up and help and soon they were all seated on the floor eating and talking animatedly about the whipping winds.

"*Bhayah…* brothers… be sure to keep the women and children safely in their cubicles and secure everyone's trunks under your bunks. There is some rope under the stairs if you need to tie your trunks to your bunks. And don't light your lamps… flames not safe in this weather. *Kala pani*, the dark water of this ocean, seems angry tonight."

In the darkness of night, families huddled together and men in their bunks hunkered down, unable to sleep as gale winds screamed by their tiny portholes and the ship was swept up and down with the waves. The single blankets were insufficient and men crouched in fetal positions shivering in the cold.

Booming thunder and flashes of lightning drew worried eyes to the securely-fixed portholes. The ship was lurching sideways and fear replaced nausea as the men huddled and held on to their bolted bunks. Suddenly there was screaming from the bunks in the middle of the quarters.

"Water!! Water coming in…"

Amir was confused. The portholes did not open.

"Where… where?" he yelled, as he leapt out of his bunk in the darkness. Men were scrambling on the floor shouting unintelligibly. Water gushed down the ladders midship. The men rushed to the ladders staring up to see frothy water flowing in from the open upper deck. The ship swayed ominously, throwing the men from side to side, banging them against bunks. Then sacks, trunks, boxes, pots, pans, utensils from under the ladder were propelled across the floor as men ducked and screamed. Children and women's voices were heard crying out from the cubicles.

"Keep the women and children in their cubicles," Amir shouted. "And don't light any lanterns!"

Bhodraj struggled toward the cubicles and held out his arms to brace himself against the walls. Children were crying, as the women clung to them and their bunks. Priests Rajiv and Sajiv were wobbling, trying to get to the main bunk area. Several metal trunks came careening across the floor. One of them came at an angle slashing into Rajiv and knocking him senseless on to the flooded floor. Bhodraj grabbed him and shouted for help. Amir and Purat took hold of Rajiv and dragged him back to his cubicle. There was blood oozing from Rajiv's belly onto his cotton shirt.

"Stay here," Amir shouted. "*Behnji*, sister, keep him calm. Sajiv help him."

Amir and Purat struggled back to the main bunk area. Bhodraj was still clinging to the wall where Rajiv had been hit.

"Bhodraj!!! You are bleeding!"

"My leg... my leg. The trunk hit my leg..."

Bhodraj's *dhoti* wrapped around his legs was covered in blood.

"Can you walk? Never mind, Purat, let's get him to the sick bay bunk."

Amir, Purat and several of the men wrapped *dhoti* cloth securely around Bhodraj's leg and Pundit Rajiv's belly and returned to the main bunk area. The floors were covered in several feet of foaming, icy water and men were being thrown from side to side.

"Grab on to the bunks... they are secured!" Himal shouted. The swell of the sea, rising and surging, battered the ship, pitching it from side to side. Gale force winds howled and whipped relentlessly. The terrified screaming of steerage occupants continued as the storm raged all through the night and into the morning. And then there was an eerie calm. Exhausted, the men stared blankly, not wanting to relax their grips, not wanting to believe that it might be over. Sunrise could be seen through the tiny portholes that thankfully were built not to open.

Slowly the men started to find their feet. Sloshing through the water, they walked with difficulty clutching bellies and aching backs. They examined the damage. All the sacks of food supplies from under the stairs were now scattered around the floor and soaking wet. Strewn pots, pans and other utensils were floating in water. Metal trunks that were no longer secured under bunks had been pushed along the aisles and were lodged, blocking pathways and causing water to collect in big pools. Amir picked his way over the debris toward the cubicles.

"How are they, Sajiv?"

"Not good, Amir. The bleeding in Rajiv's belly did not stop for many hours and he is in great pain. I held folded cloth against the wound all night and it seems to have stemmed the bleeding. Bhodraj's leg is secured and the bleeding has stopped, but he too is in pain."

Amir touched both men on their foreheads to feel for fever. Rajiv appeared to be sicker. Amir quietly went back to the bunkroom, searching for something. He lifted up several sacks and set them back down until he came to the one he sought. The wet sack was heavy as he lifted it on to his bunk opening the string.

Smaller bags of spices, some still drier than others, flowed in red and yellow streaks on to his bunk. He took out one bag and gently opened it. He thrust his hand into the bag and took out a handful of turmeric powder, bright yellow and wet. He made a ball of the wet spice and tearing two strips off his tunic he wrapped the poultice into two palm-sized packages. He walked back to Rajiv and Bhodraj and gently placed the poultices on their wounds.

He asked the helpers to secure them with cloth. Rajiv seemed to be asleep, not aware of what was going on. Bhodraj was awake and kept saying he wanted to get up and help others. Purat calmed him and urged him back down.

The rest of the men, led by Anpu and Himal had already started bailing water using the bath buckets, pots and metal bowls, carrying them into the latrines and throwing the water down the grates. The ship was steady now and trunks were returned to underneath bunks. Bhimnad was dragging sacks back to the storage under the ladder, shaking his head at Amir.

"All wet Amir… all the rice, beans, lentils, grains… all gone..."

"Never mind. At least we are all safe. Rajiv is badly hurt. I am going to the upper deck to see if I can get some help."

When he reached the top of the ladder, Amir noticed that their makeshift kitchen was no more. The stove was securely bolted, but the tin walls and roof had blown away. Through the bolted gates, Amir could see that the first class upper deck was deserted. Doors leading into the dining rooms were secured.

The few outdoor tables and chairs that remained were strewn all around the deck. He could see no one. He ran down the ladder to the very bottom deck where he and his friends usually waited for their sand, coal and sea water rations. Frothy sea water had collected in the small space at the foot of the ladder but the bailing had helped lower the level. He banged on the door, shouting for help.

After what seemed like ages the door was yanked open by two angry men.

"What do you want?"

"We need help. We need the doctor. We have two badly injured men..."

"The Surgeon Superintendent is busy. We have lots of sea-sick people he is attending to. Come back later!" The door was banged shut.

Amir and Purat knocked again and again. No answer.

They returned to Rajiv and Bhodraj and through the next several hours they applied clean poultices and watched over their sick mates. They continued cleaning up, but the floor planks remained slimy and slippery. Blankets were soaked through and Amir knew he would have to ask for permission to hang them on deck to dry, something they were strictly warned not to do. The unsightly spectacle of steerage clothes hanging on deck would be offensive to passengers taking tea on deck. Clothes in the metal trunks were thankfully dry, so the children were dressed in dry clothes, though they were still shivering and the patients needed dry blankets.

Toward evening Amir walked pointedly down the ladder again and banged on the storage door. This time Andrew opened the door. Amir was taken aback expecting the ire of the two men who had slammed the door before.

"Oh Mr. Landers... I thought... thank you, Mr. Landers. We need help. Two men are badly injured and the children need milk and food... we cannot cook... all our supplies are wet... blankets wet..."

"Calm down, Amir...come, come inside."

Speechless at this hospitality, Amir followed Andrew into the storage hold. He stared at the huge tanks, at a maze of pipes connecting to other pipes, at huge storage barrels, but mostly he stared at the dry floors.

No water had come into this secured section of the ship. They walked past the Chinese crew who were busy at wash stations and the white men, with greasy hands and faces, working in the boiler area. Andrew took Amir to a small room with a table and chair and upended a box for him to sit.

"Sir, our priest is badly hurt. He has a deep gash on his belly and another man with a large cut on his leg. The water flooded our steerage compartment and we cleaned most of it, but we need to dry our blankets. The children are cold..."

"Amir, how did the water come in?"

"Sir, the ladder..."

"Oh my G... Oh yes...the ladder... there is no door from the top deck... Oh yes I am so sorry, Amir. Come, come let me go and see."

Andrew rushed out with Amir following him. When Andrew entered the bunk area, the men who were bent over various chores, stood upright bowing their heads in greeting. Taking one of the lamps, Andrew examined the area, slipping once on the slimy floor, but quickly steadying himself.

"Where are your injured men?"

Explaining how the injuries occurred, Amir led him to the cubicles and sick bay with a few of the men following with lamps. The women and children were huddled in other cubicles as Andrew gently undid the makeshift bandages and poultices and grimaced when he saw Rajiv's wound.

"The poultices helped to keep the wounds from becoming infected. What is in them?"

Amir started to explain about turmeric and Purat hurriedly dipped his hand into the sack at the foot of Rajiv's bunk and showed Andrew.

"That's good. I will bring the Surgeon Superintendent to look at these men and I will send dry blankets for these patients and the children."

"Sir, we need your permission to hang our blankets on the upper deck to dry..."

"Yes yes… just do so around the corner away from the dining room area."

"And… Sir… we have not eaten today. Our food supplies are wet…"

"I had thought of that Amir… I will send food. Come to the storage door in an hour."

"Thank you, thank you, Sir."

True to his word, Andrew arranged to provide supplies. Two men brought a wooden crate filled with small tin canisters of soup and bread. The men carried several blankets in a stack balanced on outstretched arms. In a second crate Amir found sacks of rice and dried peas.

The supplies were gratefully received in steerage. Several canisters of soup were first taken to the children and as the women opened them their faces fell. Swimming on top were tiny pieces of meat. Amir looked knowingly at Rajiv's wife.

"*Behnji* we have to eat. The children have to eat. We have to try and feed Rajiv *Bhai*. Please… they need the sustenance."

Rajiv's wife, a staunch vegetarian, looked from Amir to Sajiv confused. After several moments Sajiv, sighing deeply, agreed.

"*Behnji* we are in a desperate place, a desperate time. We are in God's hands. This is the food in front of us. The children cannot go hungry."

Adam quietly added, "*Behnji* in Islam in desperate times we say a prayer and eat."

She walked away quietly with the canisters in hand. The children were fed and Bhodraj was fed. But Rajiv appeared too sick at first to sit up. Amir persisted and a few sips were tilted into his mouth. Sajiv, Adam and their families ate as did all the men in the bunk area. Amir called Bhimnad and a few of the other men and they agreed that at first light they would get to work on the upper deck to try to repair the cooking area and to run ropes on which to dry the blankets.

***

The next morning the gate clanged open as Surgeon Superintendent Wilkie, Andrew and several crew members entered the steerage deck. The indentured men were working on cleaning up the cooking area and straightened up as the surgeon and his group entered.

"Where is Amir?"

"Hanging blankets…there, Sir," said Anpu pointing around the corner as some of his peers rushed off to find Amir.

"Ah there you are Amir. What's going on?"

Speaking hurriedly Amir explained as he led Wilkie to the sick bay. Wilkie sniffed trying to isolate the musty smell of the wet grass mattresses.

"Yes I see… slippery here… watch. So Amir what? … blankets drying? Pots and plates okay?"

"No we are hanging blankets out now…"

But Wilkie was gingerly opening up Rajiv's wound.

Andrew said quietly, "The poultice has helped to close the wound, Sir…"

"No, no, no, no, we can't have this! The captain will have my hide! This man needs this wound cleaned. What is all this yellow stuff? Andrew hand me the carbolic solution from my bag!"

The surgeon cleaned the wound and applied a salve. Then applying fresh gauze, he bandaged the abdomen. He did the same for Bhodraj's leg. Andrew was aware that the surgeon received a stipend for each healthy recruit delivered to the British indenture office in Durban. None of the other crew knew this and he said nothing.

"I will come again in a few days. Andrew make sure these people are kept fed and dry. The captain is relying on me to get this group safely landed…can't have sick ones…"

Realizing that he could be heard and understood Wilkie led Andrew hurriedly up the ladders and to the gate. Andrew was saying, "Sir they prefer to cook their own meals…I will give them fresh provisions. Can their kitchen be repaired?"

"See what you can do, Andrew."

Amir, Purat, Bhimnad, Himal and Anpu took leadership all day encouraging their friends to work at cleaning and repairs and trying to boost the morale in steerage.

Food was cooked on the open coal stove without the protection of the tin walls despite the gusty evening winds. Next morning through the storage door came sacks of additional dry goods, a barrel of oil, a crate with tin canisters of hot porridge, brooms, mops and a promise from Andrew.

"Crew men will fix your kitchen, Amir. We are two weeks away from Mauritius where you will get fresh Indian spices…"

"No, no, no problem about the spices…we can manage…we are dry-ing some…thank you, thank you, Sir."

***

On the sixth day after the storm, the Captain and his officers walked into the saloon for their weekly meeting. They met later than usual this morning. Regular routines and cheerful chatter had resumed among the passengers. The dining room was full and some men were already in the smoking room. Servers were dashing from table to table with trays of steaming eggs, pastries, biscuits, warm bread and urns of cof-fee and tea.

"Well old chap?" The captain turned to Surgeon Superintendent Wilkie as they took their seats. The other men sat at the table with notebooks in hand.

"My dear boy! You did yeoman's duty!" The Captain slapped Wilkie on his back. "Sea-sickness everywhere, what?" His loud laughter was infectious and the men joined in. "So what still remains to be done?"

"Well, the bouts of nausea are over, Captain. Sick bays are empty, cleaned and sterilized…"

"Good, good man! We are back to normal routine then, what?"

"Well yes, mostly. The two injured men in steerage are recovering. The one had a nasty gash in his stomach…"

"Well is he not recovered? Should we be sending him back from Mauritius? Can't be delivering sick men at the Durban harbour. Not good for my reputation."

"Well…"

Andrew interrupted, "Sir, he is the priest and I have been checking on him each day as I do my regular rounds…"

"Each day in steerage, Landers? Are we not keeping you busy enough here?" the Captain bellowed.

"Yes Sir, but there was a lot of damage in steerage and I am seeing to it that things are cleaned up and repaired. You had said that you want to be sure that we deliver healthy workers to the Protector of Immigrants in Durban."

"Yes, quite. But if this man is still sick…"

Andrew continued, "Sir, the priest is recovering well. I talked to him and their lead man and they definitely want him to continue on to Durban. The men have developed friendships and are determined that the priest and his family will remain with them and they will watch over them."

"But the men could be separated upon landing in Durban."

"They realize that. But they have determined amongst themselves that whoever lives close to the priest's family will watch over them as they settle."

"You seem to know a lot about steerage, Landers. Fraternizing with the labourers?"

"No Sir…just my job, Sir."

"All right. The other lad recovered? His leg, I believe?"

Wilkie cut in, "I have been checking on those two every few days too, Captain. The lad's leg is nearly healed. A little bit of a limp, but fine."

"Let's get on with the rest of your reports."

With little damage to the workings of the ship, the reports were routine. The Captain, pleased with his team, joined them over coffee at the end of the hour-long meeting. Andrew waited for an opportunity to draw the Captain aside.

"Captain, may I have a private word?"

"What is it Landers… more requests for steerage?"

They were near the heavy tan curtains that draped over the tall windows near the door leading to the outdoor breakfast area. Andrew gestured that they go out on to the deck.

The two men walked over to the railing and with his elbow resting comfortably on the polished wood, the Captain turned questioningly to Andrew.

"Sir, as Captain you are empowered to perform marriages?"

"Marriages? No… Not for steerage surely. They have their own religions…"

"No, not for steerage, Sir… for me."

The Captain stared for a minute unsure what was being asked.

"Sir, I wish to marry on ship. My bride-to-be is Annie Booth, Major Ballantyne's maid."

"Are you mad, Landers? The Ballantynes need their maid! They are going on to England you know and you are commissioned to work in Durban!"

"Sir I have talked to another maid Laura Dunkley who is returning to England and she is happy to continue on with the Ballantynes."

"Oh! Quite... Oh well. I will need to talk with the Major. It will be another ship, different quarters..."

"Sir, the maid has talked with Mrs. Ballantyne and she is pleased for my Annie."

The men talked for several minutes and it was agreed that after the ship left Mauritius on its last leg of the journey, the Captain would perform the civil ceremony. As there was no Minister on ship, the Captain led Sunday prayers, but he did not think he could perform a religious wedding. A civil ceremony suited Andrew just fine.

***

Rajiv propped himself up comfortably on his bunk and looked tiredly at his wife and five-year-old son. It was ten days after the storm and his belly wound was healing well, though his strength was slow in returning. Namita cradled their son reassuring him that *Papaji* was fine.

"Take him upstairs, Namita. You will be all right...go see the kitchen all fixed and repaired...go, go it's okay."

"*Namasthe Punditji*! How are you today?" Bhodraj's cheery voice was a daily welcome for Rajiv for several days now.

"*Areh* Bhodraj...come, come...*areh*, look at you walking now...nice walking stick..."

"Yes...yes... Amir saved a piece from the kitchen repairs—good *nayh*? But I will be walking on my own soon...then you should use it, *Punditji!*"

"Yes...I am standing up a bit every day. You come for your lesson, *Bhayah*?"

Since he was bedridden, Rajiv had begun teaching Bhodraj to read and the two convalescing men spent an hour each morning and evening with books from Rajiv's trunk. Bhodraj relished learning the basics of reading and writing and Rajiv was happy to teach and talk about the scriptures.

Other men joined them after chores were completed. The brother-hood between priest and *dhalit* did not escape the men who were generally pleased to see it. Namita took her son up the ladder. The sight of a woman walking out alone with a child was not frowned upon as it would have been otherwise.

Here in this new world they were forging new lives with greater tolerance. The wives of the five married men often talked together and they learned about women who were indentured and sent to far-off lands to work as domestics and even in the sugarcane fields. The women offered to help with the cooking chores on deck and could be seen cleaning rice or lentils in the folds of their saris, picking off stones or tiny clumps of sand.

On the fifteenth day after the storm, lamplight along the shores of Mauritius was a welcome sight for those eagerly standing on tip-toe on the deck to watch the ship come into port. It was still early morning and orange streaks of sunrise lit the skyline behind them and twinkling lamps ahead. Port Louis was barely visible. None of the indentured labourers would be alighting there, but Amir knew that the port was a destination for the ship's maintenance and for loading mail onto ships bound for India.

"Purat, you know that the Surgeon Superintendent asked if he should send Bhodraj, Rajiv and his family back to India from Mauritius because of their injuries…"

"Yes but I agree with you, Amir, they are our brothers. They will go with us and we will take care of them…"

"Yes that's what I explained to Mr. Landers and the Captain has agreed as long as they do not show signs of illness when we reach Durban…"

"No, no, they are both so well, *Bhayah*."

The men fell silent as they watched the ship cut through the calm waters toward the harbour. They could hear the rumble of the machinery as water was pumped into the holds.

There was still no sign of first class passengers in the breakfast area on deck. Walking to the back of the ship around to the other side closer to the other barred iron gate, they found a better view as the ship approached the harbour.

As daylight broke, Amir and Purat, with Bhodraj supported between them, stood breathing in the fresh morning air, watching the approaching harbour. As the ship hugged the coast, they were interested
to see mostly lush greenery of trees and succulent shrubs but only a
few palms. They heard their friends at breakfast below, but they were
mesmerized by the sight of Mauritius.

It was an hour before the ship moored at the harbour. The men re-
marked on the familiar sight of bougainvillea bushes in the surrounding areas and noticed rustic low wooden structures built in rows close
to where the ships docked. A few fishing boats rocked gently in the
waters further away from the dock, near the sandy shoreline.

"Nice place, *nayh?*" Bhodraj exclaimed.

"Yes, I see some people like us lifting crates… but I think to other
ships, *nayh?*"

"Look at that nice church over there," Amir pointed to a white-
painted church surrounded by bougainvillea bushes and Pride of India
trees. "Smaller than the one in Muzaffarnagar, but so neat!"

Just then they noticed the Captain, Surgeon Wilkie and some other
officers walking down the gangplank that had emerged from the ship.
The men stepped on the stone platform, walked for several minutes
and then on to the stone *ghat* or steps leading up from the mooring
area. The fourteen steps of the *ghat* were made of heavy stone. The men
disappeared from sight as they reached the top.

"They must be going to file papers with the government," Amir
mused. "I heard that there are thousands of our brothers here in Mauritius too, working in the cane fields. But not all from the British Raj…"

"Then who brought them here?"

Anpu who had joined the men said, "Well south of Madras there are
lots of French people, *Bhayah*. When I made my contract with the British man there were others of our brothers talking with French officers.
So they were going to French places. Maybe this is a French place?"

"I don't know, *Bhayah*… but it looks very nice."

"*Areh* look! Look!" Purat pointed excitedly at the gate where the
Captain and his men had climbed the stone steps.

"What is it, Purat?"

"*Areh yaar*—look beside the gate… in the stone wall… flowers, garlands… *Bhayah*…it's *Ganeshji*…*Bhayah*…it's *Ganeshji*…!" Purat had his palms together, breathlessly muttering a prayer, staring… holding back tears."

Sure enough in a small broken recess in the low stone wall along the harbour platform someone had placed a clay statue of Lord *Ganeshji*. The flowers and garlands indicated that this Hindu shrine was tended, most likely by the men who worked on the wharf, as a welcome for the thousands of indentured labourers who disembarked here and were parceled off in service to the various cane fields. Amir, Purat and Anpu with their palms together prayed silently and the astonishment at such a small but emotionally significant sight stayed with them for many days. It would be years later that they would learn the name of Aapravasi Ghat, an inspiration that would serve as a reminder in the shaping of their own new communities.

***

"Are you nervous, my dear?"

Andrew and Annie were quietly working in Lord Clive's suite, helping the maid who was not well. The ship had left Mauritius at sunset and this morning Annie's roommate, Mary, woke with a pounding headache. With the Ballantynes and Clives enjoying breakfast and the beginning of the last leg of their journey to Durban, Andrew and Annie busied themselves with sheets, brooms, pails and cheerful conversation.

"Aye, Andrew… but happy. Mary worked many nights on my dress…I hope that hasn't caused her headache?"

"She will be fine Annie…and she will be a perfect bridesmaid and witness for us…I am excited my Annie."

They chatted happily about plans for their marriage that was a week away. Andrew was well liked by his staff so a small feast was being planned below deck for the special day. When they were not busy with ship's duties, the cook and the other Chinese crew were preparing food. They ironed Andrew's suit, Annie's wardrobe, and white tablecloths for the crewmen's dining area on the lower deck. Others were scrubbing and cleaning the area and had placed a small barrel of whiskey in the dining room for the wedding party.

The civil ceremony would be performed by the captain in the library beside the first class dining room. But the only guests there would be Andrew's friend William Bickerton, Annie's friends Mary Higgs and Laura Dunkley, Surgeon Superintendent Wilkie and Major Ballantyne's family.

The morning of the wedding dawned bright. The Indian Ocean sparkled in the sunshine. Whales could be spotted in the distance. Durban was still another five days away, but steerage and first class passengers had noticed the calmer waters and spotted splendid sea creatures, signaling the proximity of warm lands ahead.

Andrew, dapper in his cream suit, white shirt, and brown boots, stood before the Captain with William next to him, looking expectantly behind them at the door to the library.

Annie entered with her hand on Major Ballantyne's arm. Mary, Laura, the children and Mrs. Ballantyne followed behind. Annie was surprised when a young girl, dressed simply in a pale blue dress, began playing a harp in the far corner of the room. Startled, she caught the smiling eyes of the girl and recognized her as the teenage daughter of one of Major Ballantyne's officers accompanying him on the ship. Annie was touched by the Ballantynes' kind gesture.

"Annie, Andrew, Major Ballantyne and guests…" the Captain began in his booming voice, then quickly modulated for the small library. "I am happy to perform this civil ceremony for this young couple. As you know, there is no ring on ship… so dear boy you are going to have to buy this lovely bride-to-be a ring in Durban!" He laughed, easing the quietness in the room.

The ceremony proceeded as smoothly as the bride and groom had hoped and the genuine good wishes of the people attending brought tears to Annie's eyes. The captain entered Andrew and Annie's names into his register as a married couple, and the certificate with his signature would need to be presented at the Births, Deaths and Marriages office in Durban upon debarkation. As the bride, Annie was served first with coffee and delicate pastries and she shyly accepted. She sat at a wooden table the likes of which she shined daily in the quarters she cleaned. Andrew noticed her thoughtful expression and knew what she was thinking.

"We will make a lovely home together my Annie…" he whispered.

She smiled up at her husband, happy and content.

The raucous party in the crewmen's dining room was already underway even at this mid-morning hour.

"Hey, isn't anyone working?" joked Andrew, as he entered the room with Annie on his arm and Mary, Laura, and William following.

"Aye! We have taken the day off Andrew!" "Congratulations, my boy!" The newlyweds were surrounded by well-wishers and cups of drinks were handed around for the toast.

Andrew knew that all of them had woken earlier than usual, performed their tasks and were taking turns juggling their remaining duties so they could be here for him and Annie. The cook had prepared a sumptuous meal of roasts, Chinese rolls, lentil soup, breads and pastries which were washed down with wine and for some, whiskey.

Chapter 3

Port Natal

Ten days after the John Davie left Mauritius, it sailed smoothly along the coast of Natal, heading steadily south. Rajiv, almost fully recovered, stood between Amir and Purat. Bhodraj, fully recovered, stood at the railings with Himal, Anpu and other young men. Children bounced about excitedly pointing at the dolphins offshore and the birds overhead.

"*Areh...* careful children! Not too close to the railings! Watch them, *Bhayahs...*" Amir called to the others.

"Amir, where do you think we will be assigned?" Purat asked, as he ran his fingers over the metal identity disc hanging around his neck.

"I think that those of us who were recruited by the same recruiter might be placed together at the same farm, don't you think?" Amir looked at him quizzically.

Evening was approaching and small lanterns could be seen along the coast. The Surgeon Superintendent on his visit the previous night had said that they would reach Port Natal in two days. The men were now standing on deck looking forward to docking the next day.

"That will be good, Amir. You are my brother and hopefully we will be together. But what about the others? What about you, Rajiv, *Bhayah?*"

Rajiv looked up at Purat, "As a priest I was told that I will serve a community that needs a priest. I am not sure where that will be."

"Andrew promised that he will talk to the Captain to tell the Protector Williams that you will be with us since your injury, Rajiv."

"That will be good *Bhayah* Amir." Rajiv continued to sway his head for a few minutes lost in thought.

"*Areh…* look at that light on that tall structure? What kind of light is that? How is it so bright?"

Amir and Rajiv looked to where Purat was pointing. A lighthouse could be seen in the fading sunset and Amir and Purat were puzzled as to how a wick-burning lantern could shine so bright.

"But we saw such a tower as we left Calcutta too, didn't we?" Amir countered.

Rajiv launched into an animated explanation of his readings about the discovery of gas lighting systems that he had found in government office libraries. The men were intrigued as most streets in their towns were lit by lamp-lighters using lighting oil or kerosene lanterns.

Some of the children came around to listen with fascination to Rajiv's explanation of modern advancements. Steerage passengers had bonded on the voyage and nurtured the innocent curiosity of the children.

"*Chalo*, let's go down now to eat. The evening meal is ready, last night on this ship, *nayh*," said Himal as he gathered the children and adults and steered everyone down the ladder for their last night on board.

When the children had been guided down the ladder, Amir touched Rajiv's arm and pulled him back. Purat seeing this stayed back as well.

"*Kya baath hai* Amir *Bhai*, what is it?" Rajiv loked quizzically at Amir.

Amir lowered his voice and asked, "*Punditji*, a few of the men at the Calcutta depot talked about the *kala pani*, black water. They said that once we cross over the ocean our souls' journeys will be broken so we cannot have the same reincarnation journey that we would have if we stayed in India."

"Yes, some Hindus do believe that. But just as a precaution, both Sajiv and I packed in our trunks, a bottle each of *Ganga pani*, Ganges water. The bottles are glass with a nice cork as well as a screw on the closure. We wrapped the bottles tight with cloth too. By taking this water together with us on the ship, *Ganga Matha*, Mother Ganges, is still with us."

"*Aachah…aachah…*" Both Amir and Purat nodded with relief. Then curiosity crept in.

"Glass bottles? They are expensive, *Punditji*?"

"Yes...yes..." and Rajiv laughed. "You know, the *gorawallahs*, white folk, drink whiskey and throw away the bottles. Our temple people clean them and wash them thoroughly. Then they fill the bottles with water from *Ganga*."

"*Areh Bhayah* if we had known...*areh Ganga Matha* flows right through our Muzzafarnagar and we could have filled some of our own *dubbahs*, containers...*nayh?*" Amir looked quizzically at Purat who bobbed his head in agreement. Rajiv patted him on the shoulder and said, "Yes my bottles were filled in Meerut, close to your village *nayh?* And Sajiv's was filled from his village near Patna."

The friends joined the others at their meal, reassured that the journeys of their souls were not interrupted by this momentous journey across the *kala pani*. The conversation among all the steerage passengers was happy and everyone was chatty, looking forward to disembarking on to a new land of opportunity.

The next morning Amir, Purat, Anpu, Bhodraj and Himal were first on deck at sunrise, excitedly looking at the approach to the Durban Harbour, which was named after a local British governor named D'Urban. Again they saw a lighthouse high on a tall hill directly in front of the approaching ship. It stood on a high lush green hill on the coastline that jutted out into the sea. As the rising sun touched the vibrant green of trees and shrubs, the hill seemed to sparkle. The ship turned right slowly and moved through a cemented corridor of the dock that created a calm, protected channel and narrowed the approach from the sea. The John Davie slowly moved toward a stone wharf where several other ships were already docked. There were only a few buildings in the port area, but the men could see several cement, brick and stone buildings being erected. Labourers carrying heavy loads worked on the construction site. There were several neat, low brick buildings. One impressive two-storied white building had curved arches and windows and a flag flying on a post. Beside that building and half hidden from their side they noticed a long low narrow wood building with a red tin curved roof. Since it was surrounded by a brick wall they could see only the tops of the walls and the red roof. The ground around the dock near the water's edge was strewn with what appeared to be rubble.

Other Indian steerage passengers emerged on deck and by midmorning all fifty-five men, five women and seven children eagerly chatted on deck watching the disembarkation process. The men wore their clean white *dhotis* and white tunics, the women in colourful cotton saris and the children's bright traditional clothes matched their bubbly excitement. Trunks had been packed and stacked in the bunk area ready for the signal for the men to carry them off the ship. Over their shoulders the men carried small white cloth bags with some personal belongings, money, papers, and an extra *dhoti*. The long gangplank from the lowest hold was crowded with local Indian and African men, dark-skinned, naked from the waist up, carrying metal trunks, shiny wooden boxes, casks and barrels and some pieces of polished, carved furniture. They carefully placed the luggage and delicate items along the wharf and returned to the hold for more.

From the lower cabin level, there was a separate sloping gangplank with railings on both sides, which was reserved for white men, women and children. The women walked carefully dressed in full length gowns in soft spring shades. The men in long coats and narrow-legged pants strode ahead of them offering their hands to support the women and children as they stepped off on to the cement pavement. The children were being fussed over by other women in frilly white hats and white aprons, who had emerged with them from the ship. The steerage passengers knew that these were the English *sahibs*, their wives, children and nannies whom they had often seen in their cities back home. But as these fresh faced families disembarked, the steerage passengers looked on in silent awe.

A short while later crewmen emerged, dressed in white sailor outfits, crisp, short-sleeved shirts, comfortable long pants and small white caps. The crewmen busied themselves on the wharf giving instructions to the African and Indian porters to carry luggage on to several horse-drawn buggies. Then Amir recognized the Captain emerge with several piles of paper tied in bundles under his arm. He was accompanied by the Surgeon Superintendent also carrying files, and other officers dressed in the beige uniforms that were familiar in Calcutta. They walked toward the two-storey government building. Last to disembark, but not from the passenger gangplank, but from the lowest level of the ship using the cargo gangplank, were several Chinese men, dressed in working pants and shirt. They headed out to the wharf, walked past the frenetic activity and disappeared into the town.

The indentured Indians were still waiting on the ship and by mid-afternoon when all the white passengers had left the wharf they became increasingly concerned. There appeared to be no-one on the ship except them yet the deck gangplank was still in place. Presently they saw one officer coming back on board. As he emerged on to the deck and approached the iron gate Amir and Purat recognized him as Mr. Andrew Landers. There was a worried look on his face. Without unlocking the gate Andrew asked for Amir.

"Here I am Sir," said Amir gripping the grills of the gate.

"Amir I am sorry. The Captain and Surgeon Superintendent are still in discussions with the Port Authorities and they sent me to say that they are leaving to go to their quarters to get some rest. Tomorrow morning the Port Doctor will board our ship to conduct health inspections on all of you."

"Tomorrow only, Sir? Health inspections, Sir?" Amir's bewilderment showed in his worried eyes.

"Yes...they need to make sure that there are no diseases...illnesses you know."

"But Sir we are all healthy...you can see...look..."

"Yes I know Amir... I am sorry... it is routine."

Dejected Amir sighed, "Okay Sir, I will explain to them."

"Amir you still have supplies to cook some food?"

"Yes Sir... all packed under stairs, but yes still there...we can cook... not a problem, Sir."

Andrew left after more assurances, but the deflated group was obviously dejected, disappointed.

The simple meal of rice and *dhal* lentils was eaten quietly and as night approached blankets were unfolded and sleep finally came even to the most worried.

The next morning after morning meals, and the cleaning of the cabin and latrines the group once again packed belongings and gathered on the deck quietly waiting. Himal was the first to see a small group of white men walk briskly along the gangplank and board the ship. Himal, a muscular, athletic young man, ran to the front of the ship's steerage deck where Amir was talking to the other men. They rushed to the gate and waited, anxiously grasping the iron grills.

The Captain rattled the keys impatiently as he unlocked the gates and told the indentured group to go on back down the ladder. As the group hurried down the officers followed. Amir stood at the bottom of the ladder as the other steerage passengers stood silent by their bunks. The families were in their curtained area.

"Are you Amir? Yes, yes…Wilkie you'd better take over here…" The Captain awkwardly stepped aside in the tight space allowing the Surgeon Superintendent to come forward.

"Yes Amir…we have here the Protector of Immigrants Colonel Williams and the Port Doctor with us. We will need to examine all the passengers."

"Sir there are women here also…"

"Yes… yes …we have a nurse here…come forward nurse…"

The nurse, a small woman dressed in a plain long greenish gown with a full length white apron and a small white starched cap on her head, appeared nervous surrounded by men. Her eyes, darting from the Surgeon to the Indian men looked confused.

"Go through, Elizabeth…the women and children are through there…" the surgeon talked calmingly pointing toward the curtained area. The nurse hurried through.

"Now men….. stand beside your bunks…" seeing the startled look on the faces of the men the Surgeon turned to Amir, "Tell them Amir."

Rajiv, Sajiv, Anpu's uncle and Adam, leaving their wives and children in the cubicles, had come out and joined the men, standing straight-backed along the cabin. The inspection took several hours as each man was turned, asked to sit, stand, lie down, remove garments and prodded. The doctor and his accompanying assistants were not always gentle, but the procedure was not harsh. Finally, after three hours the officials gestured to Amir to come up to the deck.

"Like I said Captain…ship shape!!" said the Surgeon Superintendent.

The Captain slapped Wilkie on the shoulder and turned to Protector Williams.

"Yes all good. Here's Elizabeth now."

The nurse was climbing up the shaky ladder gingerly and was offered an officer's hand as she came on deck.

"All clear, Sir. Healthy women and children…well fed…good teeth… clear skins….no women's problems either…all good, Sir."

Slapping one another on the shoulder the group proceeded out of sight as the Captain locked the gate again and disappeared only to re-appear with the group on the gangplank below. They walked briskly to the two-storied building.

The steerage passengers stood quietly watching. Not knowing what would happen next they looked dazed around them at the inspectors, the lush vegetation, the wharf, the cluster of low buildings, the dark shiny skinned men rushing around carrying boxes on their backs. Then Rajiv, Adam and Sajiv suddenly remembering, rushed down the ladder to their families. The children were sobbing, their mothers comforting them.

It was midday when officers unlocking the gate caught the attention of the passengers at their midday meal. The uniformed men ordered them to clean up and line up on deck. The men hurriedly collected the tin bowls, washed them in the bath area and within minutes were climbing up the ladder to meet the officers.

"We are ready to disembark you. Form a straight line in single file..."

"Sir pardon me Sir...there are women and children below"

"What?? Yes, oh right...bring them... bring them first." The khaki uniformed officers blew on their whistles.

"Quiet, quiet...let's have some order here."

The families from below were brought up and lined up. The others mutely lined up behind, protectively looking at the children craning their necks to ensure that they were all right.

Amir ventured once again, "Sir our trunks...?"

"Don't worry about those...the Africans will unload those..." Laughing, one of the officers snapped, "You won't lose them! Now let's go."

They were led through the gate, past the breakfast area of the white passengers, down the wooden steps on the outside of the ship. They had to jump on to a narrow platform that rounded the front of the ship to the crewman's gangplank that they had seen earlier from above. On the cement wharf they once again lined up single file and followed the three officers who walked briskly along a rough, rubble-filled walkway to the brick wall surrounding the red-roofed structure that the men had seen from the deck.

There was a solid iron gate entrance with an armed uniformed guard who unlocked the gate and with a salute gestured to the officers to proceed. Rounding a corner inside the walled area, the men approached a door-less entrance to the wooden structure. Purat was first to read and recognize the words on the sign that read "Coolie Barracks." He gestured to Amir with his eyes flaming, but cautious. Amir knitted his brow but said nothing. As they entered the barracks behind the families, they recognized with dismay that this was a depot. Another depot! Visions of the Calcutta depot flooded into Amir's mind as he gasped and took in the scene.

Cots, three rows deep, lined both walls with a wider aisle down the middle. The low roofed depot was roughly a hundred yards long and about twelve feet wide. The cots along the front half of the aisle were already occupied by Indian men sitting, standing, and kneeling by the cots. The officers urged the new group to keep moving along and pointed them to the cots in the second half. By instinct the men turned to the families first, hurriedly speaking in Hindi, Tamil and Telugu, instructing the men with families to choose cots first, close together. The protective instinct for the safety of the children appeared uppermost in their minds. Amir, Purat, Bhodraj and Himal quickly found cots close to the families and watched the other men take up cots nearby. When they stood at attention after just a few minutes, almost all the cots in the depot were occupied. The officers walked slowly up and down the aisle viewing the startled men and frightened children and women. Finally, the officers left and as if all at once the hum of voices broke the silence.

Amir walked over to the front of the depot, close to the entrance and talked to some of the men already there. They had arrived on an earlier ship from Madras, had been processed and were waiting to be assigned to sugar estates. They had been in the depot for two days. Amir and his shipmates walked along the aisle away from the entrance and found at the far end another doorway leading outside. To their left against the outside brick wall were two latrines with doors. As they gingerly pushed the doors they saw that the latrines were equipped with a small stool leading up to a small wooden platform with a hole, under which was a bucket for night soil. The stench was strong but the latrine appeared clean otherwise. To the right of the exit and around the corner of the building the men came upon stacks of metal trunks pushed up against the wooden wall of the building. These were the belongings of indentured labourers from the other ship. Further along and close now to the front gate there was what appeared to be a tin tank with several large tin bowls neatly stacked one inside the other. There was a ladder attached to the side of the tank and Amir ventured up. Looking inside he realized that this was rain water most likely for the purpose of washing themselves in the morning. Walking back, they wondered aloud about what water they would drink and what food they would eat, especially the children, for whom the men had ensured milk and nutritious food on the ship. As the afternoon progressed there was nothing to do but sit and wait.

The evening meal arrived on two carts pushed by African men. Two large pots on each cart, metal bowls, metal cups and large tin cans of water were brought to the middle of the depot and left there. Men from both ship loads quickly proceeded to scoop out the thick porridge-like vegetables into bowls and handed them out starting with the children first. They ate quietly and, returning their bowls and cups to the cart, they sat on their cots looking vacantly about them wondering what was to happen next. Nothing....

Morning saw families and men lining up for the latrines and at the water tank. Ablutions completed, they returned to their cots. Amir went around the building again curious about their own metal trunks and possessions. Their trunks were there, stacked, waiting. He touched his, with his name neatly printed in Hindi, caressed his trunk, knowing that there were valuables inside and memories of home and he slowly walked back inside. Porridge was brought the same way as the night meal and after breakfast the waiting resumed.

They had not long to wait. Around mid-morning officers took the men from the first ship outside to the front gate. Amir ventured to the door-less entrance and watched as the men were grouped into clusters of nine or ten and led out of the iron gates. Then his eyes brightened as he saw a group of officers enter the gate and his heart lurched as he recognized Andrew Landers among them.

"Good morning, Amir."

"Good morning Sir!" Amir's obvious relief at seeing him showed in the full-toothed smile.

"Amir, the men who were recruited from my region will be assigned together…" He saw Amir's relief and touched him on the shoulder. "Don't worry."

The sorting of the men and families proceeded. Many of the men who had been together in the Calcutta depot found familiar faces in their assigned clusters and they were relieved. But Anpu and his uncle and family were in a cluster with others from the Madras recruitment area and Anpu seemed disappointed. "Amir, we are told that we will be sent to the south coast while your groups are going north."

"I know, Anpu, but we were all friends on the ship…all brothers *nayh*? You know all of them…"

"Yes, yes…but I wish I was going with you and Purat, and Bhodraj…"

"We too may be going to different estates, Anpu…we don't know."

The officers were speaking so the men quietened to listen.

"All of you will be taken by train to your estates tomorrow. Your trunks will be taken to the trains as well." As the information and instructions were given, translations were occurring concurrently among the various groups. The officers departed, but Andrew lingered.

"Sir…thank you, Sir, for keeping us together."

"It's all right, Amir…that is how it works."

"Sir…Anpu going south and we north…will they be far?"

"Yes, I'm afraid so, Amir. There are sugar estates all along the Natal coast. They are headed south to Umzinto and you are headed north toward Tongaat."

Amir had no idea what that meant and Andrew seeing the blank look repeated,

"Quite far, Amir. About fifty miles south of where you are going."

Anpu, his uncle and two children engaged in conversation with others in their cluster and soon, heads shaking from side to side amiably, they seemed fine. Then the waiting resumed till the evening meal and nightfall.

The next day, around mid-morning, the quiet in the half-filled depot was interrupted as several officers entered.

"As I call your name and number line up here," said a stout young man in a firm voice as he pointed to the entrance way.

Several groups were called and then Rajiv, Bhodraj, Bhimnad and Himal heard their names called one after another and they breathed sighs of relief realizing that they were in the same cluster. They lined up touching each other on the shoulders. Rajiv's wife Namita, held on to her five-year-old son Hemang with one hand and with the other hand she held the edge of her sari over her head and mouth as tradition dictated. Two more clusters were called and in the final small group, Amir, Purat and Sajiv found themselves together.

Shaking their heads amiably they formed the rear of the line, Amir's hand protectively on Sajiv's son Yathindra's head. At twelve years of age, the boy stood tall, even beside the unusually tall Amir. The boy put his arm protectively around his mother Parvati, while his father held his six-year-old sister Minati's hand. Amir looked back at Adam and his family still standing beside their cots.

One of the officers approached Adam and talked quietly after which Adam and his family joined the cluster in which Rajiv and his family were waiting. His ship friends smiled broadly as they helped Adam's children join the group with Adam and his wife following. As Adam walked past Amir, he whispered, "Shop opening contract...not sugarcane farm work." Amir nodded sideways in understanding. Adam's eight-year-old son Asif, held out his hand to Rajiv's five-year-old Hemang, happy to have his ship playmate with him while his little sister Ayesha held on to her mother Fatima's *kameez* dress.

The newly formed groups followed the officers out of the brick wall enclosure into the open gravel road. The road was wide and went past several one and two storey buildings, some of which were under construction. There were impressive brick buildings housing stores and offices and a few scattered, small red tin-roofed wooden structures. A few of the buildings had green shrubbery, trees and a few cement benches out front. Dozens of African and Indian labourers hurried in and out of the buildings carrying heavy wooden crates and other loads on their backs. The groups of ship passengers were guided toward the two-storey government building where they were met by a few white men not in uniform, but smartly dressed in long coats, tight trousers, some with monocles on their eyes. They talked with the officers and then appeared to inspect the groups of men. Amir and Purat whispered to each other realizing that these men were from the estates and they were examining people assigned to their farms.

"Why does this man not have a disc number?" a crisp-voiced, heavy set man called out pointing to Adam.

"He is a passenger Indian, Sir. Intends to open a shop to serve your coolies, Sir."

The man grunted assent and walked on to look at Bhimnad and Himal, nodding favourably.

The man examining Amir's group looked carefully at them, his piercing green eyes looking straight into the eyes of the Indians. He was tall, slightly on the heavy side, and in his mid-thirties. With his fingers twirling his ample moustache he stopped in front of Amir.

"This one is tall! Lighter skin too!" he laughed. "Where did you find him?"

"One of the officers was recruiting in the north, Sir, Mr. Harper, Sir."

"Humpf! North…that explains…lighter skin…I thought mix…" He stopped speaking in mid-sentence. Then continued, "Why the pock marks on the face? Several of them?"

The same officer responded, "Mr. Harper, Sir, those are from childhood measles or small pox. But they all have been cleared by our doctors both in Calcutta and here, Sir, all healthy, strapping young men."

Amir stiffened, but did not allow any emotion to show in his face. The heavy-set man continued his inspection, sweating around the brow even in the cool June morning. Amir averted his eyes and noticed their trunks being carried by African men and loaded on to two long carriages pulled by four horses each. After the final inspection, the white men walked briskly back into the government building and the three officers began lining up the Indians again and instructed them to follow.

They walked in clusters with the two horse-drawn carriages following. The officers had said that they would be walking to the train station, but the Indians had no idea where that was. They walked for several minutes with nothing in sight other than bush and trees and several long, low wooden buildings like store houses. Then they approached a stretch of two-storey buildings on either side of the wide gravel road. These buildings had wooden pillars and short verandahs outside their doors through which white men and women sauntered in and out. Bullock carts and small canopied one-horse carriages waited outside these shops and supplies were being loaded in sacks, barrels and boxes by Indian and African labourers. The scene was not much different than in small towns back home, but while many modern buildings were being erected here most of the existing buildings were much more rustic. In India, local labourers had worked with Raj officers to build sturdy and architecturally well-designed buildings of brick, cement and stone. The Indians noticed that here work had started, but still was not as advanced as in India. There were several crews along the way working on brick structures. The Indians' attention was drawn to African men dressed in short loin cloths and Indian men in nothing but white *dhotis* carrying loads of bricks in baskets slung on wooden rods across their shoulders to construction sites on either side of the gravel road they were traversing.

The groups walked on, attending from time to time to the children who gripped on to parents and friends when they got tired. The gravel underfoot was rough and stony in places and hurt their bare feet. After another half hour they walked past a small red-roofed brick building surrounded by a high brick wall. They could see a cross standing on a small roof pillar and a chimney with gently rising whiffs of smoke. But what caught their attention was the line outside the gate. There were more than twenty people lined outside in various positions, each appearing to be sick or in pain. There were men and women, Indian and African, some kneeling, some bent over and others standing or leaning against the wall.

"Clinic?" Purat whispered to Amir. They were familiar with similar clinics in and around Muzzafarnagar and had seen more on their long walk to Calcutta. Amir nodded and the groups kept looking curiously as they continued their walk. It was a full two hours that brought them to a small wooden red-roofed station and behind it they could see railway lines. Beside the low-roofed station, there was a huge structure being built with the walls towering above the present structure and part of the curved iron, arch-shaped roof was already in place.

The men knew that the huge train station in Calcutta looked like this one being built. There was another large building being built opposite the train station with most of its brick walls in place and the men raised their heads to admire the tall central tower which was being erected. Hundreds of workers, Indian and African, were hauling loads of brick, iron rods and other material on their backs, sweating even though dressed only in loin cloths. The groups led by the three officers were ushered into the train station. Their trunks were off loaded in the midst of the throngs rushing about outside. African and Indian men were hurriedly carrying the trunks in and depositing them beside the railway tracks.

The groups stood on the slightly raised cement platforms anxious about next steps. The children were tired from their long walk and were leaning against worried parents. A train pulled slowly into the station its steam rising in heavy smoke puffs and seeing it, the tired children perked up excitedly. The officers directed Anpu's group to get on to the front cars and they were required to load their own trunks. Anpu hurried over to Amir, Purat and the others for a quick goodbye before lifting his heavy trunk on to the car then jumping off to help his uncle and other men. One of the officers headed toward the back cars with several other white men and a few white families of women and children. That train pulled out of the station after half hour and the Indians on the platform looked briefly into the first class cars toward the back of the train, seeing just the tops of bright orange cushioned seats. The caboose looked like a little verandah and two smartly dressed white men in long pale green coats and stiff white collars smoked pipes as they chatted amiably, gesturing with their pipes.

Another long, hungry wait and then the arrival in the opposite direction of a black smoke-puffing train, longer than the first. The two officers directed the remaining groups toward the open coal burning engine car and into the third class front cars. Amir and his friends helped all the other passengers load their trunks before lifting their own on board. The families clustered together on the long, low wooden benches that stretched across the entire width of the car leaving a narrow aisle at one end. The trunks were pushed under the benches leaving little room for feet and legs. But the tired travelers were content to finally be seated cross-legged on the seats.

The children, hungry and tired, curled up against their parents and even adults leaned against one another too tired to look at the frenetic activity continuing on the platform. Amir fingered the two strings around his neck and rubbed the metal key that hung from one of them. He knew that his mother had packed a few, not easily perishable, dry lentil cakes, wheat biscuits, tamarind sweet-sour treats and sweet sugar balls. He would offer these to the children when the train pulled out.

The train puffed out of the train station heading north. Curiosity and awe replaced hunger and fatigue as the Indians stared out of the windows watching the fronts of houses for some stretches and the backs along others as the railway track wound steadily away. While some houses were small brick structures most appeared to be wooden with red corrugated tin roofs. The unusual thatched roofs on some houses caught their attention. Even brick and stone houses had these thatched roofs. Some of them had horse-drawn wagons in front of the doors. They also looked curiously at small mud huts clustered together in open areas between cement houses. There were African women seated in front of some, busily working with what looked like straw. Babies and children ran around playing naked, laughing, singing, chasing a goat occasionally. The children on the train laughed as they watched and munched on the treats that Amir had given them. When the railway track passed the ocean in one stretch, the blue serenity of the sea had an odd allure for this group of tired passengers even though their memories of crossing the *kala pani* held pain as well. The abundance of green vegetation, trees, shrubs, flowering plants and many birds were welcome sights to their tired eyes. However, exhausted from their eventful day, many of the adults and most of the children were asleep after the first hour.

Amir and Purat continued to stare quietly out at this new land. The train passed sugarcane fields on rolling hills, lush green, magnificent swaths separated by narrow pathways, stretching over the tops of the hills, forming geometric patterns like those on some saris back home. The train stopped at the large Umgeni station and two smaller train stations before it pulled into a station with a small white church abutting almost into the railway platform. Here the train driver and his soot-covered mates got off the train. The smartly dressed station guard blew his whistle indicating his request for attention.

"Avoca station!! One hour stop!"

The officers who had supervised the boarding of the indentured Indians now walked briskly along the platform into the third class car. They called out the names of the men in two clusters and instructed them to disembark. Rajiv, Bhodraj, Bhimnad and Himal's group was called and they hurriedly began off-loading their heavy trunks. Amir and Purat helped their friends and with heavy hearts returned to their seats. The groups on the platform were organized, counted and lined up by the officers. They were hauling their trunks on to bullock carts. Amir looked through windows on both sides. He smiled as he looked at the huge tamarind tree in front of the tiny church, "Just like *Matha-ji's* tree," he thought. His mother loved that tree in front of their little home in Muzzafarnagar. From the opposite window he saw a rustic tin structure just a few feet from the train track and gasped as he watched a bullock cart cross the lines behind the train and pull up by the shack with Adam and his family following behind. Now Amir grabbed Purat and together they kneeled on the benches staring. Was this the shop that Adam was being assigned? They leaned out the window shouting "Adam *Bhai*, Adam *Bhai… areh…* look Adam…*areh!! Bhayah…* brother!!"

Adam saw them waving and waved back pointing at the tin shack.

"My shop, my house *Bhayah…* mine!" he laughed.

"*Areh* good, good, *Bhayah*!! May God be with you…"

Adam was interrupted by the African men unloading his trunk and his attention was diverted as were Amir and Purat's by the officers returning on to the train.

"We have several more stations till we get to our final destination in Tongaat. Amir, your group will be getting off two stations from here at the station called Phoenix. You will first pass Inanda station, don't get off there, it's just a short stretch from there to Phoenix where your group will get off. We have a little while longer here as other passengers get off so we will start again shortly."

Some of the indentured men wandered on to the station looking for a latrine. They found one at the very north end of the platform backing on to a wooden fence separating the station from the small graveyard behind the church. The tiny latrine marked "Coolies" was similar to the one at the harbour depot and soon Sajiv and Parvati took their children too. Other Indians lined up as well.

Amir and Purat settled back into their benches, legs crossed under them, looking at the bustling activities on the platform. Beyond the station were softly rolling hills, not steep, with paths on which several carts had started moving. There were several wooden and brick houses, some small, some larger, well-spaced along the gravel road and up the slight hills. Sugarcane fields were beyond the houses and some shacks could be seen far off. They saw two horse-drawn carriages with canopies coming toward the train. The horses were guided right on to the small platform and for the second time Amir gasped. He and Purat stared at Andrew Landers standing on the platform with his arm around a small, neatly dressed white woman wearing a pale blue ankle length dress, a white shawl on her shoulder, black lace-up boots and a small blue hat. Andrew was directing the loading of two trunks and several wooden crates on to one of the horse-drawn carriages. Amir and Purat had not seen Andrew board the train, but the central station had been so busy and the first class cars stretched from the middle of the train to the back.

"That's Mr. Landers. He is getting off here!! What is the name of this place? Ahh... *aachah*, all right...this is called Avoca. So Sir will be a master here," Amir said pointing to the sign on the station. Andrew helped Annie climb into the carriage and he followed. The driver then egged the horse out of the station and Amir and Purat watched it go slowly along the dirt road, taking the fork on the right.

The third class was quite empty now with only the three small groups as the train headed out of the station. A few Indians and Africans had boarded in Avoca. They were without luggage, the two Indian men with just small string bags on their laps. As the train chugged slowly past the small tin-roofed Avoca station, it went on to a high bridge overlooking a swollen river.

"*Areh* look... look! How close to the road is the river!! And over there – look isn't that Mr. Landers' carriage?" Amir pointed to the narrow gravel road running along the river with almost no shore between road and river. Andrew's carriage was indeed moving along having gained a trot, heading west. There were tin shacks beyond the narrow road and also along the small road leading up a hill which the carriage passed. Amir and Purat lost sight of the road as the train pulled away and into dense sugarcane plantations for several miles. The river re-appeared once and then no more. The passengers made themselves comfortable some stretching out on benches now with the added space and soon the monotonous chugging of the coal-fired engines lulled them to sleep. Amir quietly looked out the window as Purat stretched out beside him on the bench, snoring softly.

Chapter 4

The Estate

For half an hour the train slowly travelled through nothing but sugarcane fields, lush and green for miles on either side of the track, on flat ground, and on gently rolling hills. That headache that had started after the storm on the ship came back this morning and Amir leaned his head on the window lost in thought about his home, his parents, his brother Gulab and apprehensive about his new job.

A river, much bigger than the first, came into sight along the left side of the train and soon the train entered the high dual track bridge crossing over the sparkling expanse. Another half hour along, still lush with cane fields on either side and the train began a slow approach to the Inanda station for a short stop. The two African men disembarked here and the train continued on to the Phoenix station. The passengers sensing the change in speed had all sat up with faces glued to their windows.

The Phoenix station was bigger than the one in Avoca. The low wood and iron station office, a little longer than Avoca's had a pleasant pole-supported sunny verandah. Amir and Purat handed their small cotton shoulder bags to Parvati to hold while they helped Sajiv with his trunk as the family disembarked. Young Yathindra held little Minati's hand and kept her close to their mother. Amir, Purat and Sajiv went back to help other passengers with their trunks.

Even though it had warmed up considerably, the rays of afternoon sun from the west were a welcome respite. The children stood on the verandah happy after their restful sleep, but they were hungry. No one had had a meal since the morning breakfast at the depot. Parvati dug in her cotton bag and gave them more tamarind balls to chew. The trunks were loaded on to bullock carts by African workmen and the group waited for the officers.

"You will be taken to the Campbell Estate by your estate manager. We are just waiting for his arrival."

The officer had a kind, reassuring manner and the indentured Indians felt at ease.

The estate manager arrived by horse and buggy a short while later. He was a tall, middle-aged tanned man with blue eyes and a short beard and was dressed in a grey long coat, starched collar, tight pants and tan boots. He shook hands with the officer and standing out of earshot of the Indians they talked for a while, exchanged paperwork and then the officer boarded the train and they watched the train leave, heading north again toward what they knew to be Tongaat.

"Right!! So you are my lot, eh!! Quite! Gather around and listen. Your trunks will be taken by bullock cart to your barracks. You will follow this man to the estate." From behind him and standing in the space between the station and some trees, an Indian man stepped out. He was dressed in western work clothes, khaki pants and shirt with a thick belt around his paunchy stomach. In the bustle of the station, the indentured group had not noticed him. Smiling, he came forward and spoke in Hindi.

"*Namasthe*. I am your *Sirdar*, Gobind. This is the Manager Mr... Walker...eh...Sir. Once your trunks are all loaded you will follow me."

Mr. Walker climbed on to his carriage and whipping the horses took off around the station to the road behind.

The *sirdar* Gobind, gesturing to the group, followed on foot, leading the group to the gravel road behind the station. Here there were several structures, some double storey, some single, some were brick and most were wood and iron with red tin roofs. They started west on the gravel road at first, but then cut behind some of the buildings and into more wooded areas along footpaths. Gentle hills and bright flowers made for pleasant surroundings and in several of the valleys they saw clusters of mud and log thatch-roofed huts with African women busy working in small vegetable gardens or creating baskets from dried straw. They walked for half hour before they saw the river that they had crossed by train. It had narrowed considerably here and a walking bridge stretched across to the other side.

"Not far now," Gobind called out smiling but distracted as he waved his stick to and fro and kept his eyes on the grass underfoot in some places. The reddish black ground was covered with brushes and grass along the footpath, but further in the bushes on either side were lush trees.

Beyond the bridge the scenery became splendid as groves of peach trees, avocado and small clusters of mango trees came into view. A manicured garden stretched as far as the eye could see on either side of them. Then a magnificent white gabled, two storey house came into view. The canvas awnings over the windows were blue and tan striped and climbing vines hugged the house on either side. So many windows! Nothing like the white officers' homes back home which were heavier brick or stone-covered sedate structures. This house had a whimsical, fairy tale look, like what Amir had imagined the hunting palaces of Rajahs would be like though he did not imagine them white-walled when his mother told him stories as a child.

He imagined them brown or tan in the jungles of India. But this structure was as delicate as a summer breeze. They noticed several Indian men bare-backed tending to the sprawling flower garden. Amir recognized the much loved frangipani tree! This one though did not have any of its delicate white flowers, perhaps June is not the rainy season here as in India, he mused. There were also several hibiscus shrubs. His mother loved to pray with those!

Their *sirdar* called out and led them on to the pathway that by-passed the house toward the back where stables could be seen further behind. A gravel road led from the stables to a public road south of the grounds. They followed this road another ten to fifteen minutes and noticed a row of small, neat brick buildings with manicured gardens and small white children playing around them. In one of the homes there was an Indian *ayah*, nanny, carefully minding two small children. Near the door of one of the homes, in a small driveway, the group recognized what looked like the horse-drawn, small-roofed buggy that the manager had ridden from the station.

Several more minutes brought the group to tin barracks. There were three rows of tin structures with small well-trodden dirt laneways separating them. The small front spaces for each tin shanty had fire pits with iron grills over them. The eerie silence caught the group's attention. It was mid-week, around four in the afternoon and no-one was around, not even women and children. The *sirdar* took the group to the back row of shanties and instructed them to occupy the shanties two people in each. Amir and Purat waited until the other people selected theirs, Sajiv's family occupying the seventh room in the row and Amir and Purat stood in front of the last one.

"You will find some rations, supplies in your room. Your trunks will be brought here in a short while. You will start work tomorrow. In the morning at five o'clock you will hear a horn and then you must start walking to the cane fields. You will work until six o'clock in the evening when you will hear another horn and you can walk back here."

Amir raised his hand.

"*Sahib* where are the cane fields?"

"Over there." Gobind pointed to stretches of fields in the distance about a mile away past clusters of huts and grassy terrain. There were cows grazing in the fields and African boys could be seen tending the cows. The sugarcane fields dipped down a small hill first then stretched both south and north of where they were standing.

"Sir, where should we go?"

"Keep walking straight from here...see that way...you will come to the cane field. I will be there and show you your sections to do your cutting. *Pangas* will be given to you for cutting the cane, but you must return them to the sugarcane carts at the end of each day's work."

"Yes Sir." The men rolled their heads sideways as they listened.

Gobind strode off back up the road the way they had come. The men looked at one another, some shrugging and some confidently entering their new homes. Amir and Purat made sure that Sajiv's family was all right, and then they returned to their room. It was small about six feet square with a dusty dirt floor, one small window and a wooden entrance door. Inside were two cots with straw mattresses and a rolled up blanket on each.

There was a small table and three rectangular wooden boxes on which to sit. On top of the table were several small hessian sacks. Peering inside the men recognized pouches of rice, lentils, flour, salt and other pulses and grains. There were no pots or pans.

They wandered outside and joined other men looking around at their surroundings. There was a well south of the barracks which had tin bowls stacked neatly. They drew some water and returned to the barracks offering it to Sajiv's family and others in the group. Wandering behind the barracks toward the cane fields the men located the latrines set back behind a small hill, but close to the winding public road. Amir guessed that it needed to be near the road so night soil buckets could be picked up as was the case in towns in India. There were three tin latrines, each with a step up to a wooden platform with a hole and a bucket underneath. There were also two small wooden structures further left of the latrines for bathing.

Amir, Purat and Sajiv wandered back with the other men in their group.

"Sajiv, you are here as a priest. What did the recruiters tell you? Will you be working on the fields? And will your son have to work?"

"No *Bhayah*. My son is learning the priesthood and my wife and daughter will be helping me set up a temple. About ten years ago, our Indian leaders in India lodged a complaint with the British Raj about the bad treatment of Indians being taken to their many colonies. They made many demands which the *goras*, white people, had to agree to because they needed Indians to work their sugar fields. Here the African Chiefs do not let their people become slaves to the cane fields so the British had to agree to some terms. So allowing priests to come was one of them. They also now have The Protector of Immigrants in each colony."

"How do you know all this?"

"Fortunately, *Bhayah*, my family back home is on good terms with the local British officers, always talking, always helping to make peace. Also, I was able to read a lot in their government offices and I made sure I asked a lot of questions."

"That's good, Sajiv. Because I am worried, seeing that there are no women or children left here in the barracks. They must be also working in the cane fields. I wonder if that is the case. Cane work is very hard."

The friends nodded and then noticed that the bullock cart with their trunks was pulling up on the road to their barracks. The men rushed to it and started to carry their trunks to their rooms. As they did so they heard the loud wailing of the horn gaining in crescendo then subsiding to a long low sound at the end.

"That must be the six o'clock siren. Our neighbours will soon be back," Amir smiled as they pushed the heavy trunks to the rooms.

The trunks were quickly opened and many of them found pots and spices inside and soon several of the fire pit grills had rice and *dhal* lentils bubbling for the evening meal.

It was more than an hour later that the indentured labourers slowly returned from the fields, hot, sweaty, tired and staring curiously at the new group. The new group stared incredulously, as they saw children as young as four years old, walking with their mothers looking tired and worn out. There were five children ranging in age from four to twelve. Amir, Purat, Sajiv and the other men jumped up and rushed with outstretched arms to their new neighbours.

"*Bhayahs*!! We are your new friends!"

Many of the men returned the greeting with enthusiasm, but some, either too tired or not interested, simply grunted and headed for the other rows of tin shacks. Amir noticed that the five children were spread among three families, two families of which had a husband, wife, a boy and girl, and one was a single woman with a four-year-old little boy. Amir had seen children working in India but here, so far from home, it broke his heart to see that little boy. Later when the new group was seated outside in a circle on the ground eating their meal, Amir asked Sajiv,

"*Bhayah* that little boy, his mother seems alone. Will Parvati talk to her?"

"*Aachah* Amir…but maybe tomorrow evening. Tonight we just need to settle down."

***

Life on the estate in those first few days was tense, tiring and hard, not because of heavy lifting but more because everything was new. They had arrived mid-week so they had only the Thursday, Friday and Saturday to work until their day of rest on Sunday. It was a strange land, with new customs and bosses whose English was hard to understand. They needed to get used to the habits of even the other indentured labourers.

Amir and Purat, both early risers, awoke a full hour before the five o'clock siren each morning. They had found wild peach trees on their way back from work on the first evening and had collected several twigs to brush their teeth and scrape their tongues. After morning ablutions, they cooked the morning porridge for their row of shacks.

"Amir, why don't they have pumps for water here like we have in our villages? There is a river nearby?"

The two were seated at the door of their shack on Saturday morning, eating their porridge.

"Yes, I don't know Purat. Did you notice that they are still building stone and cement buildings? This is a new place even for the *goras*. They are still progressing. But maybe closer to their sugar mill? I don't know if the mill is close to the river. It would need some kind of wheel, *nayh*?

These and many other questions kept the men amiably talking as the horn sounded, and with the other workers they started their nearly half hour long walk to the edge of the cane fields.

The three rows of barracks housed close to fifty labourers who were divided into three groups. Amir's group had been dispersed to other groups, but Amir and Purat stuck together. In their group, there was one family, the one with the twelve-year-old boy and eight-year-old girl. The father's name was Ramsamy, the mother was Meena, the son was named Krishna and the little girl was Devi. The children worked diligently alongside their parents.

"*Bhayah,*" said Ramsamy amiably to Amir and Purat. "Our work group must cut this block of the cane field," he gestured widely to about a five hundred square yard block of long cane stalks.

Ramsamy explained that they must chop each stalk into two feet lengths, bundle them using aloe string and load the bundles on to bullock carts.

"Where do the carts take the bundles?" Purat asked.

"*Areh*, long way… that way to the mill," he said pointing north.

"We will slowly move toward the mill block by block…you will see it."

As the group picked up their *pangas* from the cart already stationed in the field, Amir noticed that Meena took one, but the children did not take a *panga*. Ramsamy explained that the adults cut and the children bundled the stalks and loaded them on to the carts. He said that it takes each group four days to work their patch and then they are moved to the next. The first day on the job the new group brought no lunch.

They did not think of it so they would have gone hungry until their night meal. But the family shared their meagre rations of which Amir and Purat took very little making sure the children ate. Subsequently, they packed a small amount of food and water in containers scrounged from the yard and from others in the barracks. Some were fortunate to have packed tiffin lunch tins in their trunks.

The *sirdar* Gobind had come by to watch the group and Ramsamy stopped talking, busying himself in silence. Gobind just stood and watched for a few minutes then proceeded north to other groups of labourers.

"No talking, *Bhayah*...sirdar gets angry." Meena and the children kept their heads down. The sugarcane plants were tall, dwarfing the workers. The growth was thick and the walking lanes were very narrow as they worked row by row.

The children collected the cut stalks from their parents, deftly removing the long leaves off the stem and piling them to be once again cut into two feet lengths.

The children then bundled them into twenty piece bundles and tied them with strips of aloe found on the *panga* cart. The boy, like his father, wore only a *dhoti* and Devi wore a long patterned skirt and short top. Her nose and ears were pierced with rings. She worked with the efficiency of a seasoned adult.

The group worked silently until the six o'clock siren. The walk back was silent as they were all tired. That evening before eating, Amir and Purat bathed and washed their *dhoti*s with the scarce well water. Taking clean *dhoti*s from their trunks the friends set up their little prayer shrine inside their room.

There were wooden wall beams across each tin wall and choosing the wall facing east Amir and Purat reverently set the small clay *Ganeshji* statues that their mothers had packed in their trunks together with a clay lamp, a little bottle of oil and some cotton wicks that their mothers had lovingly tied together in small bundles tucked inside their trunks. They picked wild flowers growing nearby for their prayer place and felt at ease knowing that each morning after ablutions and before sunrise they would now be able to light their *dhiya* and pray.

On the Sunday morning after breakfast, Sajiv's son Yathindra went to sit and talk with Ramsamy's son Krishna. Parvati, leaving her daughter Minati with Sajiv, went to see the single mother with the four-year-old boy.

"*Areh Behn*…sister…are you there?" She called from the shack door. There was no response, so she called a few more times and the door opened. The woman, young and thin, dressed in a clean yellow sari had her hair knotted on top of her head revealing striking features and bright eyes. Unlike Parvati, there was no red dot on her forehead, which was the sign of wifehood. She was freshly bathed and her bare feet, hands and nose had tiny rings of jewelry. She stepped aside and gestured for Parvati to come inside. The little boy was sitting on one of the two cots eating a bowl of porridge.

"*Namasthe Behn*…I hope I am not disrupting…" Parvati started.

"No no…I was just feeding Ashok…it is nice to have a visitor…no one comes…" and her voice trailed off into silence.

"What a beautiful boy!" Parvati placed her hands on the boy's head and then cracked the fingers of both her hands against her temples. The young woman smiled brightly at this loving act of blessing. Parvati noticed the boy's eyes and though startled did not show her surprise. His eyes were light green.

"My name is Sibani…" and seeing Parvati break out into a wide smile she added, "Yes, I too am named after Parvati, Lord Shiva's wife!" And the two women touched each other's hand warmly.

Sibani looked quietly at Parvati for a minute and then said, "I know you have seen Ashok's eyes, *Behn*. I know you are wondering…"

"*Nayh nayh…*"

"No, its okay. I can tell you."

Sibani took a deep breath. Keeping her eyes on Ashok, she rubbed her forehead as if deep in thought. Parvati stayed quiet.

"I came here with my husband nearly five years ago. He was recruited in Calcutta. We had just been married and were living in the shanty town near a bridge by the Hooghly River. Life was very hard for a labourer like my husband and my father had used most of his savings for my dowry. My husband did day labour going to the end of the bridge and waiting for wagons to come by from rich people or construction people who needed workers."

She picked up Ashok in her arms. He had finished his porridge and she gave him the wooden spoon and metal bowl to play with and gently placed him just outside the door. The child, a worker in the field, now eagerly busied himself digging the sand and cooing, a child playing.

"One day a man, an Indian man, just like us came to that spot and instead of offering them construction work offered the group of men a chance to come to Natal as sugarcane labourers."

"But, *Behn*, I thought that they only recruited Indians from farms and cane fields," Parvati interrupted.

"Maybe so, but the recruiter saw that these were strong young men. He offered them a free passage and promised that life in this new land was rosy…lots of money…lots of opportunities. And he convinced my husband that after five years he could own land here. That was the best news and even his parents agreed that this would be the land of great fortune."

"The sea passage was very difficult. Many fights on board and the women had to protest loudly before we were allowed to have a screened off section for us to sleep in the crowded steerage compartment. But we were happy to arrive here on this estate. But that is when the trouble began…"

Sibani became silent. After several awkward moments Parvati placed her hand on hers and just sat quietly watching Ashok playing.

"I was only a bride of a few months…and when we arrived at the station I was the only woman and I could see that the white man… the fat manager who met the train with the *sirdar*…the tall one with moustache and green eyes…was looking at me strangely. But we arrived at our room and were happy to be together and hopeful to start our new life. But the next morning as we woke up in this shack…this same shack…" she started to sob.

Parvati moved closer and held her hands, not rushing her…not saying anything…just sharing her silent anguish. Sibani wiped her eyes on her sari *aanchal*, the part that went around her shoulder and regaining her composure continued.

"The *sirdar*…he told me…" She stopped. Then taking a deep breath she continued, "He told me that I could not go with my husband to the field…that I had to stay in the shack for a while. My husband protested, but he screamed at my husband to go, showing him his leather whip and lying that women only worked in the afternoons. The *sirdar* left and my husband followed him to the field."

The sobbing now was wracking Sibani's breath.

"I just sat in the room alone not knowing what was going on. Then he came..." She fell silent.

"Who came, *Behn*? Did someone hurt you?"

Sibani nodded her head gesturing 'yes' and continued.

"That white manager, the one I saw at the station... came into the shack. I screamed, but he put his hand on my mouth. He tried at first to calm me down speaking softly. But when I continued to cry and scream he became angry and shoved me on the bed, pinning me down. He said all wives must do this."

Parvati gasped, speechless. Her bright features and usually friendly eyes froze in an expression of horror. Sibani, now with steel determination continued.

"He raped me... repeatedly."

Now both women were crying, but noticing that Ashok had turned around and was staring at them, they both dried their eyes and pretended to be cheerful, calling out to him and engaging him in conversation.

Parvati quietly asked, "Your husband? Did you tell him?"

"No, not at first. How could I tell him? Such shame...I brought such shame. I went to the field that first day, but could not find him. I learned that he was on a different work crew and the other workers looked at me with accusing eyes. That manager attacked me several more times always the same story...the *sirdar* would come early in the morning... tell me to stay behind...the *memsahib* needed me...and always the same hell. Only the next four or five times the manager came prepared with a gag for my mouth so I would not scream."

She thought for a moment, then added, "What about the other women in the shacks? Did this happen to them? I keep wondering but I don't know...there were only two other women here that first year and I never found out. But there are two other barracks on this estate for Indian workers... maybe other women did suffer the same way...I don't know..." Her voice trailed off.

They heard some men returning from walks and conversations start up in the yard. But Parvati stayed, sitting quietly, not rushing this wounded soul.

"Then two months after our arrival I knew I was pregnant. I wanted so much for the baby to be my husband's…I was terrified that my baby would be the manager's. And then my Ashok was born. At first my husband did not notice his fairer skin and green eyes. Ashok was at my breast most times that my husband was home so he did not see. But I knew there will be trouble."

After a deep breath she continued.

"It was when Ashok started to sit up and look at his father…around six months old that my husband flew into a rage one Sunday. He hit me fiercely…calling me *kusbin*…bitch… and just screaming with no heed to the crowd that had gathered at our door. He then left and went for a walk. The people followed for a while, but they thought that he had calmed down so they went back to their shacks. But just as I put Ashok down for his nap my husband returned. He was holding a flaming piece of wood from the fire pit. I saw what he had in his hand and wanting to protect my baby I ran into the yard and my husband set my sari on fire jabbing the burning wood into my crotch.

"I rolled on the ground by which time other men got hold of my husband and restrained him. He dropped the firewood and ran toward the railway station. The men did follow, but they are not allowed to go further than that from the estate. The two women helped me into one of their shacks and treated my burns."

She lifted her sari and showed the severe burn marks up both her legs and one deeply gouged wound, still unhealed, near the top of her thigh close to her crotch. Parvati was stunned as she stared at that hole and saw what looked like thigh-bone, but Sibani laughed bitterly, "The burns had me confined to my bed for the next several weeks and good thing…no more visits from that bastard *gorawallah* manager."

Parvati was not smiling, shock and anger written all over her face.

"Those two women took care of me…in the morning before work and at night when they came back. The *sirdar* had arranged for the white doctor to come, but only once. It was those sisters who administered the salves and changed the bandages. They are no longer here. They were close to the end of their contracts and left after a year. I don't know where they went…probably working for some *memsahib* or maybe working in the city."

"And what about your husband?"

"I think he's dead." She looked at Parvati with blank eyes.

"How do you know, Sibani? He must have had a contract…the estate or the British officers must have looked for him…*nayh?*"

"Well…you know that the sea is only a few miles beyond the railway station…going that way?" Sibani pointed east. "There was a story… many months later, which the men in the barracks heard from fishermen in the shops by the station. There was a body washed up on the shore. They don't know who the man was. The authorities took the body away. In my gut I know that might have been my husband. I don't know if he still had his indenture number disc around his neck. I know nothing. And even if it was him would the estate owner tell us? They have deemed that he ran away…they are not paying me any money owing to him. Do they pay when a husband dies?"

Parvati looked confused and Sibani continued.

"As a woman, we get paid only half of what the men are paid. They get ten shillings a month and an extra shilling for each year of their contract. But me? I am only given five shillings…no extra shilling each year."

Ashok had stood up and he came inside wrapping his arms around his mother.

"Look at my strong boy, *Behnji*!! Ashok make *Namasthe* for *Mausi*… Aunty."

The boy hid behind his mother.

"*Behn*…when you see his little hands picking up the pieces of sugarcane and placing them carefully in a bundle…now he can pick up two! One in each hand!" Her voice trailed off, the smile that her child brought to her strained face fading slowly.

"When Ashok was a baby, I tied him on my back as I cut cane in the fields. He was such a good baby. My breast fed him until two years ago…now I take food for us to work."

The smile crept back as she said, "You know some days I still carry him on my back to work." She laughed. "He loves the ride!"

The women talked amiably for a while longer and Parvati went back to her shack promising to come back each evening.

Back at their shack, Sajiv and a few men were seated cross-legged on the ground talking. Yathindra was back and sitting on the doorstep while Minati was inside reading quietly from lessons that her father had assigned to her. Parvati averted her eyes and went inside, covering her head with the *aanchal* of her sari. After a few minutes she called out for Yathindra and sent him out with a pot of rice and *dhal* mixed together ready to be cooked into *kitchri*.

The men, understanding, left, greeting Sajiv as *"Punditji"* and wobbling their heads amiably, they walked to their various shacks where many chores awaited them on this their only day off. Parvati busied herself at the fire pit not saying anything at all about her visit. That would have to wait until their children were asleep.

Chapter 5

A Community

That first Sunday, Amir and Purat ventured back toward the train station following the same path that they had taken upon arrival. The reddish black earth felt good under their bare feet and they strayed from the footpath in places to go nearer the trees placing their work-worn hands reverently on the trunks, rubbing the bark and feeling the leaves between their fingers. It had rained a little the night before and the smell of earth… of nature… after gentle rain was intoxicating.

"Now it's June…maybe they don't get the monsoons like we get at this time, *nayh* Amir?"

"I don't know, Purat. I think their summer will come many months from now…maybe then?"

The friends chatted as they approached the foot bridge. They did not step on to the bridge right away, but walked along the water's edge bending and cupping water in their hands and washing their faces reverently.

"Ahhh…*pani*…water… Purat…flowing gently…I love rivers, Purat. I remember the river near Muzzafarnagar. That same river wound up in your part of the village too, you were so close?"

"*Areh*…yes…we were rascals. Once my friends and I jumped in naked! We did not know some girls were peeping from behind those bushes, until they stole our *dhoti*s and hung them on trees further up the hill!"

Amir laughed at his friend and Purat slapped his back as they walked over the bridge. The walk was more relaxed than the week before as they were able to see far on either side of the footpath. There were many different kinds of houses, some brick with curved front windows and others were more rustic wood and iron structures. These were lined on either side of the winding road on which bullock carts and horse-drawn carriages slowly moved along. There were front gardens with roses, agapanthus, and hydrangeas and around the homes closer to the river they admired what looked like white lilies, different from the water lilies that they were used to back home. As they neared the top of the gentle hill approaching the railway station, there were large patches of well-tended vegetable gardens. Succulent green cucumbers on long tendrils stretched all the way to the footpath.

At the top of the slope, they stepped on to the road that had lines of shops on either side and across from the railway station. The road was busy with people, mostly Indian and a few Africans, carrying baskets, moving from shop to shop. Some shops were shuttered and closed. Amir and Purat instinctively felt the cloth of the small white bags slung over their shoulders to feel for the few coins they had brought.

These were British coins for which they had exchanged rupees in India at the recruitment office. Even though the white people were using British currency, rupees were still used in villages back home. The indentured men were told that British coins will be needed in Natal. Amir and Purat knew that since they had arrived mid-month their pay from the sugar plantation would only be five shillings at the end of the month rather than the ten shillings promised per month.

"*Bhayah*, let's go see what is in some of these shops," Amir tugged at Purat who was taking in the street scene.

The shops were mostly tin structures, but a few had been improved with brick extensions on the side. Some shops had a second storey that looked like homes with curtains on the windows. A little further northward were some even better structures with curved arches at the entrances. Some had little pole- supported verandahs like the ones they saw in town when they had first arrived.

They ventured into one of these stores. The inside surprised them. Rows of vegetables in wooden crates lined one wall and two aisles to their left. On the right hand wall, on wooden crates and shelving, were Indian pots, pans, bowls, brass prayer *lotas*, urns in different sizes and so much more. At the back wall of the store, sitting low to the floor was a young Indian man with two sturdy money boxes on a low table.

"*Namasthe Bhayah, Namasthe Bhayah*...hello brother," the young man called out to Amir and Purat and gesturing to a young girl much younger than him to take over the money box, he rushed toward the friends. He looked the same age as Amir and Purat and the girl could have been around fourteen.

"Welcome, welcome...*aiyeh*...come, come. My name is Prabhu. Come."

After introductions, Prabhu took Amir and Purat around the store showing his wares as they wove their way around other customers.

"And this is my little sister Bhagirathi." The girl pulled her shawl across her mouth and lowered her eyes. "*Areh...Namasthe bolo*...say hello," he exhorted his sister laughing, but the girl looked sideways shyly.

Prabhu explained that the store was his and his father's. His father Ranjith Singh had come almost twenty years ago and was one of the first labourers in the sugar estates nearby. After his indenture had ended, he was allowed to stay and was given a piece of land in exchange for the free passage back that was due to him. Over the years, his father had bought more land piece by piece and now he had a large market garden from which he supplied fresh vegetables daily to his own store and to several white stores.

He proudly touched and picked up bunches of fresh green onions, marrows, bright yellow pumpkins and squash, eggplant, and Amir's favourite okra.

"Your father could buy more land?" Amir asked, thoroughly engaged by this friendly young man of his own age.

"Yes... he and my mother worked hard to cultivate the land and as they acquired more they employed a few Africans who liked to work the land and many Indians too."

As the store became busier, Amir and Purat let Prabhu see to his other customers and using a small part of their money they bought some okra, a few potatoes, onions, oil and other supplies. Bhagirathi took their coins shyly and when the men were not looking she stole a look at them and giggled when they caught her eyes! They laughed amiably and started to walk out. At the door they asked Prabhu where he got his pots, pans and other dry goods.

"*Areh*...there are lots of merchants in the city. We take the train some Sunday afternoons and go to Grey Street. That is where there are bigger stores that supply us smaller shop owners."

"Where do they get their goods?"

"On the ships that come from India. These larger merchants bring everything from India - spices, pots, pans, prayer goods, even the Ramayana and other religious books. Lots of Muslim merchants too, they bring the Quran, clothing...everything"

"*Aachah*! You have lots of customers...all here from the barracks. Where are the white people?"

"On Sundays they go to church in the mornings and in the afternoon some take the train to town. Others take their carriages or the train to the next station called Mt. Edgecombe. There is a Roadhouse Inn where there is a bar. They drink and eat meals cooked by Indian cooks there."

"Oh. Indian cooks. Lots of different jobs for Indians then, *Bhayah?*"

Amir and Purat were impressed. They left and walked past several shops that were closed and came to another open store with an older bearded Muslim man wearing his white prayer cap standing at the entrance.

"*Aiyeh...aiyeh...andhar aiyeh*, come, come, come inside, *Bhayah*... come, come," he beckoned to the friends. Many other shoppers were entering and leaving and the friends shook hands with the man and were guided into the store. This one was a fragrant oasis of spices. Sparkling clean metal trestles, lined up in several rows from door to the back wall, held dried chilies, cumin powder, coriander, cinnamon, turmeric powder and every Indian spice one could think of. Amir and Purat still had spices in their trunks and did not need any, but the aroma in the store was pure intoxication.

They breathed in the flavours of their beloved India and rejoiced in finding a little India here. They noticed a small box with writing paper and pencils selling for a penny each. Both Amir and Purat bought a sheet and pencil each.

"*Bhayah*, how do we send letters back home?"

The man quickly came over to the friends, eager to explain.

"There is a post office near the railway station in town. Many people give their letters to me and when I go to town once or twice a month I take them to the post office. They give me the three pence for mailing. Then the ships take them home."

"You go to the town?"

"Yes, yes…our Muslim brothers are building a big mosque in town… in Grey Street. *Bhayah*, it is going to be beautiful. You should come with me…they have started it and it is half way up…such beautiful arches and the minaret? Oh, for that they will bring special builders from India." He was gesturing enthusiastically seeing the mosque in his mind's eye. "*Bhayah*, my name is Ebrahim. I came ten years ago…one of the first passenger Indians…I am from Delhi…I came to start this shop."

The men once again engaged in animated discussion and discovered that there were several estates close by. Next to their Campbell estate, there was the Acutt Estate and a little further north there was the larger Phoenix Estate. Hundreds of indentured Indians worked on the estates, but also on agricultural and dairy farms, road and railway construction. As well they worked in the white homes and a white roadhouse bar several miles up the main North Coast Road. Fascinated, Amir and Purat shook hands with Ebrahim and agreeing to go to town in two Sundays' time they parted as new friends.

Going home, the friends decided to take the main road rather than the footpath. On either side of the road were several homes, some with small yet exquisite front gardens. This main road gently sloped down the hill and divided into two, one leading toward the footpath and the other winding down and around toward their estate. On the left side, they passed a small white church with a large, well-tended front garden. Many white families were gathered in small groups chatting while children played in the yard. The people walking along the road were quietly respectful as they passed. But at the gate, stood a line of young Indian boys and their fathers. The boys ranged in age from around eight to twelve and they were dressed in sparkling white *dhotis* and loose white tunics. Their fathers in white *pugris*, turbans, light tunics and loin cloths, *dhotis*, stood holding their sons' hands. Curious, Purat asked one of the men why they were there.

"*Angrezzi* English lessons for our sons."

Amir asked who taught them.

"Church *memsahib*…every Sunday after church prayers."

Pleasantly surprised and curious, Amir and Purat waited with the men. Presently a matronly, smiling faced middle-aged white woman dressed in a plain, light blue ankle-length dress, a small blue hat and soft black shoes came to the gate.

"*Aiyeh…aiyeh…*come, come…" she led the boys to the back door of the church and seated them in a semi-circle around her low stool. The fathers followed as did Amir and Purat and all the men sat on their haunches several yards back on the grass at the back of the church. The teacher raised her finger to her lips asking for quiet and then said,

"Good morning, boys," which the boys echoed in unison and then she instructed, "Ready for the Lord's Prayer?" At this all the boys together with the teacher recited,

> *Our Father, who art in heaven,*
> *Hallowed be thy Name.*
> *Thy Kingdom come.*
> *Thy will be done on earth,*
> *As it is in heaven.*
> *Give us this day our daily bread*
> *And forgive us our trespasses,*
> *As we forgive those who trespass against us.*
> *And lead us not into temptation,*
> *But deliver us from evil.*
> *For thine is the kingdom,*
> *The power and the glory,*
> *For ever and ever.*
> *Amen.*

The teacher then looked up and gestured at the fathers,

"*Jhawo…jhawo…ek ghanta…ek ghanta,* go, go now…one hour…one hour."

The fathers stood up wobbling their heads from side to side saying "*Aachah…aachah…*yes…yes…" and walked out to the gate. Amir and Purat were stunned that the woman spoke Hindi and also that these Indian children, some of whom were Hindu and some Muslim were reciting the Lord's prayer. They both recognized the prayer that was said in the little church back home, but they did not recite it at their little school in India. One of the fathers explained.

"*Areh Bhayah*…any prayer is good, *nayh*? But our boys know that our prayers at home are the important ones. But this lady teaches our sons the language and to read and write and to do some arithmetic."

Amir and Purat took their leave at the gate while some of the fathers again sat on their haunches to wait for their sons for an hour, while others walked toward the shops.

A little further down the road from the church, Purat pointed to two farms where there were several cows grazing. In the one closer to the church, there were two white men on horseback slowly moving among the grazing cows supervising several Indian labourers. There were sheds toward the back of the property and Amir could see cows being tended and milked.

The next farm, separated by a wooden fence was much smaller and its field stretched down to the river. On this farm, to the surprise of both the friends, they saw an Indian man on horseback. There were a few cows grazing and the stable was closer to its modest wood and iron house.

"This must be one of our Indian brother's farm, *nayh*…" Purat wondered.

Amir nodded, looking eagerly as he walked and feeling a sense of pride and hope. They walked along the carriage bridge careful to hug the side as bullock carts passed them.

Across the river still on their left hand side there was a low grassy patch at the bottom of a gentle hill. There was a circle of African men and women dressed in long white, full-sleeved robes and the women wore an additional blue tunic over their white gowns while the men wore short green tunics. The men's heads were covered with straw hats while the women wore white cloth turban-type headdresses. They were chanting together and rising and squatting in unison. The sound of the chant was pleasant to the ears of the pedestrians and many stopped on the bridge to watch.

"Prayers…this must be like an African church…but no building?" Amir turned to Purat wondering.

They stood for a while drawn into this service, each thinking back to their parents, their homes, their communities and momentarily lost in the memories of their own *hawan* prayer ceremonies back home. They remembered the aromas of *ghee*, butter, being poured into small ceremonial fires by *pundits* like their friend Sajiv here. After a while they resumed their walk on the gravel road and the homes of their masters came into view clustered together on a branch road.

They walked slowly along to their barracks. Their fellow labourers were busy washing clothes and hanging them on strings between trees, their meagre belongings placed outside while the insides were being cleaned.

The afternoon, pleasant and sunny, smelled fresh and felt peaceful. Amir and Purat cooked their vegetables and shared with Sajiv and his family and then they proceeded down the same path they followed to work each morning toward the cow fields.

Each gathered cow-dung in discarded tin containers and coming back to their room, removed their beds and belongings outside and proceeded to wet the dung and spread it on the floor. Cow-dung floors were warm and smooth rather than the dusty original floors in these shacks. By late afternoon the friends were sitting outside chatting to a few other labourers, the few who had not gone into town on the train. Supper was soon to be cooked in the freshly cleaned outdoor pits.
***

Parvati and Sajiv were sitting quietly on their doorstep. It was growing dark and the children were asleep. As a Hindu wife, Parvati did not address her husband by name.

"*Bapuji?*" She addressed him the same way her children did. "Dear respected father." Sometimes, she addressed him as "Yathindra's dear respected father."

"*Haanhji?*" Sajiv turned to face her, "Yes, respected one?"

"I…eh…today…"

"*Bolo bolo*…say… go on speak freely." Sajiv gently touched her hand.

Parvati slowly, very quietly related to her husband Sibani's story. Sajiv listened with his head bowed. As a priest he had heard many stories back in India about women who were abused, not only by their spouses but also by in-laws and occasionally even by their adult sons. Here during his first week of talking to some of the other labourers he had heard a few stories of conflicts, verbal disagreements and fights and had been asked by two men for advice on prayer and meditation. But this report from Parvati, he knew, would be the first of many stories he would hear that would cause him anguish.

"I will think of a way to give her solace…through you Parvati…we will think of a way." They remained quiet, then he mused, "I have been talking with one of the white managers…I hope it wasn't him…but there are two or three of them…I don't know." They sat together for a while and then moved inside.

"The manager said that we could have a bit of land to build our temple. I will ask for a piece by the river, *nayh?*" Parvati's eyes brightened as she nodded. She checked on her children one on each bed, prepared their own bed on the floor and they turned in for the night.

As darkness fell, Amir and Purat brought their furniture inside their room and lighting their small kerosene lantern placed it on their up-turned wooden box-table. Tired from working on their dung floor, the friends were preparing for bed. They each carefully counted the little money they had and locked some in their trunks and some, wrapped in small pieces of cloth, they inserted into two little holes in their tin wall and extinguished the light on the table. Amir's headache was back and his head was throbbing. He had been making cinnamon poultices from the spices his mother had packed and holding one now to his forehead he fell asleep. The letter to his family back home would have to wait… maybe later in the week.

The five o'clock horn came too soon and so began another week of work. Ramsamy and his family now regularly caught up with them and walked and chatted on the way to the fields. The cane stalks were very tall in these mature fields and the lanes between them loomed dark early in the morning before the sun had fully risen. Behind them in the fields already harvested other men were clearing the dried leaves and debris to start planting new crops.

When their first quadrant was completed midweek, they were assigned their second quadrant, which brought them closer to the adjoining Acutt estate to the west. The heat on some days was quite strong, but with water from their tins it was bearable and their cutting had become faster and more efficient. The following week their assigned quadrant took them much further from their barracks. They needed more time to walk to work as it was further north and very close to the sugar mill.

"Look...look just as you said, Purat...look at that water wheel!"

The mill was a long low structure in front, but high and impressive toward the back. The whole structure ran parallel to the river that was fast flowing in that area. The huge wooden water wheel right next to the river was turning slowly pumping fresh sparkling water first from vane to vane then into pipes which led inside the mill. The sound of the splashing water, together with the sound of the slowly moving vanes around and around created a whispering symphony, calm and serene.

Right outside the huge double doors of the mill there were two upright water pumps with short, curved pump-handles. Several Indian men were carrying buckets of water into the building, while others were lifting bundles of sugarcane off the line of wagons and hauling them inside. Sluices of whitish water could be seen running back into the river. The two men were momentarily mesmerized.

The crack of the whip cut through the silence and Purat's scream was immediate. The second whirring of the whip was interrupted in the split second by Amir's hand shooting upward, gripping the leather which wrapped itself around his palm. Purat was bent over in pain yelling "*Ayee, ayee*," as Amir pulled on the whip and stared into *Sirdar* Gobind's expressionless face.

"No talking...no talking...get back to work!!"

Amir, stoic and silent, pulled the whip out of Gobind's hand and unwound his own palm. He said nothing, just stared with gritted teeth and instead of getting back to work as commanded he bent over his friend. The deep gash on Purat's back was bleeding, but Purat had stood up, the muscles in his strong arms rippling, his legs steady and tall and his head held upright.

"*Aachah, Bhayah*? Are you okay, my brother?" Amir asked quietly.

"Your hand, Amir...it's cut...blood!" Purat tore off a piece from the bottom of his cotton *dhoti* and started to wrap it around Amir's hand.

"*Nayh...nayh*...no...no...its okay, *Bhayah*...it's okay. Let's get back to work."

Sirdar Gobind strode off down the long cane path. His portly frame and upright back could be seen as he marched, whip in hand swinging it with confidence. Other workers looked on afraid to come closer. The friends knew that these men too had suffered a lashing and both just nodded their heads sideways indicating that they were all right. Work resumed.

Picking up their *pangas* they continued cutting the stalks from the roots, chopping them into shorter pieces and wincing with pain as they did. Ramsamy and Meena, obviously concerned kept stealing glances at their work mates, but stayed their distance exhorting Krishna and little Devi to get busy. The six o'clock siren was a welcome relief and the walk home was slower today, but Ramsamy's family stayed with them as the other few men in their group walked ahead. Their path back from work took them past the little shack at the edge of the fields that Gobind used as his office.

Each morning he counted the workers, checked off their names on his list and each evening he did the same. His little office was furnished with an old desk and proper chair and his neat desktop had the trappings of comfort like a tea pot, a cup, a tiffin lunch box and a covered brass urn. Across his chair back was a checkered African blanket neatly folded. This evening as he sat checking off the worker's names he averted his eyes as the last two stopped to have their names called. As was his usual habit, he stayed at his desk after all workers were counted and even as the workers were over the first hill on their way to their barracks. They often looked back to see that he still worked at his desk.

"A lonely man," Ramsamy started, but Amir cut him off with a grunt.

"No! An evil man! He does not have to be cruel to get us to work!"

"He sits there until late into the evening. I have made out his form sometimes at his desk, when I use the latrine as the daylight disappears."

Amir and Purat said nothing, just walking faster now to get to their shack.

At the barracks other groups had already arrived and there appeared to be a commotion in the middle row of shacks. Tired and hurting, Amir and Purat reluctantly joined others to see what was going on. Two of the labourers were screaming at each other, fists lifted and other men were holding them back. Seeing that they were restrained and having seen other arguments and fights before, Amir and Purat turned back and slowly walked to their shack.

"Another fight?" Sajiv looked up from stoking his fire and then realizing that his friends were hurt he sprang up. "What happened?"

"It's nothing, *Bhayah*. Other men suffer worse."

Sajiv sat them down at his fire pit and calling out for Parvati shook his head in frustration.

"We have heard from other men who were beaten and we have tended to some of them, but how do we make this stop?"

Parvati had run back inside and returned with rags, water in a dish and some poultices. Sajiv proceeded to tend to Amir and Purat.

"*Bhayah*, don't worry about us...we will take care of ourselves..." But Sajiv was muttering and dabbing at their wounds and finally wrapped Amir's hand in a clean cotton bandage ripped from his own garment.

"You will eat with us tonight. Sit...sit...be comfortable."

As they ate their evening meal, Sajiv told them about the piece of land he was negotiating for their temple and this took the men's mind off their injuries.

"The manager has said that I can have a piece by the river close to the foot bridge. There is a worker on the neighbouring estate who has helped with building temples in his village back home. The manager here says he can ask that man's manager to release him to build the temple for all three estates."

"We can help too, *Bhayah*...that is wonderful news!" Amir and Purat were excited about this welcome good news.

And so it was that over the next several weeks, work commenced on the first temple for the community. The piece of land released next to the river was really of no use to the Campbell estate. It was not suitable to cultivate cane and the river was too shallow in that stretch for any other technical use. The temple would face eastward toward the river. The Campbell patriarch whom none of the workers had seen close up had apparently told his managers to advise the workers about the acquisition of tin, wood, nails and building materials as well as advise them on proper foundation laying.

The managers, always eager to keep the Protector of Immigrants satisfied, complied. From time to time, old Mr. Campbell or his son could be seen watching from the back garden of their white gabled house at the top of the gently sloping hill above the footpath.

At first Sajiv thought that the temple would be a wood, iron and tin structure, but as the trenches were dug, the builder from the next estate, Gopalsing, advised that some bricks should be used for the front and back walls. The managers agreed since the building, being visible from the main house, had to be aesthetically pleasing to the masters.

Chapter 6

Durban Town

The visit to town with Ebrahim was delayed for several weeks. The men found out that indentured labourers needed permits to venture beyond two miles of their estates. Amir and Purat were not going to ask Gobind. But Sajiv advised that they should in fact swallow their pride and ask. That conversation was to be had at the request of Sajiv who asked to meet Gobind at the temple site. As Amir, Purat and other labourers spent another Sunday morning clearing the ground, Sajiv talked quietly with Gobind. They both walked over to Amir.

"Your permits will be ready next Sunday," Gobind spoke to Amir, but averted his eyes, still remembering Amir's simmering anger. Amir said nothing, but as promised Gobind brought the permits to the site the following Sunday. It bore their names, their indenture numbers and a government stamp.

The men had no idea how the process worked, where the nearest government office was, and who facilitated the permits. For the moment they did not care. They accepted the papers from Sajiv and thanked him, not looking at Gobind at all.

It was on a Sunday two months after their arrival that Amir, Purat and Ebrahim set out to the train station for their trip to town. Tickets purchased, they sat in their third class compartment chatting amiably. By now the friends had received wages twice. For the first half month they received only five shillings and for the second month they received their full ten shillings.

Amir carefully divided his money into three separate cloth pouches, one for his parents, one for his savings as he had vowed to buy land as soon as he could and the third and smallest amount was for his own use.

It was from this pouch that today he carried two shillings to spend.

"Ebrahim *Bhai*, how can I send money to my parents back home?" he asked as the train chugged across the bridge spanning the huge river that they remembered from their first train ride to the estate.

"*Bhayah*, you should not send a lot of money home. We cannot trust the mail. We do not know who handles the mail. I will show you to-day…I have some letters from people to take to the post office by the Central Train Station. You can try…but maybe just send a little and when you know that they get it then you can trust better, *aachah*?"

"Yes…yes…*aachah*…*aachah*," both friends agreed.

The train moved at an even pace for the two hour ride to town. The men chatted animatedly admiring the rich green sugarcane plantations on both sides of the tracks.

At the brief stop at Avoca Station, they peered at Adam's shop with its tin fence, but nobody was in sight. After Avoca, the sugarcane plantations gave way to more developed and inhabited areas as they had seen on their first trip. Some canefields did appear, but not as large as the ones further north.

"*Bhayah*…not much sugarcane fields now?" Amir enquired.

"*Nayh*…these areas are changing to more businesses and houses… you will see white people's nice houses closer to the ocean when we are nearing the town."

"But some of our shipmates went to other sugar estates…"

"*Haanh…haanh*…yes, yes. There are large sugar estates south of the Durban town…big…big… and even bigger estates north of where we live, *Bhayah*. Even one Indian buying sugar estate!"

"*Areh…suchh? Nayh*… true?... No! Indian buying sugar estate?"

"Yes, his name is Bodh Singh. He came almost twenty years ago, first group of indentured. And when he finished his contract he started buying land and planting sugarcane north of where we are…way north…in a place called Stanger."

Amir mused, and rolling his head he said, "*Aachah…bohoth aachah*… good…very good…an Indian…a Singh…*aachah*."

At the Central Railway Station, the three men stepped on to a busy platform. Ebrahim led them briskly to a station office. Because it was Sunday, the only day off for labourers, the government had set up a make-shift office for multiple government-related purposes. There was a line of men and women waiting patiently to reach the one service window.

"What are they doing?"

"They are here for many reasons. Some have complaints that they need to file about their estates..."

Before Ebrahim could finish his sentence both Purat and Amir stuttered together,

"Complaints? The labourers can file complaints?"

"Yes a decade ago the government set up the Protector of Immigrants Office, but on Sundays that office, near the harbour, is not open. The white people go to church on Sundays. But two officers are stationed here. They receive those papers, but it is very hard for labourers to file complaints. They cannot speak English very well and some can only write a little bit and only in Hindi or Tamil or Telugu. So they come with helpers. I have helped a few people in our community, but I cannot always be available, I have my shop."

"Yes, yes we can understand."

"The reason why I am showing you this station office is that you can also drop off mail here to be sent to ships going home. Since the post office and all government buildings are closed on Sundays, the officers do multiple tasks. They collect and load the bags of letters on carts and when they return to their office by the harbour the bags of letters are sent to the ships. So you see, after this office, we don't really know for sure the route of our letters."

The men stood watching for a while and Ebrahim led them outside and across the street to a two storey structure with a flag on the roof.

"See here," Ebrahim pointed to a large structure being erected next to the smaller post office building. "This is going to be the main post office and next to that the town hall is being built."

Amir and Purat had seen these structures on that first day when, tired from the walk from the pier, they had boarded their train.

"Occasionally, especially when I have my own letters to send home and orders for my shop to mail, I come here on a week day to use this main post office. I know my letters are reaching home and the orders for my shop are being filled because I am receiving return letters and also getting all my products from India for my shop. So I trust this main post office."

They stopped outside the post-office building at a public water pump.

"*Areh*! Nice water pump, *Bhayah*. See…just like Muzzafarnagar!" Purat drank first excitedly, his strong body bending over the pump as Ebrahim pumped, gulping the water as it fell into his cupped palms. Their thirst quenched the men continued walking.

"Yes, we have two pumps near the shops where we are going and one near the mosque…for us you know to do *wuzoo*, you know, wash before prayer."

"Yes yes, *Bhayah*…that is good…Purat and I were wondering why there were no pumps on our estate."

"The merchants told me that here in town a British man named Currie built a huge water pump, near the big flower gardens about five years ago."

Amir interrupted, "*Areh*, curry is what they call our *tharkari*…is this man an Indian who built the pump?"

"*Nayh…nayh*…he is a British man…an engineer I think. Only five years ago, so the pumps are quite new. On your estate there is no pump, but on the bigger estates just north of yours there are water pumps. Our river is very good, *nayh*…so more pumps will come, *Bhayah*."

Ebrahim led them past the closed building and headed west through a crisscross of gravel roads busy with pedestrians. Some were wider than others, but all had bustling shops from which people emerged carrying goods. Carriages were trotting by and Amir and Purat were surprised to see Indian people in some of these carriages.

The men were dressed in smart long *kurta* shirts with veiled women next to them, alighting together at shops. It was several streets later that they arrived at Grey Street as Ebrahim excitedly announced to them. The men's faces broke out in smiles. Here was India!! Horse drawn and bullock drawn carriages all along the wide street, shops on both sides, food stalls and tea stalls all along the side of the road. Standing tall half way down the street was the imposing new mosque that looked about three quarters complete.

"Look…look there is our mosque! The smaller one down past it… see there, over there…that is the one we are attending now. But this one…*Bhayah*…this one will be our pride."

The first two levels of the mosque were complete. The majestic curved entranceway built with fine bricks smoothed over with cement bore intricate patterns, delicate, almost filigree-like patterns crafted into the cement. The second floor had a dome situated on the right side, but as Ebrahim explained this was not the main dome. That would be housed on the next floor up, which was still to be constructed. That would form the crown of the building. Across a wide street from the mosque, there were one and two storey red roofed buildings with verandahs bustling with shoppers. A light standard with a lantern on a tall pole stood in the middle of the road.

"How do they get up that pole to light that lantern?" Amir asked as they walked by.

"Gas, *Bhayah*…" Ebrahim laughed, "Yes, some streets now have gas street lights."

Amir and Purat wobbled their heads smiling, remembering that the priests on the ship had explained to them about gas lamps in the lighthouse on the hill as their ship had entered the harbour.

The three men walked from shop to shop peering in or walking into the stores, amazed at the wares on display. There was everything they would need, a home village away from home! Spices, clothing, pots, pans, urns, even furniture from India. As well there were western wares that they recognized from the British Raj back home, tables, assorted western-style chairs, lamps and even western clothing. On side streets there were sprawling outdoor stalls filled with fresh vegetables and fruits. The friends marveled at the freshness and bright colours and chatted excitedly with the men and women vendors.

Ebrahim took them for lunch to a small eating house close to the second, smaller mosque.

"Come come…all *halal* here."

The men were seated at tables and chairs in the crowded room and men in traditional Indian shirts, tight trousers and slippers served them food ordered by Ebrahim. Fresh fluffy *chapatis* and *chana* curry. Amir and Purat noticed that Ebrahim also ate vegetarian, most likely in deference to them.

At the end of an enjoyable morning, the men headed back to the train station for their two hour ride back to the estate. This time when they passed the Umgeni River little more than half hour from town, they noticed another green-domed mosque to their left and to their right along the river was a Hindu temple with a bright red dome and brightly painted avatars along the outside walls. The train chugged along not giving the friends enough time to see these properly.

The track then cut through steep cliffs on either side and Ebrahim explained that these were stone quarries. Stone was needed for the buildings being erected all over the city, especially around the harbour which was being expanded to accommodate more ships stopping in Durban for trade and to bring labourers like themselves.

When the train stopped at Avoca station both Amir and Purat stood up excitedly to look out through the side windows.

"Look, look...Adam's house. *Areh...Bhayah...*now we can see some people...two months and look he has expanded."

Approaching it from the town side, they got a brief glimpse of Adam's property, but the train passed and now they could only see the back. Adam's little shack was now much bigger. It appeared that several rooms had been attached on either side of the original shack and people were crossing the tracks precariously to walk to his shop.

"Amir...that can't be the main entrance to Adam *Bhai's* shop...it looks small."

"Maybe the other side...there...there is a big road...maybe that side is the main entrance," Purat pointed toward the main North Coast Road now behind them.

Ebrahim joined in their discussion and pointed out the road crossing the railway tracks alongside the shop that would be the frontage of the shop. He took them to the left hand window and just behind the train he pointed at another shop with a verandah also facing the main road, but with another entrance at the side road running parallel to the train.

"That shop is also owned by an Indian like your friend Adam. That family's name is Suleiman. It is a big store...big things like wheels for carriages, cupboards, beds...he sells those."

As the train pulled away both Amir and Purat were happy, happy that Indians were everywhere, happy that so many of their countrymen seemed to be successful. They were encouraged that they could be successful too someday.

That afternoon both Amir and Purat sat cross-legged on their beds to write their long overdue letters home. It had been nearly two months and now they were comfortable that they could give their parents heartening news about the new community they were helping to grow here. Each enclosed two shillings, a smaller amount than they would have liked to send, but they heeded Ebrahim's advice. They walked their letters over to Ebrahim's shop knowing that he might go into town again in the next week or two.

Chapter 7

Working Life

The following months took on a routine at the barracks, hard work every day, clearing and building at the temple site on Sundays, occasional fights in the barracks in the evenings, and the children growing in age and confidence. The weather was windy through October and much hotter in November. The fieldwork, difficult though it was, became routine and on some Sundays the friends went to the shops. They had become friendly with Prabhu. They bought vegetables from him and enjoyed their chats. His sister Bhagirathi was happy to look after the sales while they chatted. Amir asked Prabhu about the *Angrezzi*… English lessons at the church and about The Lord's Prayer.

"*Areh…haanh…haanh…yes…yes.* I went there too from the age of eight till I was nearly twelve. My parents don't mind the Lord's Prayer…but it was important for me to learn *Angrezzi* and to learn the arithmetic." Then laughing, he continued, "Every Sunday I'd come back here to the shop, sit my sister Bhagirathi behind the cash box table and teach her too! I would pretend to be the teacher and make her recite the prayer too. My parents just shook their heads, but Bhagirathi enjoyed learning to read and write and especially the arithmetic. That's why she enjoys handling the money for me here at the shop."

The temple foundation was built and in addition two small houses were being built on either side, one to house Sajiv and his family and the other to house temple helpers or, as was customary in India, to offer shelter to desperate people in various circumstances.

Parvati worked alongside her husband and children and she was happy to see that Sibani joined her every Sunday with Ashok along to play at the water's edge. The women had agreed that since Sibani's indenture was in its final year that she would be a temple helper, cooking daily meals for worshippers, cleaning the temple, washing robes, scrubbing urns and sweeping the yard. Sibani was overjoyed at the prospect. It was a good future for her Ashok.

The heat on some days was oppressive with the sun blazing down on sweating bodies and the summer rains waiting for night to fall. The men shortened their *dhoti*s and worked shirtless, several of them thus exposing large slash wounds on their backs. Amir and Purat looked at these signs of abuse and wondered if the men had been slacking or if these were signs of power and control from their bosses. The women hoisted their saris higher and wore blouses with shortened sleeves exposing their arms, not caring about cultural norms for women's attire. The cane stalks were so tall, twice as tall as the men and for the women it felt like they towered above them.

The thick lush growth formed oppressive walls of vegetation around them as they cut away. In the completed work quadrants, the managers often used African men to help them light fires to burn off the debris and prepare the fields for the next crop. These fires added to the unbearable heat. By the end of the day the workers dragged themselves back to the barracks, exhausted, wilted, thirsty and many of them irritable. Some had started drinking cane spirit each night to drown their emotions. They picked up discarded or rotting stalks along the way back, peeled, chopped and boiled them, fermenting the juice for days to make a strong, mind numbing brew. Amir and Purat watched them, not partaking, but knowing that there would be fights ensuing. Sajiv tried counselling but that was a losing battle.

In the middle of December, after a particularly hot day, as the tired labourers worked their way back through the narrow darkening lanes of the cane fields Amir and Purat, without thinking, walked ahead of Ramsamy's family. They always walked behind them, but today the children, Devi and Krishna, being tired and straggling, Ramsamy let the friends pass. Too tired to chat, the workers plodded along. It was the rustling of sugarcane stalks that caught their attention before little Devi's screams. She was snatched and in the split second all they saw were her flailing legs, barefoot, with ankle bangles clanging and skirt flying. Her father dove into the thick growth trying to grab her foot, but missing it by inches as her screams were muffled by something on her mouth, sounds escaping in spurts. Amir and Purat dove into the plantation and confused at first by the darkening sky and mercilessly thick growth, they momentarily lost sight of the girl. Brushing the stalks frantically, they heard the child again some distance into the plantation, but it was hard to know which way. They needed to hear her. Ramsamy was weeping, shouting, thrashing. Amir caught a hold of him and put his hand over his mouth quietening him. Picking up sounds ahead, he and Purat ran, wild with fear. The assailant had tripped and fallen, the child's screams clearly audible now. Amir was first to reach the child who had been flung on the ground as her assailant ran off deeper into the cane field. Picking her up, he thrust her into her father's arms and he and Purat ran toward the rustling stalks.

Amir and Purat together flung their large, muscular, iron-fit bodies into the familiar rounded back of Gobind's body and pinned him to the ground. They flipped him over and with his knees against the assailant's chest, Amir started punching his face, over and over again while the man covered his face with his hands. Purat kicked and screamed at him and all Gobind kept repeating was, "Not for me…not for me…"

"What is this *behnchod* saying? What is this bastard saying?" Amir wasn't even aware that he was asking this monster a question while pummeling him. Other men had arrived and pulled Amir up forcing him to stop.

"Amir, Amir…don't…don't…they will hang you if you kill him."

"We have seen the hanging tree. Amir…Amir…stop!!!"

Purat stopped first and pulling Amir up shook his head.

"It's right what these men are saying, Amir."

Breathing hard, spittle and sweat dropping all over the pathetic sniveling man on the ground, Amir lifted himself off.

"Not for me…not for me. The manager…the Sir… wanted her!" Gobind whimpered still covering his face. At this Amir let into Gobind again.

"I will kill you. I don't care if I hang…I will kill you."

Gobind struggled to sit up, his face was bleeding and his arm looked broken. The other men dragged Amir away. Flailing angrily at the sugarcane stalks, Amir and Purat were dragged back to the lane. The men continued to pull the friends along toward the barracks. Amir and Purat were both shouting, "Kill him…kill the bastard."

At the barracks, hearing the shouts, workers had gathered as the group entered the yard. Ramsamy and Meena were clutching eight-year-old Devi to their bosoms and with Krishna, they were squatting by the fire pits weeping. Sajiv, Parvati and Sibani jumped toward Amir and Purat and forgetting gender roles the women pulled Amir and Purat toward the cooking fires and sat them down. Parvati rushed inside to find poultices and bandages while Sibani cleaned their cuts with the *aanchal* of her sari as Ashok clung to her.

"I will kill him," both Amir and Purat were still delirious with anger, flailing and yelling. Sibani carefully caressed their wounds, calming them. Other women had also arrived with bowls of water and helped clean and calm the men. They also gently led Ramsamy's family to their shack and offered them their evening meal. The family ate some, but still weeping they went inside and closed their door.

Later when the men had calmed down, most of them returned to their own cooking pits to eat. Amir and Purat remained outside quietly talking with Sajiv while Sibani and Parvati sat on the doorstep with the children. Two of the white managers arrived at the barracks and strode up and down the rows of shacks asking what had caused the noise. Men just shook their heads in ignorance and ate their meals. They stopped at Sajiv's shack knowing that he spoke English. The taller manager, a heavy set man with a moustache, knelt by the fire pit and even in the fading light, his green eyes seemed to penetrate Sajiv's face as he questioned him. The other manager, shorter and younger, remained standing.

"Sajiv, what happened here? What was the screaming and crying we heard?"

"Oh nothing, Sir, Mr. Harper...nothing at all... it's okay...just the usual misunderstanding among the men. I will talk to them again...will calm them down. Not to worry, Sirs."

None of the friends noticed that Sibani suddenly picked up Ashok and rushed into Parvati's shack, away from the managers. Sajiv had had previous interactions with these managers when he had discussed his temple plans with them. So he knew the green-eyed Mr. Harper, who was now kneeling beside him, and Mr. Walker who was standing holding a log book. The managers stared at the group, and Harper gestured to Walker to check off their names in the log book. Mr. Walker called out and noted Sajiv's name, then Amir, Purat, Parvati and when Sibani re-appeared at the door with Ashok in her arms her name was called and noted in his book.

The managers strode off to the other groups and together they checked off names of Indians seated at the fire pits. They knocked on some doors and continued their checking. Ramsamy answered his door and using his limited English indicated that his family was asleep.

The managers left appearing satisfied not to have to do anything more. But instead of turning toward their homes they lifted their lanterns to light their way toward the cane fields and Gobind's little office. The summer sun was late in setting, but the light had started to fade. A while later the group watched as the managers' lanterns emerged again and Harper and Walker strode up the road toward their homes.

Amir and Purat sat chatting with Sajiv and a few other men. Amir remembered that the tall, heavy set manager with the penetrating green eyes was the same one who had examined them at the wharf. He remembered being poked and prodded by this man, but he was too tired to bring that up, yet too riled up to go to bed. The men just sat talking around the fire while Sibani and Parvati chatted quietly and Yathindra held Ashok on his lap.

When Parvati took her leave to get her children to bed, Sibani asked her if she would keep Ashok for a while. She had to get herself cleaned up and wanted a few minutes to herself. Parvati readily agreed and Sibani left, returning an hour later to pick up Ashok who had curled up and fallen asleep with Yathindra. As Sibani went inside with Parvati, Amir and Purat took their leave of Sajiv and went into their shack to sleep.

"Leave Ashok, *Behn*, let him sleep. He saw too much today... he is tired. And tomorrow that monster will be too swollen to scold you for not bringing him to work. Ashok can stay with my Yathindra."

Sibani was reluctant at first to leave Ashok, but when she saw her little boy peacefully asleep snuggled up with Yathindra she relented and went to her room. Exhausted, she fell asleep.

***

The five o'clock siren woke the barracks up and by six the workers filed down the footpath toward Gobind's office for roll call. Amir and Purat with Ramsamy's family and Sibani were grouped toward the back of the line of workers. The first scream was a woman's voice at the front of the line.

"*Aiyo...aiyo...* and she ran up the line screaming, flailing her hands. The men at the front of the line then followed suit screaming, "He is dead! He is dead!"

By the time Amir and Purat reached the front of the line, they were caught in the throng of men rushing forward. The sight that met them was bizarre. Gobind's body was slung over his desk still seated in his chair. His eyes were open, shock registered in them. There was a neat slice across the side of his neck and blood had congealed all over his desk, thick and black, not red, and not even looking like blood any more. Everything on his desk was still in place – his extinguished lantern, his teacup with tea in it, his pencil neatly sticking out of his closed log book, blood-covered but undisturbed and his blanket neatly folded behind him.

The workers stood transfixed, mute. A few men had run back up to the barracks to fetch Sajiv but before Sajiv arrived one of the white managers rushed down the path together with the worker who had dared go to his house to wake him. It was young Mr. Wilcot who had been polite when Amir's group had first arrived at the barracks. He pushed past the workers and arriving at the little entrance he stopped short, visibly shaken by the sight. Without a word he entered and examined the scene, the silence unbroken. He did not touch anything but bending over the body he muttered, "Must be ten to twelve hours ago... blood congealed."

Turning to the workers he asked, "Anyone know what happened?" They all just stared. Sajiv had arrived and Mr. Wilcot sought him out. Sajiv briefly explained what had happened in the field last night and concluded by saying, "Sir, the other two managers did come last night and checked that everyone was okay at the barracks. And then they came toward this office too."

"What time was that?"

"I think...the sun was setting, Sir...they used their lanterns, Sir, so maybe about eight o'clock, Sir?"

Wilcot carefully opened the log book to the place where the pencil was stuck and bending his head read sideways muttering, "Yes...yes... here is the entry...ten past eight...Mr. Walker, Mr. Harper... all right

Sajiv, will you make sure everyone goes back to their shacks. I will inform the authorities."

"No field work, Sir?"

"No. Everyone back to their shacks and stay there."

Half a day passed with uniformed white men trampling up and down the footpath. The managers, Wilcot, Walker and Harper made several trips back and forth. Finally, the covered body was brought back on a stretcher carried by two uniformed Indian men, a rare sight for the workers. Uniformed police officers accompanied by Mr. Wilcot, spent the afternoon talking to the workers in groups. They finally looked for Sajiv toward late afternoon.

"The officers think that someone here must have done this..." Mr. Wilcot addressed Sajiv.

Sajiv interjected, "But Sir, the managers came as I said around eight, they checked and everyone was here. They entered all our names in their book, Sir. And all the men hand back their *pangas* every evening after work in the field. No-one here has a weapon."

"It was not a *panga*, Sajiv. The force of a *panga* would take off the head," Wilcot winced at his own words. "No it was a clean slice, the kind made by a long sharp sword-like weapon."

"But Sir, no such weapon here. The only knives we have here are the small serrated knives for peeling vegetables."

"Yes we know, Sajiv."

After some minutes of silence, Wilcot turned to the two uniformed police officers.

"Mr. Walker and Mr. Harper checked that all the workers were in their shacks and as you saw they also recorded in their log book that they talked with *Sirdar* Gobind at just past eight o'clock. Gobind's log book also shows that. Mr. Walker and Mr. Harper told the authorities that they stayed at the top of the road talking for a while and would have seen the lantern if anyone from this barracks had gone down in the fading light."

The week passed, work resumed and another *sirdar* was appointed, who was an experienced man a year into his tenure. His name was Poonsamy, a gentle man from the first row of shacks. A uniformed officer on horseback came to the managers' homes several times that first week, but the Indians heard nothing from their bosses. A second week passed, still no word. No one from the barracks had been taken in and the workers finally began to think that the murder would not be solved. One evening as groups of workers sat eating their evening meal Amir finally spoke up.

"Sajiv *Bhai*, I did scream that night, several times, that I would kill that bastard and I would have with my fists if the men had not stopped me. I would have liked to kill him, but I didn't."

"I know Amir. You were here with us at the time that Wilcot says it happened. The authorities looked at the congealed blood, the stiffness of the corpse…" Sajiv swallowed, completely uncomfortable with the topic, "and he said that it happened very soon after the other two managers had left Gobind's office. Gobind had entered their visit into his log book too. You were here with me and Ramsamy was with his family… so no one knows what happened."

"*Bhayah*, you are a man of God…I swear I did not…I want you to know."

"No, no, *Bhayah*…I know you did not. I know. You were with me. I know. This is a mystery."

By the end of December, life once again took on a pattern on the estate. No one was charged. For all they knew the case was closed.

Chapter 8

News

Work on the cane fields remained hot and difficult, but the new *sirdar* was a kinder man, kind but firm. He ensured that workers were working, but appeared less hard on the children. Ashok accompanied his mother, but on one of his rounds Poonsamy touched the child's hands and wobbling his head said to Sibani, "Don't worry…don't worry, if he wants to play… *aachah… aachah*," and smiling he went on to the next group. The little *sirdar*-office at the entrance to the cane fields had been demolished and he had built another small tin structure several yards away from there, along the cane field footpath. He placed a small wooden table and a wood box to sit on and once his morning and evening roll calls were done, he immediately strode off with his log book and locked his office.

Work on the temple was progressing well in January despite the heat. Workers were volunteering their Sunday mornings and some stayed on for part of the afternoon too. They were not only contributing their labour, but each month Mr. Campbell was garnishing a shilling from their pay packets to pay for the building materials. The workers had agreed to this and assured Sajiv that they were committed to the temple. Gopalsing had supervised the cement foundation and the front and back cement walls were half way up.

Amir and Purat helped every Sunday morning, and Purat, true to his name which meant temple garden, stayed on Sunday afternoons as well to work. But Amir went to the shopping area to talk to other folks. He was not so much interested in buying goods from the stores, but thirsty to learn about business. He met with Prabhu's father Ranjith Singh who took him to his large vegetable farm a short walk from the shop. Amir was impressed with the neat rows of peas, beans, carrots, eggplant and so much more. African and Indian workers were employed to plant, tend and harvest the crops. Ranjith Singh explained that water was drawn from the river, but they were now working on irrigation sluices to bring water closer. His small modest house stood facing the road while his market garden stretched down the slope to the river. As they walked back to the shop, Ebrahim called out to Amir from his shop door. Excusing himself, Amir went in.

"Amir, a letter for you!! A letter came for you in the mail which I picked up in town on Thursday. I will fetch it. Come… come… inside."

Amir recognized his brother Gulab's Hindi writing and with a wide smile and heartfelt "thank you," he hugged Ebrahim. Clutching the letter, he ran back down the path to the temple site to show Purat who was working alongside Sibani pressing bricks and cement on the steadily growing back wall.

"*Bhayah…Bhayah…*a letter…a letter from Gulab."

Purat who had also received a letter from his family the previous week was pleased for Amir. Together the friends found a rock to sit by the water and opened the letter.

> *My Dear Bhayah Amir,*
>
> *Namasthe from Mathaji, Bapuji and me and also Chacha and Chachi, uncle and aunty, from next door. With God's grace we are all well. Thank you for the two shillings you sent and Mathaji says you don't need to send more as you promise in the letter. She wants you to eat…*

"*Areh Mathaji* always remembering to feed me," Amir laughed.

> *Bhayah, the monsoons were not too heavy this year and our crops did well. But Bapuji says he is getting old now and has agreed to sell most of our plot to the zamindar who has been pestering him for a while now. Chacha has helped Bapuji to negotiate a good price so don't be alarmed. Remember that I was good at school, Bhayah, and I too have looked at the papers and they are good. Bapuji has put the money in the post office so he and Mathaji can draw a little each month.*

They have also kept a small piece of land to continue to grow
some vegetables. I know that they will be fine and Chachi next
door is so good to them.

But Bhayah, they want me to come to Natal and be with you.
They had me read your letter over and over and were amazed and
happy to hear about the good money you are earning, the lush cane
fields, your friends, the food, the Indian merchants and farmers and
the good weather. So I will be going to the Gorawallah's recruiting
office in Muzafarnagar this week to sign up. I will send you a letter
when I know which ship I will be on. Wish me luck, Bhayah, and I
hope I will see you in a few months.
Your loving brother,
Gulab

Amir and Purat sat quietly for a while confused. Amir was happy
that his brother was coming, but disheartened that his parents would
then be alone.

"It's okay, Amir. Gulab did say that your aunt and uncle next door
were taking care of your parents. And I will write to my brothers to
watch over them too, they are close by…"

"Yes…yes, I know Purat."

He turned the letter in his hand and Gulab had dated it 'November
the twelfth.'

"It took two months for this letter to arrive Purat. He might even be
on a ship already!"

"Do you think so? After we were recruited it took us months to receive our numbers and many more weeks to travel to Calcutta. The
ships take over a month to arrive…don't worry, *Bhayah*…he will send a
letter before he sets out."

Preoccupied, Amir walked back to the barracks and Purat returned
to work with Sibani on the wall. But Amir's mind was racing. How will
Gulab know to ask to be with his brother? Who would be the recruitment officer that will handle his file in Muzzafarnagar? Gulab was only
sixteen years old, his little brother, will he be all right? Suddenly he realized that the shops will be closing at sunset and it was mid-afternoon
so he raced back to Ebrahim's store and bought two more sheets of
writing paper and an envelope. He asked Ebrahim if he could borrow a

pencil and sitting on the floor of the shop behind Ebrahim's cash table he wrote to Gulab. The words flowed, the name of the estate, his identity disc number, the name of Mr. Campbell, the name of the Phoenix train station and everything he could think of that would help to bring his brother to him and not to another estate in unknown parts like Anpu and his group. He also told Gulab to make sure that *Mathaji* and *Bapuji* would want for nothing and that *Chachi* and *Chacha* will definitely care for them. He also wrote down the particulars of Purat's family, a short way up-river from his home and asked Gulab to go and see them so they too could check on their parents. Reading over his letter, he nodded his head from side to side contented, addressed it and gave it to Ebrahim.

"Ebrahim *Bhai*, that letter you gave me, it was from my brother…he is coming."

Elated, Ebrahim slapped Amir on his back and shook his hand. Taking the letter from Amir he carefully placed it in his mailbag with other letters.

"I will be going to town on Friday, *Bhayah*…first to the post office and then to mosque. Your letter will go with me."

Taking his leave, Amir walked slowly back to the barracks along the footpath, his head rumbling with mixed thoughts and his heart beating with mixed emotions. That headache was creeping back as he entered his room and, unusual for Amir, he flung himself on his bed with a cinnamon poultice on his head and fell asleep.

Amir need not have been concerned as two months later another letter arrived from Gulab. He had been to the recruiting office in Muzafarnagar and was told to come back in six weeks. The office was closing for the December Christmas season so he would have to go back in January. That letter was dated December the first. Amir was pleased since that would mean that Gulab would get his letter before he left home.

***

It was early March and Amir and Purat were working much further west of the sugar mill in a particularly thick and tall growth of sugar. Work was much more pleasant under *Sirdar* Poonsamy. Although he was strict about quadrants being completed in the allotted four days, he was gentle on the working children, which pleased the parents. He also insisted that people work hard and non-stop so that they would not need to work during the short lunch break to catch up. He said it was important to stop and rest and eat lunch sitting down. He checked on work groups every day and had completed his round with Amir's group on this hot and humid Friday. So they were surprised to see him return in the late afternoon.

"Amir, there is someone with Manager Wilcot at my work station and he wants to see you."

"Who…who is it Poonsamy?" Amir wiped his face on a rag, looking bemused.

"It is a white man…a Mr. Landers."

Amir's face broke out in a smile.

"Mr. Landers? *Areh*…Purat, Mr. Landers is here!"

Hurriedly Amir straightened up and briskly followed the *sirdar* on the long walk along the cane path back to Poonsamy's little log-in station. And there he was! Mr. Landers stood with Mr. Wilcot. Bowing his head, Amir waited to be addressed before greeting them.

"Ah, Amir. Nice to see you again."

"Mr. Landers, Sir, thank you, Sir."

"Come back to the barracks with us, Amir. Nothing to worry about… we want to talk to you," Wilcot spoke as he led them up the footpath back toward the barracks. Poonsamy turned back into the cane fields and walked off. Amir wondered what was going on.

They walked past the barracks, the two white men chatting and Amir following. At the top of the gentle hill, beside the gravel road there was a small two room wood and iron house with a pointed roof which Amir knew to be Poonsamy's new home as *sirdar*. His family had tended a bright, small garden with a few flowers and vegetables. They walked to the other side of the road where the managers' brick homes and lush gardens were located. Still further on this road they came to small, low, square brick building set a little back from the road. There were two horse drawn carriages out in front. A sign by the door read, "Managers Only."

Inside the building were three large desks and comfortable high backed upholstered chairs. Against the front wall and large window were several wooden straight backed chairs. Mr. Walker sat behind one of the desks, but Mr. Landers gestured to Amir to sit on a wooden chair and he sat beside him on the next chair while Mr. Wilcot returned to his desk.

"Amir, I have come to ask you to come and work with me on the Harrison Estate in Avoca."

Amir's pleasure was immediately seen on his face.

"Sir...yes... yes, Sir."

"But it won't be for some time. I had to ask for you and Mr. Walker has agreed. The British Office will provide other workers for Mr. Walker, but I needed someone I know works well with people, and I saw the way you led the people on the ship."

Mr. Walker spoke for the first time. "Your *Sirdar* Poonsamy has told us about your hard work here too, Amir. We know that the previous *sirdar* did some things that we...that I did not like...but...anyway...go ahead, Mr. Landers."

"Our sugar estate is small and the canes do very well on the west, north and south sides. But the east side has not been good for sugarcane. We are trying coffee crops on that side and we need a *sirdar* to help us on that side. My sugarcane *sirdar* cannot do both."

"Sir...I can help...but I have not grown coffee, Sir."

"That is all right. Our other managers have some experience with coffee in Kerala...in south India and they will work on the planting side and will tell you more if you agree to come as our *sirdar*."

"*Sirdar*, Sir?"

"Yes I am asking you to come as our *Sirdar*, Amir. We will pay you twice what you are earning here...a *sirdar*'s wage."

Amir rolled his head smiling. "Yes...yes...Sir...thank you, Sir."

"And Amir we need one more thing. Our sugar mill is very small. It is near the river and we have some small machinery. But to the west of our plantation are very large wattle fields." Seeing Amir's confused look, Landers continued.

"Wattle are thin, tall trees that estates grow for their wood. With our growing colony we need lots of wood. The problem is that right next to our mill on the Umghlangane River, the government wants to build another railway bridge to reach the other side to the wattle plantation. You saw the river?"

"Yes Sir, our train crossed over that river to come here."

"Yes, this is north. They want to extend the railway to the west. All this will take time, but the building of the bridge will affect our work at the mill. We are thinking that we would like to send our sugarcane here to the large mill that serves the three estates here. So I will need someone to start that operation of loading the sugarcane onto carts, taking the loads to our train station and bringing the loads here."

Mr. Walker looked intently at Amir, "What about your friend, Purat?"

Oh yes…yes…Sir. My brother Purat is a very hard worker…very strong…big muscles, Sirs"

The white men smiled. "Yes, quite!! Amir, he is your brother?"

"Sir, we became brothers on the ship, Sir."

"Oh yes, I understand," Mr. Walker nodded his head.

"Amir, the *sirdar* we have is not very well and we don't have experienced men to take over," Mr. Landers looked intently at Amir. "You will need to help with the sugarcane plantations on his side as well on the days that he is sick. He is close to the end of his contract…"

"Yes, Sir…I am strong…Purat and I are strong…we will serve you well, Sir." After a few more discussions between Walker and Landers, Amir was dismissed just as the six o'clock siren sounded. Amir walked back a little dazed. He went to the well, drew water, bathed and lit his *dhiya* again and prayed at their tiny *Ganeshji* shrine, thanking God for this opportunity. With extra time today he decided to make *chappatis* on the open grill and they were hot and ready with spicy beans when Purat walked toward their fire pit, forehead creased with worry.

"What happened, *Bhayah?*"

Amir related the story excitedly to his best friend. Sajiv and his family returned tired from the temple site and Purat related the story to him as they all shared the evening meal.

"Areh…that is so good, Amir. As *sirdar* you will be earning twenty shillings a month! And you will have your own house like Poonsamy. What about Purat? What will he earn? Will he have a house too?"

The men laughed together. So many questions and no answers to all, but the well wishes were genuine.

Chapter 9

Two Weddings

Amir wrote another letter to Gulab telling him of his potential re-location and the following Sunday the friends dropped off their letters to Ebrahim and went to work on the temple, the construction of which was moving along well. The little shack on the left side was complete and Sibani and Ashok now lived there. Sibani's indenture was completed in February and Parvati offered her the shack for which Sibani was grateful. Ashok thrived among the volunteers from all three of the Campbell barracks, people that Amir and Purat also got to know and like. After work, tired but upbeat, the friends lingered by the water's edge sitting on rocks, their feet in the water.

"Amir *Bhayah?*" asked Purat and then fell silent.

"*Bolo Bhayah*...say...what is it?"

"*Bhayah*, I am going to get married," Purat blurted out and turned to Amir grasping his shoulder. "My brother...give me your blessings!"

"*Areh*...of course, Purat...this is good news! Who are you marry-ing?"

Purat shifted and fidgeted and then continued, "*Bhayah*, I am going to marry Sibani."

The shock on Amir's face showed involuntarily, but he quickly re-gained his composure.

"Purat, you mean Sibani, Ashok's mother? Have you asked her? Have you talked to *Punditji* Sajiv?"

"No not yet, not to either. I wanted to talk to you first. Amir as we worked on this temple, Sibani and I have become close. I know she is our own age...that is all right...and I want to give Ashok a good fu-ture. You don't know how it broke my heart to see him working on the field…a baby, *Bhayah*…a baby. And she… alone. She told me her story, Amir. That Gobind was a bastard! He procured the workers' new brides for that evil green-eyed Harper and then started snatching girl children as young as eight like Devi from our barracks, but also from the other barracks. We have friends now from those barracks who have been telling us. But *Bhayah*, Sibani told me her story…remember that evening when I was late coming back from here? She and I sat here…on these rocks and she sobbed telling me what happened to her."

Purat slowly related Sibani's story and Amir's reaction, like Parvati's, was shock and anger. Dusk was approaching, but the friends sat talking while the other workers went back to all three barracks to prepare their evening meals.

"Purat, does anyone from the other barracks know who killed Gobind?"

"No. The word spread that he was sliced with a sharp, smooth *talwar*…sword. No one amongst us has a sword. We would not be allowed to keep one. Soldiers and white officers back home carried them, but not people like us here."

"But it could have been a small dagger too, couldn't it?"

"But even those daggers, *Bhayah*…our shacks are searched by managers from time to time as Sajiv told us he sees during the day when we are at work."

The friends mused for a while then shaking off the gloom Amir perked up.

"Purat, I am glad you are going to marry. We are now twenty-three years old, it is time." Then Amir had his own story to tell.

"Purat…you are my brother. I was keeping this to tell you when I gathered enough courage to proceed myself. But…I too want to be married before we move to Avoca."

"*Areh Bhayah*…that is good news!! Who are you thinking about?"

Amir laughed nervously and he too fidgeted before answering.

"You know Prabhu? The vegetable shop? You know that bright girl… his sister in the shop?"

Purat smiled a broad smile and Amir continued, "I don't know if her father *Bapu* Ranjith Singh will accept me…I am just a laborer."

"But you must ask Amir. You have been to his farm…he likes you *nayh*?"

And so it was that Sajiv, Amir and Purat, dressed in clean *dhotis*, white tunics, manicured moustaches and hair glossed down and combed, with clean pale yellow *pugris* wrapped on their heads, walked the following Sunday to see Ranjith Singh at his farm up along the North Coast Road. Sajiv was the one who spoke once tea and vegetable *bhajia* fritters were brought by Prabhu's *sari-aanchal* veiled mother. Sajiv had arranged this meeting, so the shop was closed for the afternoon. Prabhu sat with his father while mother and daughter were busy in the kitchen.

Sajiv spoke.

"*Bapuji*…Amir has brought a proposal for your daughter Bhagirathi. He is leaving soon to be *sirdar* on the Avoca estates not far from here… only two train stations."

Amir intercepted, "*Bapuji*…I am not wealthy…I have saved most of my pay these past nine months. I am frugal…but I can give your daughter a good life. I have been promised a small house. I will work hard to give your daughter a good life."

"Amir is a *chatriyah* like you, *Bapuji*…brave, strong," Sajiv added.

They stopped as Ranjith Singh put up his hand, took a deep breath, looked at all the young men in the room and then spoke. His eyes revealed his pleasure.

"My daughter is fifteen, a good age to marry. She was born here in this new country and I named her after our beloved River *Ganga* so close to my village Bhojpur back home. She, our *Ganga*, and Prabudha, our Prabhu, our wise and learned son, are the hopes for our generations to come. I knew you are a good boy…a good man, Amir… when you came to meet me here to see my farm. You showed respect not only to me, but to my farm workers too…Africans and Indians…men and women. *Beta*…son…you remind me of myself. I came here as a labourer on these harsh sugar estates and after my indenture I was given this small piece of land in lieu of a passage home. I bought more and more land and I grew it. I know you will do the same. My daughter will be in good hands."

The three friends laughed, clapped their hands, slapped Amir on his shoulders singing, "*Shabash! Shabash*, Amir…congratulations." Amir, his tanned face flushed, stood up, then crouched and touched his future father-in-law's feet. Ranjith Singh lifted him saying, "*Aachah Beta…ootoh.. ootoh..*rise up my son." Then he called to his wife to bring Bhagirathi.

Dressed in a long frilly, gold patterned, bright blue skirt and matching short *choli* blouse, Bhagirathi came in slowly with her face covered in a see-through long *dupatha* scarf. She shyly placed a tray of cold *lassi*, sweet yoghourt drinks and bright orange homemade curly-cued *jalebi* sweets on the low table. Seeing the spunk she showed at the cash table in the store, Amir caught the fleeting smile on her face before she was ushered away by her mother back to the kitchen. Ranjith Singh broke off a piece of the orange *jalebi* and placed it in Amir's mouth as a sign of sweetening his mouth and welcoming him to their family.

Amir and Purat received a message a few weeks later from Mr. Landers instructing them to come to Avoca at the start of May. Mr. Wilcot had come to his room with the news after work and Amir explained to him that he and Purat were both getting married the following Sunday so the timing worked well. He hesitantly invited Mr. Wilcot to the temple wedding and the polite young man accepted congenially. The preparations for both weddings were proceeding and people from all three barracks were helping as a community.

The night before the wedding both Amir and Purat reverently unwrapped the special packages their mothers had placed among their clothes in their metal trunks. As Amir opened the parcel his fingers lovingly caressed the exquisite *haar* – a heavy gold chain with intricate gold filigree patterning around four gold coins that hung interspersed on the front of the chain.

Amir and Purat's mothers had wrapped their own gold wedding *haars* inside new simple saris, then wrapped them again in red cloth and then tightly tied the parcels with cloth strings. Both mothers knew that with their sons going to a new land for a five-year indenture, they would marry far from home and these heavy gold necklaces were their gifts to their daughters-in-law, whom they may never meet, but to whom they were entrusting their next generation. Amir, true to the name his parents had given him, which meant rich, had carefully continued to add his money from each pay package into the three little bundles stowed away in his walls. With these savings he had gone to visit the jeweller in the shop on the hill. Jumnadas was a middle-aged *bunya*, a businessman and jeweller, whose small shop, secured with floor to ceiling heavy iron bars, contained the modest gold jewellery that poor labourers and struggling free Indians could afford. Amir and

Purat chose simple gold filigree bangles for their brides.

The last Sunday in April dawned bright and sunny. The temple was completed and several avatars of the various manifestations of God, ordered by Sajiv and donated by temples in India, had arrived by ship. Lovingly installed inside the entrance chamber of the temple were tall white marble statues of Ram, Sita, Hanuman, Krishna, Radha, Shiva, Parvati, Ganesha, Durga and numerous other avatars, some in orangey clay and others in brass. Just beyond the entrance chamber was a smaller enclosure with a curved entrance where Sajiv had arranged seating for a few congregants on low stools around a small fire pit in the centre.

Purat, Sibani, Amir and Bhagirathi sat on the stools facing Sajiv as he chanted from scriptures and dropped *ghee*, clarified butter, into the fire. Each couple was instructed separately on the wedding rites and each couple separately walked around the fire seven times. The grooms, using the tips of their forefingers, each placed a red *sendhoor*, a spice paste dot on his bride's forehead.

Bhagirathi dressed in a traditional red and gold sari and Sibani in a gold-flecked, pale yellow sari, both bedecked in the gold wedding *haars* and gold bangles, shyly held their grooms' hands as their saris and the grooms' matrimonial shawls were tied together by Sajiv.

Ranjith Singh, as the bride's father, paid for the food and for his daughter's bridal clothing, but he also insisted on doing the same for Sibani. He knew that she was a widow and that it was unusual for an Indian widow to be getting married in this way. But this community, brave and different in so many ways from villages at home, was giving Sibani a new start, a new life, and the men who carried Ashok on their shoulders saw their 'sister' happily married to Purat.

After the ceremony, as they walked out into the temple garden beside the river they were pleasantly startled to see a hundred happy, swarthy faces greeting them and in the midst of these workers they were speechless to see Mr. Wilcot and his young wife. Many of the guests had brought *dholaks*, Indian drums, and the women had formed singing groups. Songs and drums accompanied the newlyweds to the river side where flowers and beetle leaves holding clay *dhiyas*, lamps, were released into the water. Lunch, cooked on the large temple cooking pits was served by several men stirring large *dhegs*...ceremonial cooking pots with long wooden spoons. The rice, *dhal* and vegetables were served on lush green banana leaves and it was a joy for Amir to see the worker-children of all ages seated on the ground by the river eating, laughing and giving meaning to the charitable sentiments of their new temple. The presence of Ebrahim, his *kameez-shalwar* clad, veiled wife, brought Muslim, Hindu, *chatriyah*, *dhalit*, *brahmins* and the white Mr. Wilcot all together on that bright, sunny Sunday.

According to Hindu tradition, the brides returned to their homes that evening, Bhagirathi accompanying her parents and big brother to their home and Sibani returning to her little temple shack where Ashok was already asleep watched over by a woman from the next barracks. The conjugal ceremonies would occur the following Sunday when a groom is required to come to claim his wife from her parents' home and take her to their new home. Amir and Purat sat with their friends for a while and then both went to Ebrahim's store to write letters home to their families about the wedding and also stressing to their families back home that all future letters were to be sent to the Harrison Estate in Avoca.

The next day, Mr. Wilcot, on his routine monthly trip to the British Office at the harbour, included in his pile of papers, two forms requesting the Protector of Immigrants to certify the marriages of his servants Amir and Purat, whose weddings he had witnessed.

There was no problem getting Amir's registration signed, but Purat's was rejected until proof could be provided that Sibani was a widow. Returning to his office that afternoon, Mr. Wilcot found a death certificate in the office files, declaring Sibani's first husband dead by drowning. Purat's marriage registration would have to wait until Manager Wilcot's next trip to town.

Part 2
1884 – A New Life

Chapter 10

Starting Over

The following Sunday, Bhagirathi prepared to leave her parents' home for her husband's home. Had it been in her parents' village in India, a short way outside of Calcutta, Bhagirathi would have had many friends, cousins and young village girls giggling and fussing over her as she decorated her feet and hands with henna. She reverently placed her red dot on her forehead and dressed in a fine blue sari and *choli* blouse ready to be claimed by her groom.

In spite of their few numbers, the girls from the barracks and other free families looked forward to the small feast and the hilarious game of *dwar-rokai*, door-blocking.

In the game, the girls would block the entrance door to the bride's house and refuse to let the groom claim his bride until he paid them a few symbolic coins. Amir's friends egged him on at first. The girls laughingly refused to let him in until they had amassed several coins in their palms. Then he and his friends were allowed inside the bride's home to join the guests in a small feast.

The same custom was playing out at Sibani's little shack as well, though in Sibani's eyes, there were quiet tears of joy as she placed her red *sendhoor* proudly on her forehead. The *sendhoor* is a symbol of marriage as long as her husband lived.

After the morning meal for the guests gathered at the temple for Purat's ceremony, and at Ranjith Singh's home for Amir's, the married couples and Ashok prepared to go to the railway station. Four metal trunks were loaded on to bullock carts and the couples bid farewell to family and friends. Bhagirathi and her mother clung to each other weeping, and Ranjith Singh kept saying,

"*Areh*, she is only going to be two train stations away. *Areh*... let her go...let her go happily."

Finally, they were boarded, trunks were stowed under the wooden seats and the train slowly pulled out of the station heading south toward the Inanda station. Ashok, never having been on a train before, kept bouncing and squealing from lap to lap, thirstily taking in the lush scenery on both sides. The sound of the whistle and chugging of the engines, *kook-chook-chook-chook-chook* became a song for him with his laughing new family of four adults, spoiling him with sugar tamarind balls and loving hugs... a child at last. As they left the Inanda station, Amir became quiet and reflective, his eyes glued to his window. The rolling, green, verdant sugarcane hills of Avoca came into view, endless and beckoning. Amir felt a stirring in his heart, a visceral call that this was going to be home, a home with his wife, a family of new brothers and maybe children in the future. Thoughts of his mother, father and brother swept in and out of his consciousness, but the fields held him in their grasp. They passed several clusters of African huts with thatched roofs and bright paintings on their walls. Then the river came into view again and they crossed the bridge into Avoca station.

Amir and Purat hurriedly lifted all four trunks on to the platform – heavy trunks that contained all their worldly possessions. They gathered on the platform in the comforting May sun, holding on to Ashok for his safety as the train slowly pulled away.

"Purat, I know which direction Mr. Landers' carriage went that day and we can hire a bullock cart to take us, but I really don't know where we would be going."

"Yes, that's true *Bhayah* and I have my little son..."

"Why don't we leave the women and Ashok with our trunks at Adam *Bhai*'s house and then we go and find Mr. Landers' office?"

Purat waited on the platform with the women and Ashok while Amir carried the first trunk on his shoulder and walked across the tracks to Adam's house at the back of his shop. A high tin fence encircled the property and Amir approached the back gate. With the trunk on his back he called out,

"*Areh* Adam, Asif...*areh Bhayah*...*aiyeh*...*aiyeh*...come, come!"

It was Asif who first saw Amir and came bounding out from under the guava tree where he was sitting with a small workbook. Nine years old now, Asif looked strong, healthy and happy, laughing out loud and hurriedly lifting the latch to let Amir in. He hugged Amir's waist and Amir put one arm around the boy and wobbling with the weight of the trunk put it down and lifted the boy into his arms. Fatima and little Ayesha hearing the laughter came out of their kitchen and seeing Amir, Fatima hurriedly pulled her *dupatha* scarf over her head and mouth.

"*Bhayah...salaam*...come, come inside. Ayesha go and get your father!"

"*Asalaam Waleikom Behn*...peace be upon you my sister. How are you? How is the family?"

Chattering excitedly, they went inside and Adam, dragged by the hand by an impatient Ayesha, met them in the kitchen which was at the back of the large wood, iron and tin structure.

"*Areh* Amir, my *Bhayah*, welcome, welcome to our home! *Areh* how wonderful of you to come...bring some drinks Ayesha...come ... come!"

Amir explained about their trunks and about Purat and the family waiting on the platform and Adam immediately called out to his two African helpers in the shop to accompany them to the platform. After hurried introductions on the platform, Amir lifted the next trunk, but the African men interceded and carried two of the trunks while Purat lifted the third on his shoulder and the group walked across the tracks to Adam's home. Over cold drinks, Amir and Purat excitedly related their news about their jobs and weddings while the women shyly listened, sari *aanchals* and *dupatha* covering their heads and pulled over their mouths. Adam insisted that they should all have an afternoon meal together, but both Purat and Amir were anxious to go and find Mr. Landers. Promising to return as soon as they could, they left their families chatting with Fatima. Adam walked with them to the platform briefly telling them about their shipmates in Avoca.

Rajiv and his family were given a small home by the Harrison estate not far from Adam's shop on top of a gentle nearby hill. He had started helping the indentured labourers with their spiritual needs. Bhodraj worked on the sugarcane fields for the first few months, but then Rajiv convinced young Mr. Harrison Junior that the children in the village needed to have a few hours of schooling. So Bhodraj was released to help Rajiv teach and was given a small shack next door to his friend

Rajiv. Adam's son attended this school for three hours each day. Bhimnad and Himal were still on the estate and every Sunday all of the shipmates gathered in the open space near Adam's shop, in front of the little church, under the tamarind tree. On the railway platform, Adam called for a horse-driven carriage to take the friends to the Harrison Estate along the river's edge, past the dirt road leading uphill and along the foot of the west side of the hill toward the Harrison barracks and the brickyard near the river.

Meanwhile, Fatima showed Bhagirathi and Sibani into the kitchen to start preparing the meal and she went into the shop to look after the shop's money transactions. Asif was instructed to have an African helper catch one of the fat hens, clucking in the backyard, read the prayers to make the slaughter *halal*, and prepare it for the women to cook for their meal. The backyard had several patches of vegetables and a wire-mesh-enclosed hen and rooster coop constructed out of tin. Ayesha crawled in, careful to avoid the smelly droppings, to fetch eggs in her little basket. When Adam returned to the shop, Fatima joined the women and children in the kitchen and they prepared a small feast, all the time chatting about Fatima and her family's life on the ship, Sibani's work on the Campbell Estate and Bhagirathi's life being born in this new country.

The meal was like nothing Amir and Purat had had for a whole year in their barracks, nothing like Sibani had had for many years, nothing like Ashok had ever had in his young life, and one that reminded Bhagirathi about her meals at home with her parents and Prabhu on some Sundays. As late afternoon approached, Amir and Purat returned from the Harrison Estate. They all sat on Adam's large mat-covered kitchen floor, enjoying the sumptuous meal. As they ate chicken curry, eggplant, okra, *dhal*, boiled egg curry and rice followed by sweet *jalebis* and *burfi* sweets, Amir stole a look at his bride and at Purat's son, Ashok. He vowed that this new family of his would never want for good food. Yes, he would continue to be frugal and careful about money, but his and Purat's family would never go without nutritious food ever again.

***

Before that family meal, Amir and Purat had taken a comfortable ride in the horse-drawn carriage that Adam had summoned for them. They paid the Indian driver from the pennies they had in their cloth bag and told him where they needed to go. The driver knew the Harrison Estate well. They followed the same dirt road that they had seen Mr. Landers take a year ago, close to the edge of the Umghlangane River. When they passed another dirt road branching left and up a hill, the driver said that Mr. Harrison had named that road Avoca Road after a place in his home country Scotland. Amir and Purat admired two plots of neatly cultivated land on their right hand side close to the river bed.

"These are very nice vegetable gardens...and small fruit trees growing in those buckets. Look at those flowers! What are they? We don't have those tall stems with the bushy red tops." Amir was interested.

"There are two men in the barracks who got permission to cultivate these plots and other free Indians buy from them. Many Indians have homes nearby."

They trotted past Avoca Road and continued along the river. The carriage hugged the base of the hill, which was thick with lush, tall sugar-cane. They approached what looked like a brickyard and the man explained that brick was made in this large factory using stones from a quarry half way to town near the Umgeni River. Many African men, with their skin and loin cloths covered in red dust, carried loads of stones into the low red roofed buildings while others were pulling skids of perfectly formed rich red bricks toward the dirt road. These, the driver explained, would be loaded on to long horse drawn carriages to be taken to the train station.

"The Harrison barracks are just up this road. There is a small sugar mill too, so we just call this road Mill Road," said the driver laughing.

The barracks were nestled close to the sugarcane fields, hardly any space separating the last of the three rows of shacks from the first row of tall cane plants.

Mr. Landers met them as they alighted. He was dressed in khaki slacks and a blue short-sleeved shirt. He directed them toward a small office up the road away from the barracks. The windows of the office overlooked the brickyard while the entrance faced the gentle slopes of the cane-covered hill. Without much small talk, he directed them to follow him and he talked as they walked up the hill along narrow fertile paths cut between rows of cane.

"This is one of three hills that we are cultivating. The two hills on our right... see over there...those hills are doing well. This hill...this side of this hill is very good for sugarcane as you can see."

They walked up the hill and nearing the top, still nestled in the fields they came by three well-tended homes, one much larger than the other two. The large house had a circular driveway and flowers and fruit trees in bloom all around it.

"That is Mr. Harrison's house. He is not well and his son now runs the estate. The other two houses, one is mine and the other is Mr. Donaldson's and his family."

The large two-storey, white painted house was much like that of the owner of the Campbell Estate. The gabled roof had intricately carved wooden panels all along the sloping edges of the roof and a large wraparound verandah extended along the front and two sides of the house. The large front windows were shaded by white curtains and the side windows with blue and white striped awnings. The other two houses belonging to Mr. Donaldson and Mr. Landers, though smaller than the Harrison Estate home, were large, red brick single storey, gable-roofed homes, with large wraparound verandahs on the front and one side of the house. The garden on one of the manager's homes was being tended by a *pugri* turbaned, *dhoti*-clad Indian man.

Amir and Purat listened and nodded, but did not take the liberty to talk. At the top of the hill the land was still fertile, but less so than the lush fields they had just walked through on the west side of the hill. The land on this east side seemed to be dry, rough cane fields. There were a few small tin shacks along the road to their left leading down what the driver had called Avoca Road.

"These tin shacks belong to labourers who have finished their indenture with us. Come let's go down this other side of the hill."

He led them down the east side of the hill and Amir and Purat saw what he had meant by struggling cane fields. The stalks were short, the leaves a dull green. As they walked down the narrow winding pathway, Amir saw that the soil was more shale-like, rocky in places, but still with patches of good fertile soil. There were tall berry trees, similar to those they had seen near the shops by the Inanda and Phoenix stations. The men there called them sling-berry trees probably because children used the berries to shoot from their stick and rubber sling-shots. They passed a huge fig tree growing majestically, its branches and succulent leaves providing shade along the hill. They continued down to a stream separating this hill from the next one rising toward the east. That hill was verdant, covered in wild flowers and trees.

At the stream they turned right and came up to a large, tall tree, filled with ripe, purple fruit. Along their pathway lay a single row of barracks. These shacks seemed larger and better built than other barracks they had seen, with their front doors facing the rippling, clear stream.

"Amir, Purat, we had this row of homes just built this month for the two of you and a few of the other families who have finished their indenture, but wanted to stay on to help develop this troublesome side of the hill."

They entered the first home and were pleasantly surprised. There were two large rooms. The front room would serve as dining room and sitting area, and the inside room as a large bedroom. There was a window in each room and even a small opening in the tin roof of the front room to allow smoke to exit and air to circulate. The cooking pits were just outside the front door, close to the stream.

"Thank you, Sir...thank you. We are married now and have families. This is very nice, Sir."

Mr. Landers briefly took them to the next three tin homes that also seemed large, but not as large as theirs. Amir and Purat greeted the men and saw wives cooking at their fire pits and several small children frolicking at the water's edge.

One of the men ventured, "Welcome *Bhayah...Sirdarji*...Nice place here...fresh stream...*jamun* tree... sweet fruit," he pointed to the fat purple fruits hanging from the tree.

Amir and Purat both raised clasped hands in greeting and smiled.

"Let's go in here a moment," Mr. Landers indicated the first house. There were some upturned wooden boxes on which they sat.

"As you saw, young Mr. Harrison has been experimenting with different crops on this side of the hill. The coffee trees are not doing well. The berries come out with black spots. A few fruit trees have been tried. The narchees are not doing well, but the mango trees are flourishing and the guava trees are coming along, but not too good."

Amir spoke up, "Sir...yes, Sir...we noticed that the few trees are struggling. But the soil is good in some parts...we will take a look."

"Yes, the *sirdar* we have is sick now and...well...I will be honest...he is not well liked. Whipping workers is not something I approve of…but I have seen the lash marks. Now that he is sick I have talked to young Mr. Harrison and we will pay him for his remaining few months and send him back to India."

Amir and Purat said nothing. They nodded, but stayed silent. Andrew continued.

"Amir, will you be okay looking after both sides of this hill? The other two smaller hills, closer to the Effingham Estates are doing well and our *sirdar* there is good…he gets good work from his labourers and the crops are always green." He saw Amir agreeing and turned to Purat.

"Purat, your job is new. We will provide more horse carriages with longer beds to carry the cane from all the hills to the road to be taken to the station. A small amount can still be processed at our own mill, but our machinery is small and we will be closing that mill in a few years."

"Yes Sir, Mr. Landers. I will work hard for you."

"And for Mr. Donaldson and for young Mr. Harrison, of course. Old Mr. Harrison's health is not good. He will be returning to Scotland in a few months."

This was a lot of information to absorb, but both Amir and Purat were confident that they could do the jobs expected of them. They were pleased too about the twenty shillings a month that was promised to them. They walked back over the hill and back down to Mr. Landers' office where they took their leave. They promised to start work the next day.

Chapter 11

Reunion

After their delicious meal with Adam's family, the newlyweds loaded their trunks on to a rented bullock cart and headed to their new home. Their route took them south from the station and past the right hand turn-off they had previously taken along the Umghlangane River. They rode up a gentle slope past the two small houses that Adam had pointed out from the station as belonging to Rajiv and Bhodraj. The cart easily traversed the slight downhill slope and on to another dirt road along a stream.

"This is the same stream that flows by our new house," Amir explained, then he added excitedly, "I'm sure it joins the big river...*areh*... must be where we saw the very small very low, stone bridge we passed just before that road that the driver called Avoca Road!!"

A little further along the bumpy road they came upon a long, low-roofed, yellow, tin structure piled with what looked like pulp bundles tightly wrapped with aloe strips. The bullock cart driver told them that was a paper mill.

"Pulp...pulp factory...*girmit* workers...government permit holders... *aparawallah*...people like us work in that factory."

"Where do they live?"

"Barracks behind the factory."

"The water pump here by the road...for factory?"

"Yes, pulp factory uses lots of water. These pumps on the road are for everyone. We all use."

The family was pleased to see the water pumps. Beyond the pulp and paper factory, there were several more pumps with people gathered around filling large *lotas*, urns, with fresh water to carry back to their barracks. The women carried them on their heads, steadily, without spilling. Most of the men tended to hold the large *lotas* by the rim or against their sides with an arm wrapped around the urn.

They came up to the *jamun* tree. It was tall with large branches spreading wide and pregnant with luscious, purple fruit. It was not possible to get the cart across the stream, even at the narrowed part which had stepping stones. Green and brown frogs jumped off the rocks into the water as the family got off the cart and Ashok, the first to see the frogs, ran headlong, screeching and laughing toward them. His mother scooped him up.

The men from the barracks came running to help with the trunks. The women from the barracks fussed over them and called out to them pointing at the evening meal cooking at the fires. It was sunset and the barracks families were ready to eat. Full from their meal at Adam's home, Amir and Purat's family however, did not refuse the offer of a meal as that would be impolite. Chatting happily, getting to know their neighbours, they sat until the sun set. Ashok, exhausted from his full day, fell asleep in his mother's arms lulled by the sound of the stream and the chirping of crickets.

The newlyweds said their goodnights. There were knowing smiles from the women who were left sitting at the fireside. As Sibani put Ashok to bed on rolled out blankets from their trunk, she could hear the women singing softly in a familiar chorus and recognized them as marriage songs. She smiled as she removed more blankets from Purat's trunk and made their own bed on the floor against the opposite wall of the room. Soon darkness fell and even the crickets were silent. The only sound was the gentle rippling of the stream.

***

The work week began in earnest. Amir and Purat rose early as usual, washed their faces at the stream and cleaned their teeth and tongue using the twigs from the *jamun* tree. They had seen wild peach trees along the way and decided they would pick twigs from those, knowing that they were better scrapers for teeth and tongues. Bathing was at night after work and they both commented on how refreshing it would be to bathe in the stream, unlike before when they had to use a bucket of well water. There was a slight bend in the stream past their shacks where tall reeds grew and they had noticed women and children going there the night before to bathe. So Bhagirathi and Sibani would also be pleased with that privacy.

Amir and Purat sat by the waterside tying their yards-long *pugris*, turbans, around their heads, then set out barefoot across the river on to the dirt road to fetch water from the pump near the paper factory in large *lotas*. This they left on their doorsteps for their wives to use for cooking. The porridge cooking on a low flame was ready, so they ate. Afterwards, they started up the hill and down the other side to the Harrison barracks. They got there a few minutes before the six o'clock siren.

Amir and Purat spent the first few days getting to know the workers in the barracks. They were mostly men, a few with wives and only a handful of single indentured women. The children who were working looked older, certainly over the age of twelve. Amir remembered that Adam had told them that Mr. Harrison had agreed to allow younger children to attend school. The work assignments were similar to their previous estate, with each work group being assigned a patch to cut with *pangas*, then chop, bundle and load on to carts. Smaller crews cleared the land, burned the debris, and planted new crops. On the third day, Amir and Purat came upon the crew on which Bhimnad and Himal served and the pleasant surprise on all their faces was followed by hugs and enthusiastic greetings.

"Areh...areh...Bhayah...Bhayah...where did you come from?" It was noisy Bhimnad who found his voice first.

"Bhimnad!! Himal!! *Areh*...we were wondering where you two were! We went through the barracks..."

"No, no we are not in the barracks. Young Mr. Harrison gave us some land by the river to experiment with some vegetables, flowers and trees...*areh haanh*...yes... yes...we have our own homes side by side over there!"

"*Aachah*...oh...yes...yes. We saw those. Are those yours? *Aachah*... so nice!"

Amid hugs and back slaps the bonds, formed on the ship, gelled again. That evening after the six o'clock horn sounded, Amir and Purat accompanied Bhimnad and Himal on their walk back along the dirt road by the river to their shacks near the foot of Avoca Road. Amir and Purat had heard that at the end of indenture, workers were permitted to have fifteen acres of land in exchange for the cost of a passage back to India. But Bhimnad told them that these experimental plots were not part of the fifteen acres' settlement as the two friends were still on indentured *girmits*, contracts. These two small plots of land were given by the Harrisons to the men to come up with crops that would thrive on the fallow side of their hill. Judging from the healthy, robust plants, Himal and Bhimnad were doing well. It was mid-week and getting late, but after admiring the crops, all four men continued walking along the river road and turned right at a small grassy fork to approach Bhodraj and Rajiv's small homes. They were seen before they called out and Bhodraj came running out to meet them, a slight limp still visible in his gait.

"Areh…who are these…*Areh Bhagwan*…oh…Lord…we are blessed… Amir *Bhayah*…Purat *Bhayah*…" Tears welled up in Bhodraj's eyes as he hugged his friends. "I wondered when we would see you." A woman clad in an orange sari watched from the doorway then ran to the house next door. Rajiv, Namita and Hemang rushed outside and clasped their mouths in surprise. Rajiv, slightly bent over on his left side where his wound had been, held out his arms and embraced both men at once.

"Come…come inside…" He led them into his little home. It was dark now, but the kerosene lamps burned bright and the clay *dhiyas* burning softly at the two little shrines in his front room made the atmosphere serene and welcoming. Hemang bounded about excitely.

"Beta…Beta…son…sit down by your mother." Namita gathered He-mang, taller now, into her arms. They were seated on the floor on woven mats and cushions. The orange-saried young woman hovered at the door and Namita beckoned to her.

"Bhabhi…sister-in-law… *aiyeh…aiyeh…bayto…aiyeh*…come…come… sit…sit with us. Don't be shy…these are our brothers…from the ship. *Bhayah*, this is Indira *Bhabhi*."

"*Areh* Bhodraj…tell them!" laughed Rajiv. "Our Bhodraj is married, *Bhayah*. Indira *Bhabhi* is from near here…along the main North Coast Road. Her family has a vegetable and dairy farm…long time…her parents are here long time!"

Indira came in quietly and holding her sari *aanchal* to her mouth she sat next to Namita, taking Hemang into her lap. The men talked excitedly catching up on a year's worth of news. However, not wanting to keep their wives waiting and worrying, Amir and Purat took their leave, cheerfully promising to meet again on Sunday.

***

The work on the estate was not easy. Most of the men were hard working but there were several who were hard to control. Swearing, yelling and throwing blows at one another were not uncommon and many nights Amir would be late coming home because there would be fights to be mediated at the barracks. Many groups of men in the barracks collected discarded bits of sugarcane and boiled and fermented them into crude, intoxicating spirits. Some had become addicted to this alcohol. A recurring problem, because of this and because of the shortage of women, was the defiling of women by drunken men who ignored boundaries of marriage. In one instance a husband took a burning piece of firewood to the face of the violator and then to his own wife who was thus twice victimized. Amir calmed both men and instructed other women in the barracks to treat the burns on the woman's face. He himself applied poultices to the other man's face. The two men could not be left in the same barracks so Amir took the sex-offender with him to the next barracks and talked to the second *sirdar* there to accommodate him.

But returning to the barracks, Amir found that the husband was still in a rage and was refusing to allow his wife back into his room. Talking with the wife in the presence of the other women, Amir asked the wife what she wanted to do. She said she wanted to get as far away from both men as she could. Amir realized he would have to talk to Mr. Landers in the morning. Meanwhile, he instructed her to stay with another woman worker. He couldn't help wondering how often that woman had been violated as well.

The next morning, Amir went to see Mr. Landers who, while expressing sympathy, shook his head.

"Amir, the divorce bill failed to pass into law last year. So they cannot divorce. They are married and must remain that way."

"But Sir...the man is in a rage...it was not her fault..."

"I know, Amir. But there is nothing we can do."

The barracks was quiet. All workers were out in the field. Even the injured woman was nowhere to be seen. Amir did his rounds of the work crews and saw the woman, still bandaged, head down, chopping stalks with a work crew. But the husband was not in any of the crews. He asked but no one knew. At the end of the day, he reported the missing man to Mr. Donaldson who was in his office.

"I will make a note, Amir. Sometimes they come back. Maybe he will. He cannot work elsewhere because his permit is with us."

Weeks went by and Amir believed that the man would not return. He wondered if angry men like him joined underground work crews, doing other odd jobs and hid under the radar until their indentured years were over, then blended in with workers doing other jobs. But Amir could not spend more time on matters like that. His workload was huge and with the troubled, infertile side of the estate requiring his attention he did the best he could to keep the workers content, spending one night a week having mediation meetings and a group meeting where grievances were aired and solutions sought.

So the months took on a routine. Purat's duties of loading the cane stalks on to carts synchronized with Amir's work crews and both men found themselves working even after the six o'clock siren every night making sure that bundles were stacked on the fields or loaded on to carts ready for the morning ride to the train station.

One of Amir's duties as *sirdar* was to pick up the mail from the managers' office and deliver them to the indentured workers. There was a small post office at the train station and the Harrison Estate letters were picked up weekly by the managers.

One morning in September 1884, four months after his wedding letter home in May, Amir was pleasantly surprised to see a letter from Gulab telling him how pleased his parents were about the wedding. But it was Gulab's next letter, several months later that worried Amir. It was a blazing hot morning in January and Amir opened the letter during his lunch break while he sat alone in the middle of the cane fields. The letter started with bright sentiments about how happy his parents were that Amir had a wife for company in a new land, but it ended on a note of some concern. Gulab was once again postponing his application to work in Durban because of *Mathaji* and *Bapuji*'s health. Gulab's words kept reassuring him that there was nothing to worry about, but Amir read between the lines. His headache once again returned and that evening Bhagirathi rubbed it with oil and massaged the pain away as she did many nights, but the worry lingered. His work was extensive and he was now nearing the completion of his second full year into his indenture contract. He could not think of going home to check on his parents. So Amir did what he did best, he immersed himself in his work.

The soil on the east side of the slope did have potential. Some of the plants that he bought from Bhimnad and Himal were thriving in the months that followed. The best ones to thrive were the red roses. These were not the long stemmed variety, but the bushy, thornier kind, which did not seem to mind the rocky soil and even the shale conditions of the soil. He took flower cuttings to the two managers whose wives loved them. The mango trees thrived and the clusters he planted in various spots began to grow. It would be years before they would begin to bear any fruit but patience was a virtue that Amir did possess.

One of the other plants that Amir bought from his friends was called red-hot-poker, the bushy succulent red flower cheekily swaying on top of a long green stem. This one he decided to plant across the river from his front door at the base of the next hill arising eastward from there. That hill was not cultivated. It lay lush with grass and healthy trees, but no particular crops. There was however, wild aloe, its multiple, fat, succulent stems with thorny edges, growing richly in clumps. Amir cultivated these perennials, dividing them at the roots and planting them in a row going half way up the hill. In several weeks, Amir noticed that the red-hot-pokers and the aloes had flourished with little water. Both species had actually started to multiply into more clumps. He examined the soil and was encouraged by the rich, moist texture. He bought fifty more red-hot-pokers and continued his experiment. He was now nearly a year into his job as *sirdar* and had gained the trust of his workers and managers.

He approached Mr. Landers and asked about the new hill on which the red hot pokers were thriving. Mr. Landers said that hill was not assigned to any estate. There was no interest in planting sugarcane there. But he would approach young Mr. Harrison to see if it could be assigned to the Harrison Estate to use. That process took another few months, but in June the permission came through. By then the red hot pokers had proliferated and the harvest was excellent. The aloe stems could be cut and stripped into long strings for tying bunches of flowers. Mr. Landers gave Amir permission to see if he could sell the flowers.

Amir approached Adam first and placed some bunches in his shop, but found that local Indians did not buy flowers. They grew them in their small gardens and mostly carnations, marigolds and hibiscus for prayers. The little church took a few bunches, but the old white pastor there was preparing to leave and go back to England at the end of the year and couldn't promise a regular order of flowers. There were very few white parishioners as Avoca had mostly Indian and a few African families. So Amir decided that he would take the bunches of roses and pokers on carts two miles south on the North Coast Road to the homes of the white *memsahibs* who lived in sprawling homes in the place called Red Hill, named after its rich red soil. At first he cautiously approached these properties, many of which were guarded by dogs. He would stand at the iron gates and call out for the servants.

"*Areh Bhayah…areh Bhayah…aiyeh…*brother…come."

"*Namasthe…kiyah baath hai*? Hello, what is it?" they would ask and small conversations would ensue.

These were mostly Indian men who were the gardeners and Indian women who were nannies and cooks. Thus he slowly established a clientele. But this work was in addition to his work as *sirdar* and had to be done once a week on Saturdays. He diligently handed over the few shillings to the office and Bhagirathi, who was used to the business operations in her family's store, kept a record of the number of bunches tied, the number sold and the money given to the managers.

On Sunday mornings, Amir and Bhagirathi worked on their own vegetable patch. She was pregnant with their first child and he was protective so he did the heavy hoeing and allowed her just to water and tend to it lightly during the weekdays. Also during the week Bhagirathi accompanied Sibani, pregnant too with her second child now, to walk Ashok slowly to Bhodraj's school for his two-hour morning lessons. He happily held on to both their hands, his mother gathering him up in her arms from time to time and covering his face with kisses as he wiggled and giggled. He was thriving, studying English and Hindi and had made new friends. He had helped his father build a little cart, and even though he was eager to get back to it at home, he was good about concentrating on his lessons with Bhodraj. Purat had found four old carry-cot wheels at Suleiman's shop and using a piece of wood as a seat he had secured the wheels on two iron axles and attached a string in front for Ashok to steer it. Ashok gave his friends turns to ride it careening down to their stream much to the heart palpitations of his mother.

Walking to school with his mother and his *Kaakiji*, respected aunt, as he addressed Bhagirathi, was a special time. While waiting for Ashok, Sibani and Bhagirathi spent the time with Indira or helping Namita prepare the prayer goods that her husband needed for any prayer *hawans*, ceremonies that he had to perform. At other times they went to see Fatima if she was not busy helping Adam in the shop. During the week Sibani also took in washing from the few white families and free Indians in the area, but now that she was pregnant she allowed the women next door to take that *dhobi* job since it gave them a little money. The stream was a good opportunity to expand their *dhobi* business and Sibani did not mind.

Sibani and Bhagirathi also started a sewing business. Purat and Amir were both making twenty shillings a month, but the extra money earned by the wives was important for household expenses. Purat and Amir had bought a second-hand sewing machine for each of them from Suleiman's shop and a small table each to set it on in their front rooms. The sewing machine was a curved block of wood on one side connected to a metal shaft on the other that held the thread on top and a needle at its base. It was turned by a small wheel on the right. Sibani and Bhagirathi did the large seams by machine, but the more delicate stitching they still did by hand. They would sit outside watching Ashok, now six, playing by the stream with other children, and leading them into mischief around the *dhobis'* washed clothes that were drying on the rocks. Sibani and Bhagirathi also had irons which rested on the fire pit grills to heat and after a garment was finished they ironed it before giving it to the client and collecting the shilling or two in pay. The women who brought them sewing orders were mostly from among the free Indians, but also a few of the indentured women.

Sunday afternoons were spent mostly at the gathering place outside Adam's shop, in front of the little white church under the tamarind tree. On the first Sunday after they had arrived, Amir and Purat bought simple beds, tables and chairs from Suleiman's shop, which was across from Adam's shop and took them by bullock cart to their homes. But subsequent Sundays were spent enjoying the camaraderie of friends and making new ones. Some men engaged in friendly stick-sword fights with others yelling encouragement and children played *dunda-gholi,* with a twig across a little hole in the ground and another twig to flip it to see how far it would land. Little girls sat in the dust playing with five stones thrown up in the air which they would dexterously catch in one hand while singing play-songs. The church allowed them to use one of the latrines on the edge of the horse and bullock fields that abutted the church property. That latrine was used by their African caretaker and gardener. The children loved watching the horses and bullock grazing in that field, waiting to be saddled or hooked on to carts when required. Food was brought and shared picnic-style under the tamarind tree. Bhagirathi and Sibani saw many of their own creations worn by the children and women, and mused on ways to expand their offerings. Fatima told them that she sold saris in her store and Bhagirathi bought one with an idea in her head. The saris were imported from India by merchants in town and Adam in turn bought them and sold them in his shop. Each sari was six yards long, meticulously embroidered by garment workers in India.

Bhagirathi cut four lengths, two for skirts or *langas* and two smaller pieces for blouses or *cholis*. She gathered the skirt lengths at the waist with a little slit on top tied by a thin cloth string and sewed the seam at the back down to ankle length. For the *cholis* she designed a fashionable round neck with buttons down the front and hand-sewed some beads picked from the reeds growing at the water's edge. The *choli* was short, ending just before the waist, above the *langa*, leaving a modest, traditional inch of midriff showing. On her monthly visits home, she took her creations to Ebrahim *Kaaka*, Uncle Ebrahim, whom all the children in the area had always addressed respectfully as *Kaaka*, father's brother. Ebrahim agreed to show off her creations in his eponymous store that sold everything. Soon Bhagirathi brought orders from women there and so their business increased.

The local Indian midwife who had a shack close to Rajiv and Namita's home, checked on Bhagirathi and Sibani regularly for half-a-shilling each time, but the government had also recently started sending a doctor on horseback once a month to check on Indian communities at government cost. Durban's Medical Officer of Health and the Inspector of Nuisances whose job it was to monitor sanitation, came to Avoca from time to time. The Doctor checked the workers in the barracks. The main concern was the spread of diseases like dysentery, but he also checked the health of women workers and did drop in to check on Bhagirathi's and Sibani's pregnancies, not by touching them, but just by asking questions.

Purat's work was also busy and becoming more stressful. He had been assigned a few Indian and African workers to load the cane stalks on to the carts, off load them on to trains at the station and then off load them again at the Phoenix station where they would be transported to the huge Phoenix sugar mill. Both Purat and Amir had started learning and speaking the local African language, Zulu, as each had African men on their varied work crews. Purat saw Sajiv, Parvati, Ebrahim, Prabhu and other friends frequently in the Inanda and Phoenix estates.

The station masters at Avoca station and Phoenix got to know him and both white men looked upon him to translate and help as issues arose. From time to time there would be Indian railway workers brought to those stations to repair or extend lines and when arguments arose, Purat helped to calm things down. As Mr. Landers had said a year ago, building had started on the extended railway toward the wattle plantation west of the Harrison estate. A bridge was being built just yards from the estate and brickyard. Purat was often called upon to settle disputes there as well. More than a hundred Indian workers from railway barracks at the large Umgeni station and even as far away as the barracks serving the harbour were brought in to build the bridge and the extended railway. Purat was finding that his services were being requested more and more by the railway. There were huge railway barracks between the main railway station and the large Umgeni train station. These barracks, called the Magazine barracks, were often erupting with conflicts. Also, the Inspector of Nuisances had to go in often to supervise sanitation concerns. The bucket system for collecting night soil was being implemented across Durban and urgently at all the barracks to curtail the habit of defecating behind bushes and along rivers, which thousands of Indians in barracks had been forced to do since no sanitary system had been previously provided. So Purat was taken as translator and peacemaker and was released to the government on those instances by the Harrisons.

Bhagirathi's baby girl was born in May of 1885 and Sibani's little girl was born in June and both women were assisted in birth by the midwife. The husbands, pleased with the midwife's work paid her over and above the three shillings' fee. With religious flexibility, the baby naming ceremonies were held together eleven days after Sibani's baby was born. Rajiv had opened his sacred scriptures and recommended the letters or sounds that the baby names should start with and sitting by their stream at a little fire, with fruit trays as offerings to the gods, Amir and Bhagirathi named their little girl Jaldhara, meaning current of water. Both parents loved the quiet dignity and calming sounds of rivers and streams. Sibani had whispered to Purat that she wanted her daughter to be named Nina, meaning beautiful eyes, as her bouncy daughter looked at her parents with her sparkling black eyes and chubby cheeks. Bhagirathi's parents and all of Amir and Purat's friends were there and Sajiv and Parvati played the role of Sibani's brother and *Bhabi* in place of her parents as required by the ceremony. The little religious shrines inside the two homes were taken outside, cleaned, washed and replaced with new tray cloths, new flowers and fresh *dhiyas* were lit.

With new babies to fuss over, in addition to their work, the women and neighbours were kept busy over the next weeks as the men returned to their dawn to dusk jobs. The cooler mornings and evenings in the months between June and October were always welcomed by all. The indentured workers, railway workers and African labourers had to lift huge rocks to build the new bridge. By October, Purat was seconded more and more by the government and found that his job had become very diverse. But the Harrison Estate still held him to his contract as was required for the five years of indenture. He was helping at the bridge site as supervisor and at times was called to settle disputes at the wharf where labourers and stevedores were often at loggerheads.

Chapter 12

Changes

Over the next several months, Amir's weekly trek to the white *memsahibs'* homes with bunches of flowers was yielding good money for the Harrison Estate. He learned how to steer a bullock cart and was able to rent one every Saturday for a shilling plus a few pennies for feeding the animals. Pleased with his excellent service, the white women spread the word and his client list increased in number to over fifty *memsahibs*.

One Saturday, as Amir slowed down his bullock cart, cognizant of the quietness of the tranquil neighborhood, he noticed a small bank with a sign that read The Natal Bank. It was located on the main North Coast Road at the corner where the main road intersected with the smaller road that led up the hill to the *memsahibs'* houses.

Amir hopped off the cart and walked up to the signboard to find out the hours of operation. The bank was closed as Saturdays were half days for banks. He decided to come an hour earlier on Saturdays to deposit the company's money at this bank so it would be separate from his own money, which he still kept at home in three parcels in the chinks in the walls of his house.

Subsequently, each month he withdrew the company money and gave it to Mr. Landers with a clear hand-written *hisaab*, account, written out by Bhagirathi, showing total bunches of flowers sold and money earned, minus the cost of renting the cart and feed. Bhagirathi showed Amir that the money he took out of the bank at the end of each month was a few pennies more than the money he put in and she explained the concept of interest to him as explained to her by Prabhu. She urged Amir to trust The Natal Bank with their money too. She showed him the *hisaab* that she was keeping for their own personal money. He was pleasantly surprised by her meticulous account keeping. He drew his fingers across the lines showing the four pounds he had saved from the Phoenix indenture, plus the eighty pounds' *dowry* that they had received from Bhagirathi's father, plus the ten pounds six shillings saved since he had become *sirdar*. In another column, she had subtracted their modest expenses plus the three shillings a month they were sending home to India. When they took out the little cloth packages from their walls and counted it all up, their total savings added up to ninety-six pounds and six shillings over the two years since Amir's arrival. He agreed to put ninety pounds into the bank in a new personal account. The remainder and the few shillings she earned from sewing would be for food and household expenses.

Rajiv had started a fund for the building of a temple in the future. Unlike the Campbell Estate where Sajiv was able to negotiate a piece of unused land, here in Avoca the Harrison Estate was locked in several different negotiations regarding crop variety, difficulties with the mill, and the building of the railway bridge.

Rajiv had not found an opportunity to discuss temple plans with the managers. But the free Indians as well as the indentured labourers contributed whatever they could and the money in the temple fund was slowly growing. Amir and Adam talked Rajiv into using the bank to keep that money.

Religion continued to play an important role in the lives of all the Indians. Most Indians in the area were Hindus who observed their private prayer ceremonies in their homes and once a year they celebrated the festival of lights, *Diwali*. This year, 1885, Ashok and his friends were looking forward to *Diwali* in November. Amir and Purat made sure that their families had new clothes and the children had one shop-bought toy from Adam's or Suleiman's shop. Dozens of clay lamps or *dhiyas* were purchased from Adam's shop. These would be lit up on *Diwali* night and placed all around the houses. Amir and Purat sat Ashok and the other children beside their stream on the preceding evenings and explained the significance of *Diwali*.

"*Papaji*, tell me the story again," Ashok exhorted his father.

"*Aachah…Diwali* marks the conquering of the evil Ravana by Lord Rama…"

"No, no tell the whole story! Tell the whole story, *Papaji*!!" Ashok knew that this was an action story with intrigue, war and fighting and the good men won.

Laughing Purat began. *"Areh...aachah Beta...aachah...yes,* all right my son...all right!"

Not only the children, but everyone in the shacks gathered around the night fire to listen. Purat started the story where Lord Rama was about to be crowned King of Ayodha by his father King Dashratha who had three wives. Rama was the eldest wife's son. The third wife, jealous of Rama, tricked Dashratha into exiling Rama to the forest threatening suicide if he didn't comply. Distraught, Dashratha granted her wish that their son Bharatha would be crowned. Rama, his wife Sita, and his youngest brother Laxman went away into the forest to serve their fourteen-year exile. A few days later, Dashratha died of sorrow. Bharatha was away on a journey, but when he returned he became furious with his mother. Loyal to his brother Rama, Bharatha refused the throne and set out to find Rama in the forest.

Rama insisted on carrying out the promise he made to his father. Bharatha returned home, but simply began to look after the dynasty until Rama's return. While they were in the forest, evil Ravana came from the island of Lanka and kidnapped Sita. Rama and Laxman frantically looked for her and they were befriended by a race of human-like monkeys who promised to help. One of the leaders, a mighty monkey named Hanuman, found a way to go to Lanka and he discovered Sita wasting away, frightened and alone in a small temple on the grounds of Ravana's palace. Overcoming huge obstacles, Rama's army of monkeys and bears crossed the ocean and landed on the island of Lanka, killed Ravana and his ilk and brought Sita back. Since their journey from Lanka took them through South India first and then back north to Ayodha, the Tamil Hindus in South India celebrate *Diwali* a day before north Indians. They lit millions of *dhiyas* to light Rama's journey from South India to the north all the way to his palace in Ayodhya.

Ashok and his friends interrupted Purat several times wanting to know about the actual fighting and the next day the boys reenacted the fights between good Rama and evil Ravana using sticks and slings. For a week the games continued in anticipation of *Diwali* night.

This year *Diwali* was in early November. The Harrison Estate allowed two days off for *Diwali,* the Tuesday and the Wednesday. The

Tamil Indians originally from South India celebrated a day earlier than the North Indians. The latter visited their homes and shared in a feast. The next day the other Hindus reciprocated. Sibani, Bhagirathi and their women friends cooked up several pots of vegetables from their modest gardens, *roti* and sweets and a steady stream of visitors enjoyed the on-going feast laid out by the stream. At night the homes were turned into a wonderland with dozens of small clay lamps lined up all around the shacks and along the stream. Children went to bed late, bellies full and minds and hearts filled with joy.

The Muslim religious observance of the Islamic New Year was celebrated in a different month each year and was called *Muharram*. Coincidentally, this particular year *Muharram* too was to fall in November a few days before *Diwali*. This would be the first year that Amir, Purat, their families and all the other Hindu families in the village would celebrate it with Adam and Suleiman's families. Adam explained that floats, known as *Tajiyas*, had been built by Muslim families, mainly in town and these floats on wheels would be brought to the Umgeni River where they would be immersed, some soluble pieces left to float into the sea while the actual pagodas were taken back and stored for the following year. On the Sunday preceding their *Diwali* celebrations, a large group of Hindus accompanied Adam, Suleiman and their families by train to the Umgeni River to participate in the *Muharram* festivities. After the *Tajiyas* were immersed in the Umgeni and prayers were read, there was music, food and dancing into the night and many Hindu-Muslim friendships were formed.

But the government had put a curfew on *Muharram* celebrations and all indentured labourers had to be back in their barracks by 9 o'clock at night. Force was being used by police mounted on horseback against some of the reveling men, so Amir, Purat, Adam, Suleiman and their mates gathered their families and guided them back to the train station before any trouble began. Not only was Ashok asleep in his father's lap on the train ride home, many of the other children and some of the adults as well dozed off from sheer exhaustion.

***

It was December of 1885 and with their baby seven months old, Bhagirathi was two months pregnant again. The pokers flower hill was thriving with a rich swath of orange-red spreading across nearly half the hill. The plants that Bhimnad and Himal originally sold to him were of two varieties, one that bloomed in summer and the other, a hardier variety, bloomed in winter, offering Amir blooms all year. The red roses on the original hill were thriving too and Amir needed more help. As *sirdar* he diverted two more workers to the flower side of the business and then approached Mr. Landers.

"Sir, the flowers are doing very well, Sir. I have transferred two more workers to work those hills. They are walking each day from the barracks. Sir, I want them to stay in the houses you have so kindly provided for Purat and me and with four rooms I could have four new workers there. I need to move Purat's and my families out of those barracks by the stream and build two houses further up the hill, by the fig tree, Sir."

"Amir, you are the *sirdar*, you can do what you see is necessary. And yes, you are right the flowers are flourishing. Young Mr. Harrison has mentioned it too. Mr. Harrison Senior has gone back to Scotland leaving the running of his estate to his son. We are relying on you to expand the flower business."

Amir rolled his head and waited for a response about the houses he wanted to build.

"Where will you build Purat's house?"

"Sir, there are two flat spots, one under the fig tree and one across from it on the pathway near the narchees trees."

"But I know how much you like the stream, Amir."

"Yes Sir…but it's only a very short way down the hill, Sir. Also the water pumps are there too and we can still go to the stream to bathe and to the pumps to carry water…it's all right, Sir."

"*Aachah*…okay, good Amir…we are counting on you…"

Mr. Landers reflected and seemed like he was going to say more, hesitated and then simply said, "It's all right, Amir. You go ahead and do what you think is necessary." He stood up to welcome two white men who walked into the office, men that Amir had seen several times before on the estate with Mr. Harrison and the managers. Amir bowed and left, careful not to touch the men as they shook hands with Mr. Landers.

Since Amir and Purat's shack could each accommodate two men, Amir transferred four men from the sugarcane fields to the flower hills.

But first the two additional shacks had to be built. Amir explained to Purat and together they each designed the two shacks as simple square structures with four small rooms and an outdoor latrine. Amir's shack under the fig tree was ready in two weeks with the help of the four men and two additional African men, whom Purat had brought from the railways, working from sunrise to sunset. The tin, wood, nails and other materials were bought by the estate, since the men were still indentured. The shacks still belonged to the Harrisons, but Amir and Purat had control over their building plans.

Amir's and Purat's families both moved in together in Amir's shack, while Purat's shack was being built. In another two weeks when Purat's shack was ready the families began to make these new shacks their homes. Vegetable patches were dug, outdoor fire pits and cooking grills were set up and Bhodraj brought cow dung from his wife Indira's father's dairy farm to plaster the floors. Bhagirathi brought two small *tulsi* plants from her father's large *tulsi* bush, which he in turn had cultivated from seeds that he originally brought from his village in India. She gave one plant to Sibani and they each planted one in front of their homes. They surrounded the little plant with small rocks and designated that as the place where they would say their morning prayers to the sun and pour a symbolic small *lota* urn of water, before going inside to light their household *dhiyas*.

Amir's days were long and hard, every weekday spent on the sugar estate and flower hills. Saturday was spent in flower sales to the white clients and even Sundays now were not days of rest. He rarely accompanied his family to the gatherings outside Adam's home and he and Bhagirathi had not been into town for months. Bhagirathi saw how gnarled and broken the skin on his hands and feet had become. She pounded pieces of aloe and mixed it with mustard oil and a little turmeric powder to make a paste. She massaged this on his hands and feet once or twice a week in the evenings.

With continued problems at the sugarcane barracks, Amir's evenings were often spent settling disputes. The African railway workers camped near the bridge that they were building beside the river. At night they made alcoholic brews and had a little *shebeen*, a drinking shack, where they boiled and brewed strong spirits. The Indian workers, in addition to their own cane spirits, were also joining the railway workers at night and fights that started at night would spill over into the mornings and on to the cane fields. Amir's headaches came and went and when he was in pain with a severe headache, Bhagirathi rubbed his head with salves that she pounded on her homemade mortar and pestle using a clean large rock as base and a smaller smooth rock to pound. After massaging, she wrapped clean cloth around his head, covering his eyes, as the light hurt his eyes increasing the headache.

In late January 1886, the Christian Mission that ran the little white church made some changes at the church. The old priest left and Pastor Mohan arrived from a small village near Madras. There were very few white families, only the managers' families and the station master, but they all now mostly went to an all-white church in nearby Greenwood Park. There were no Indian Christians in Avoca yet, but Pastor Mohan was given a different priority. He was tasked with providing a school for all the Indian children in the area. Pastor Mohan busied himself with turning the entrance half of the church into a mission school while the original chancel area, pulpit and three front rows of pews remained intact for future Sunday service. The remaining seven pews were moved back closer to the entrance and designated for student seating. Local Indian men helped to build low long tables to be used as desks for students. The day after Pastor Mohan arrived Rajiv went to greet him. Together they discussed the mission of the church.

"Mohan *Bhai*, almost all the Indians here are Hindus and I perform all their religious *hawans*, ceremonies, baby naming...everything."

"Don't worry, *Bhayah* Rajiv. I am from Madras...I know about *Punditji*'s work. I am not here to convert ..."

"*Nayh...nayh....*" Rajiv was embarrassed, but relieved. Mohan and he had strolled out of the church and were looking at the grounds, stopping to smell the flowers that the church gardener was tending in the front yard.

"*Bhayah*...the *gorawallahs*, white folks, are recruiting more and more workers from around Madras. There will be some Tamil Christians who will come. But I am also interested in making sure that our children here are given an education. I was happy when I was offered this post."

The pastor reassured Rajiv that he was not there to convert Rajiv's Hindu flock. Rajiv apprised Pastor Mohan about the skills and successes of Bhodraj as the village school teacher. So it was that Bhodraj became the first school teacher at the Mission. The Indian community rallied around Pastor Mohan and helped him plant flowers and Indian vegetables at the small house that he was given across the street, close to Suleiman's shop and home. This was the same house that had been used by the previous pastor.

Ashok now nearly seven years old was a confident student and numbers were by far his best area of learning. He loved math and it was a joy for Purat to see him trying to teach his baby sister and Jaldhara numbers on their plump little fingers before they could even say their first words. The walk to school was a little longer from the fig tree where their new homes were located, but several of the women walked together with Sibani and Ashok. Bhagirathi watched both babies Jaldhara and Nina until Sibani returned and they resumed their sewing. Sibani no longer did the *dhobi* washing of clothes leaving that to the women by the stream. Their sewing business was thriving, not only machine sewing but they also started doing delicate hand smocking on baby clothes as well as lace and embroidery work. Even the managers' wives liked their smocking and embroidery on children's clothes. The extra money was a welcome addition to both families' savings.

It was in early June of that year, 1886, that Amir received the letter from Gulab that broke his heart. Amir had delivered all the indentured mail that cold morning, but did not open his letter until the end of the day. It was a Wednesday and as was his custom he finished work on the sugar estate and stopped to look at his roses and pokers. At the stream, he sat under the jamun tree and opened his letter.

> Dear Bhayah Amir,
> It is with a heavy heart that I write this letter. Bapuji and Mathaji both passed away within two days of each other after a severe illness struck our village. The visiting doctors called the disease dysentery and Bhayah they both suffered two weeks of very bad health with vomiting and worse. Bapuji went first and Mathaji gave up her fight and went two days later. Chachi tried to help but her husband too was ill and preceded our parents in departing this earth. Bhayah, I performed the funeral rites by our beloved river and scattered their ashes. Chachi has gone home to Calcutta to her

brothers and like her I am selling our home and our piece of land to the zamindar. Bhayah, I am coming to you. I have been to the recruiting office in Muzzafarnagar and I am told that once my health tests are completed I would be able to go on a ship called the Umvoti which is to leave here in early September and will arrive in your Durban Harbour in late October. Please forgive me for this news Bhayah, please forgive me.
  Your brother Gulab

Amir sat stunned and then the tears came. He held his face in his hands and cried, his bare feet in the stream and his *pugri* dismantling from his head, tangled in his fingers. His gasping brought one of the men from the stream shacks running to his side, but Amir was inconsolable. The young man, Ajit, ran the short distance up the hill to Purat's house and both hurried back to Amir. Between wracking sobs, Amir gave them the news. They simply sat with Amir not saying much and it was an hour later that Purat instructed Ajit to go and tell Bhagirathi and Sibani who would be worried as darkness had set in.

Even in his grief, while sitting quietly with Purat, Amir asked about Purat's family.

"*Nayh Bhayah*...they are all right. I just received a letter from my brothers a few days ago."

"The sickness?"

"*Nayh Bhayah*...they are upriver, little ways from your part of the village. My brother said that some people did get sick, but he did not mention that anyone had died...my *Maaji*, *Papaji* and brothers are all right. Now let's get you home, Amir *Bhai*...let's go home."

The next evening after the end of the work day, Rajiv came to Amir's house to perform prayers and read scripture. The letter having arrived in June meant that his parents had died two months prior, though Gulab had not indicated a date. Nevertheless, Amir's family and friends gathered for the solemn prayers under the majestic fig tree. Bhagirathi, now heavy with child in her eighth month of pregnancy, was assisted with the preparations by Rajiv's and Sajiv's wives and by Sibani, who was herself in her early months of pregnancy. Ashok and his friends kept the babies occupied dragging them back and forth on the dirt road in his cart. Amir, eyes red, hands shaking, performed the prayers at the *tulsi* shrub, but even in his sorrow his heart rose to see so many of the sugarcane workers silently standing in his yard, just there to show support. There was nothing left now for him in India.

"This here is home, these are my extended family now," he thought as he prayed.

***

The next few weeks saw Amir immersed in his work. Bhagirathi bought woollen socks for his tattered feet and when she was visiting her parents' home in Phoenix, she also bought Indian *chappals*, sandals, for both Amir and Purat so that they did not have to go barefoot into the fields. In addition, she bought each of them covered shoes to protect their feet especially during the colder June and July days. One Saturday as Amir was delivering flowers in Red Hill in his rented bullock cart he noticed an unusual sight. He clutched the ornate iron entrance gate to one of his client's homes and called out,

"*Areh Bhayah*!!! *Bhayah*…what are you doing…why are you throwing out those plants?"

"Too much, too wild…*memsahib* likes clean garden…not too much of one kind," the gardener said pointing to a large pile of agapanthus plants that he had dug up and thrown outside the gate. It was late June, winter, so there were no blooms on the plants. But Amir remembered seeing the exquisite head of dozens of tiny blue bells clustered into a magnificent crown on the apex of long green stems in the hot summer months. The gardener had planted the agapanthus all along the inside wall of the property close to the gates. Culling perennials was a wise practice especially in a garden where diversity was the focus and the gardener was now piling up the discarded clumps outside the gates.

"*Bhayah*…don't throw them away. Can I take them?"

"Yes, yes, help yourself," and the man helped Amir load close to a hundred of the plants on to his cart. Paying Amir for several bunches of roses and pokers, the gardener hurried to the house to give the housekeeper the flowers to be arranged in several vases throughout the rambling house.

Elated at his find, on his way back home Amir took a detour and went to Bhimnad and Himal first. They were excited about Amir's find and gratefully accepted several of the agapanthus to cultivate.

"*Bhayah* Amir, you will need to use fertilizer to cultivate these."

"Well that hill of flowers is very large...we ferment our own vegetable peelings to make fertilizer for our small vegetable garden, but..."

"Nayh...nayh...you will need proper fertilizer...let us show you."

Bhimnad and Himal walked Amir to the back of their garden sheds close to the river. They had stacked dozens of large paper bags of what looked like cement.

"This is professional fertilizer," explained Bhimnad.

"*Areh?*"

"*Haanh...jihaanh...*yes, absolutely yes. And you will never guess how it's made!!" And both gardeners laughed uproariously.

"Your night soil...all of our night soil..."

"*Areh chee...chee...chee,*" Amir shook his hand, expressing disgust.

"No...no... it is fine and very good. There is an estate not far from the Umgeni River...it's owned by a white man...Mr. Clare. The government transports all the buckets of night soil that they collect from all over Durban and dumps it on his huge estate. He has a large crew of Indian and African labourers led by white men, engineers, who use chemicals on that waste and put it through huge machines and turn it into fertilizer that is used for crops."

"*Areh...nayh...nayh,*" Amir could not believe what he was hearing.

"Come, come look." Himal cut open a bag and apart from a strong, but not too offensive smell, the fertilizer looked like garden soil.

"When you plant your agapanthus use a spade of this fertilizer at the roots of each plant and water it regularly at first. After it takes, the rain will be enough to water it."

Amir planted and fertilized the agapanthus on his poker hill, above the bright red swath of red pokers, toward the top of the hill and each day his workers carried buckets of water from the stream and hand watered the plants.

***

Bhagirathi's second baby girl arrived in late July of 1886. They named her Sookdhay, the giver of joy, an apt name during Amir's mourning for his parents. Amir happily joined in the prayers and the small feast, and the children were excited to welcome another baby amongst them. The women were now very busy with babies, vegetable gardens, sewing orders and Ashok's schooling. Amir and Purat too, immersed themselves in their twelve-hour work days. Ajit, a short dark-skinned young man, emerged as a leader amongst Amir's flower crew and took admirable responsibility for the red-hot-pokers, the roses, the aloe and the fledgling agapanthus crops.

Ajit was a strong bodied, amicable young man not yet eighteen years old. Having come from Madras, he spoke mainly Tamil, but had learned Hindi while still back home. He had picked up English as well while doing odd jobs for white officers in the Madras area where his parents still lived. Amir was grateful for Ajit's leadership since more and more of his time was being spent resolving issues in the sugar estate. The managers had downloaded more responsibilities on the two *sirdars* while they seemed to have meetings two or three times a week with other white men who came to their office. Amir was not sure what was transpiring, but he was too busy to give it more thought.

The Umvoti was due to arrive at Durban Harbour in October. So a month before, Amir kept an eye out for Mr. Landers so he could speak to him. Early one morning he succeeded.

"Sir…Mr. Landers…" Amir shuffled into Andrew's office just as Andrew was settling at his desk.

"What is it, Amir?"

"Sir…there is a ship…Umvoti arriving next month?"

Andrew pulled out a large notebook from his side desk drawer and flipped through the pages.

"Yes…here it is…the Umvoti…due to arrive here on October 26, 1886. Why do you ask, Amir?"

"Sir, my brother Gulab…he wrote to say that he would be coming…"

"Oh…Amir…I am so sorry…I have been so busy with meetings…the other *sirdar* told me about your parents' death…I am so sorry."

Amir rolled his head muttering thank you, but said nothing else. Andrew had started to run his fingers down the page.

"Ah yes…here it is…Gulab Sing…yes I do remember. Your brother had given the Muzzafarnagar office your name. We try to keep families together, Amir, so yes he is coming here. You must be happy about that?"

"Yes, Sir…yes…happy, Sir."

"Quite! Tell you what…I will be meeting that ship the day after it docks…you can come with me to the docks…would you like that?"

"Oh…thank you…thank you, Sir!!" Amir's face broke out into a rare smile.

Amir left Andrew's office with an unusually light step. Smiling and humming songs from his wedding chorus he returned to the fields. Andrew worked on a stack of papers and decided to go home early for lunch. He walked up Mill Road and turned left just before he reached Avoca Road, on to the small side lane leading to his house. He nodded to the gardener and tiptoed on to the verandah. He opened the door gingerly and entered quietly, not wanting to disturb the babies.

Annie was standing in the dining room engrossed in something that she was reading on the large, oval, mahogany table, one hand resting on the smooth wooden back of the velvet covered chair. Andrew walked past the ornate sitting room, careful not to brush against the intricately carved hand rests of the burgundy couch.

The clock on the mantle softly chimed the hour and moving softly on the Indian carpet, past the filigreed side board, lithely stepping around the silk screen separating sitting room and dining room, he tiptoed smiling into the dining room.

Reaching her, he silently embraced her from behind placing his palms on the gentle bump of her belly. She turned and put her arms around his neck, kissing him gently.

"How is our baby boy in here?" he smiled with his hand still on her stomach.

"Aye, Andrew…a baby boy, you think? How do you know she is not daughter number three?"

"Annie, I am outnumbered! Two beautiful daughters and my charming wife! I need a son to start my football team!"

Laughing, he guided her to the more comfortable, smaller, muted burgundy couch in the sitting room and stuffed a plush cushion behind her for support.

The parlour off to the side had a small fireplace and Andrew could see their *ayah*, children's nanny, busy with their two daughters, aged one and two. *Ayah* was feeding them from a bowl and with the spoon in hand was following them as they went from toy to toy. She cooed and talked gently to them in Hindi.

"I see Nora and Lilian are giving *ayah* the run around," Andrew whispered to Annie.

"Aye. Cook has your lunch ready, dear. Wash up and I will join you."

The large kitchen toward the back of the house had a small adjoining breakfast room. With the fireplace kindled beside the carved wooden table and two low-backed chairs, it was ideal for the couple to eat undisturbed. Cook had laid the table with the everyday china plates, silver ware and short drinking glasses.

"Cook has prepared roast lamb today. I notice from the aromas she has added some of her Indian spices. I hope it is not too spicy, can't tolerate too much spice recently."

"Ah, I know but she always caters to your delicate tastes, Annie."

Cook entered just then with two small platters and placed them on the table. The one in front of Annie was glazed and had a warm smell of cinnamon wafting. The platter she placed in front of Andrew smelled of curry flavours.

"Ah, thank you Cook Mary! Sweet lamb for Madam and spicy for me, thank you!" Like all the Indian Marys in all the colonial households, Cook smiled and nodded and continued to move serenely between kitchen and breakfast room bringing in other small delicacies. She left these on the ornate, wood-carved tall-boy cabinet against the wall.

After lunch, Andrew and Annie spent time with their two little girls in the parlour. At nap time, *ayah* took the girls to their nursery, down the hall to the side of the house, two rooms away from their parents' bedroom.

"Annie, come and sit for a bit." Andrew drew Annie to the two light green high backed chairs in the parlour, but Annie chose the soft pale green couch instead and sank in, drawing Andrew next to her. Andrew, now twenty-six years old effused confidence as plantation manager. With a growing family, he was firmly established as a well-respected peer among British officers and a solid family man. He had also earned a reputation as a smart businessman, ensuring best prices for cane, but also in negotiating business deals for the Harrison Estate.

"My love, shall we still pursue the hotel idea?"

"Aye, Andrew. I know we can do it. Your contract here ends in two years doesn't it? Do you want to continue here? Our independent business would be better wouldn't it?"

"Yes, true. I was just checking, Annie. It's a big decision. We are saving well from my fifty pounds a month here on this estate. In our three years here we have close to twelve hundred pounds saved in the bank. Also, even though my salary in India was half of what I am making here, I saved most of that money over my five years there. As officers of the British Raj, we did not need to buy food or pay rent in India. So I have a little over fourteen hundred pounds in that account. I am sure George Donaldson and his Beatrice have similar amounts to go into partnership."

"Aye...yes. What will that hotel cost, Andrew? And...and are you sure those men are contemplating selling it?"

"It's a small hotel and the officers at the club there heard it from a good source that the owners want to retire. I can make some inquiries. It will probably be a year or two down the road, but I do have two more years in my contract here. We will have saved more, my Annie."

"Aye...most of this furniture though will stay since it belongs to the estate...but I would want our own few pieces...especially our babies' nursery..."

Andrew kissed Annie on her forehead, "You are way ahead, my Annie...so organized as usual." He thought for a moment, "If we do buy that hotel, we will have to live in it for a year or so before buying our own home."

"Yes. But we can do it...I know we can succeed."

"When it comes time to buy in two years, we may have to borrow a small amount of money from the bank."

"Aye. But that is what people do Andrew. You and I know about this business...we can make it work, I am confident."

"All right...George and I will continue planning for it. You just take care of yourself, my dear."

The housekeeper stood quietly at the door. When Andrew looked up, the small Indian woman, dressed in her uniform of long blue dress and small cap, broom still in her hand, spoke in almost a whisper, "Sir there is a man here from the office...says that there are problems by the bridge."

"Oh, all right, thank you, House Mary. Tell him to go back, I am on my way."

***

The weeks that followed were pleasant for Amir and Purat's families. Purat, who was like a brother to Amir, was overjoyed with the news of the family reunification. As the two families sat on the ground around their fire pits and ate supper together each evening, plans were made for Gulab's arrival.

"Gulab *Kaaka*...does he look like you Amir *Kaaka?*" Ashok was also caught up in the excitement.

Amir laughed.

"*Haanh...haanh*...yes...yes. Gulab *Kaaka* looks like me...only more handsome, Ashok *Beta*. But smaller moustache. Not nice like mine, *nayh...?*" and laughing, he gathered Ashok up in his arms and tickled him. "*Areh...* you are getting heavy..."

"*Kaaka*, I am a big boy...I am nearly eight years old now!".

"And so good at numbers, my boy! We are all so proud of you. You will be the rich money man!" And the adults laughed out loud. They chatted animatedly, listening to the birds in the fig and surrounding trees, like a mini-forest. The fire was allowed to simmer down and they all retired indoors to prepare for bed. They awoke early each morning to the musical chatter of birds, to wash, pray, cook breakfast and start their chores.

The pruning of the roses, digging to air the soil around all the perennials, cutting back poker and agapanthus leaves, tending to the aloes and cutting greenery from tree branches to make bunches of flowers took the family late into the nights.

Friday nights were especially busy as they tied bunches of flowers and stood them in buckets of water to be taken to Amir's clients each Saturday. Ashok stayed awake with the adults and helped happily, knowing there was no school the next morning. But for the adults, waking early in the mornings before five became the norm. Long days of work, interrupted occasionally with severe headaches for Amir, defined their days and nights.

Tuesday, October 26, 1886 dawned bright and sunny but windy. October was always windy but this day was particularly so. Amir washed in the stream very early and by 4:30 had drawn water from the pumps and was on his way up the hill to his fig shaded house when he noticed that Purat too, having risen early was on his way down to the stream.

"*Areh* Purat *Bhai*...so early?"

"*Jihaanh*, yes, Amir *Bhai*. I have lots of nonsense going on at the bridge with some workers and I still have to load the sugarcane too. If I get more loads taken today, then Mr. Landers said I could come with you tomorrow to meet the ship."

Amir put down his buckets of water and hugged Purat.

"*Bhayah*…thank you. *Areh* look…Ashok is awake too?"

Ashok was carrying his little sister Nina, who was fussing and squirming.

"He is helping his mother…Nina was awake several times last night and Sibani is now heavy with…"

"*Aachah… aachah*…good boy, Ashok."

The wind continued sporadically all day and through the night and the next morning saw a struggling dawn. The usually orange east sunrise, to which Amir prayed each morning as he offered his small *lota* of water over the *tulsi* bush, today was shaded behind heavy dark clouds.

The wind swept up leaves and debris and swirled them around the yard which Bhagirathi was already sweeping so early in the morning, bending low over her bunch of corn-husks which she used as a broom. She had readied Amir's simple breakfast of tea and *roti* as well as some porridge. Today was going to be a special day for the extended family. She and Sibani had planned their cooking and had told their friends at the stream to come and join in for supper that evening. Lots of work to do!

Purat and Amir did their rounds early on the cane fields making sure that the few bleary-eyed, hung-over workers were on the job. Amir gave Purat and his team a hand to move as much of the cut cane stalks toward the lanes for easy loading. Around mid-morning they hesitantly approached Mr. Landers' office, neat and ready to make the journey into town and to the docks to meet the Umvoti. Andrew was ready and gestured for them to hop on the back of his horse-drawn carriage driven by his driver, as he rode in the covered cabin. At the station Andrew bought his ticket and walked briskly to the first class section. Amir and Purat went to the smaller window that served Indians and Africans and waited to buy their tickets. The train had pulled into the station by the time they were served and they ran to their third class seats just as the train started to pull away toward the town.

Amir and Purat chatted excitedly as the train went from station to station. Amir had not had a chance to go into town for months. He knew from the excited updates provided by Adam that the large new Grey Street Mosque had been completed over a year earlier. Adam's profuse praise for the new structure with minarets and arches and room to seat two hundred worshippers was always a pleasure to hear. The large mosque had replaced the small brick and mortar *Jamaat Khanna* or gathering place for Muslims that had space for less than fifty people.

"*Bhayah* Adam took me to the Grey Street mosque and from the outside it is beautiful. But *Bhayah*, I want to show you a surprise at the main central station!"

"A surprise?"

"Wait till you see!' and Purat laughed hanging on to his secret.

At the Central Railway Station, Purat who was very familiar with the place, ushered Amir toward the first class carriage to meet Mr. Landers. On the days that he went to the government offices in town or at the docks, Andrew dressed in his officer's uniform, which was crisply pressed, gold-buttoned khaki jacket, leather-belted at the waist, neatly pressed pants and a small beige cap, cutting a smart picture of a handsome, clean-shaven, mustachioed officer who elicited second glances from the few, elegantly attired white women on the platform. Andrew informed Amir and Purat that he had to pick up some paperwork across the street at the new post-office and city hall and he would see them at the government building at the docks in two hours.

"Yes, Sir. We know the building where we were brought…" Amir stuttered and Purat assured Mr. Landers that he was familiar with the docks since he worked there a day or two each week.

They watched Mr. Landers cross the street to the impressive, dome-roofed main post office and government buildings and Purat drew Amir toward the main passenger exit gate. And there, right at the busy entrance to the station, on the meticulously clean sidewalk was a huge flower stand. Rows and rows of flowers standing in silver buckets, each row raised above the first on elevated benches. Amir recognized daisies, dahlias, roses, gladiolas, orchids, strelitzias, and so much more in swaths of breathtaking colours! He was dumb-founded.

"*Bhayah*, you can bring your flowers here! These men sell these bunches to train passengers, but also to the small flower shops near all of the white areas all across the city. They also deliver to homes…"

Amir stared open mouthed, "But I deliver to my customers…"

"*Nayh…nayh…*they won't steal your customers. *Bhayah*, you are still the man who turned our Avoca into *Pulwa Gaon*…our flower village. Your flaming hills changed our Avoca. But no, these men will not take your business. They will buy from you! You will still deliver door to door to your customers in Red Hill. But this way you will be able to sell a lot more. Look…they don't have red-hot pokers. I don't see agapanthus either. And your shorter shrub roses are cheaper than these long stem roses…more of a market for them."

Amir swayed his head in agreement and as they walked retracing those first steps from over three years ago, they made their way toward the docks. The friends marvelled at the progress. Buildings that Amir had seen just started three years ago were now complete and bustling with the business of government and sales. There were still several structures being built and they nodded at the familiar sight of *dhoti*-clad Indians and loin-clothed African men carrying bricks and building supplies on their shoulders.

It took an hour and half, walking briskly, for the two of them to reach the government building at the docks and Amir and Purat sat on the stone steps for a while. Several officers walked hurriedly in and out of the building and their curious stares made the friends uncomfortable. Purat gestured to Amir to follow him and they walked on the gravel road, smoother now, toward the boom gate that led to the cement wharf where several ships were docked. Purat chatted with the two men at the gate and being familiar with his work among the stevedores they lifted the boom gate and allowed them in.

Purat pointed to the middle ship which had the word Umvoti printed in large black letters on its side.

"See *Bhayah*…there…there's Gulab *Bhai's* ship."

Amir squinted against the sun and holding his hand above his eyes he stared. Indian men in white *pugris* headgear could be seen on the deck, reminiscent of the day they too stood awaiting inspection and disembarkation. Of course, no-one could be seen clearly. The wind was still brisk and being October it felt cool as it always did close to the sea. After a while, Purat suggested they go back and wait for Mr. Landers.

Andrew came down the steps holding several ledgers under his arm. He nodded at Amir and Purat but did not say anything. His face looked serious. He walked toward the barracks where the labourers would be brought upon disembarkation and disappeared inside the gate. They could barely see him entering the low red-roofed barracks and then he disappeared inside.

Another hour was spent waiting and then Amir and Purat saw labourers lining up at the boom gates, clad in nothing but white *dhotis* and white turbans. Andrew and two other khaki-uniformed officers walked briskly to the boom gate and showed the gatekeepers some paperwork. The boom was lifted and a row of around fifty labourers, mostly men, shuffled behind them to the barracks. At the distance they stood, Amir and Purat could not make out anyone who might be Gulab but it was difficult to discern from the steps of the government building.

After another hour Andrew alone emerged from the barracks. The other two officers remained inside. The friends remembered that when they arrived they had to spend two nights in the barracks before their trip to the estate the following day. They were discouraged thinking that Gulab too would have to spend two nights and they had come all this way for nothing. But the two other officers were still inside, maybe they were sorting the labourers into groups to be transported to estates like they had been, so maybe these labourers did not have to sleep overnight in the barracks. The friends watched Andrew walk quickly up the front steps and disappear inside the government building. He did not say a word to the friends.

Another half hour of waiting and then Mr. Landers emerged from the front doors. He gestured to Amir and Purat to follow him inside. Bewildered the friends followed. The front door opened into a huge vestibule with a large dome-shaped roof intermittently fitted with stained glass allowing rays of sunshine into the foyer. There were benches all along the walls and a flurry of activity all around. White men in officer uniforms and white women wearing long skirts were scurrying around from office to office and several rushed up and down the wide staircase leading to the next floor up.

Andrew led the friends as far as he could go in the foyer and gestured to a wooden bench nestled under the staircase. He asked them to sit and sat next to Amir. He turned troubled eyes to face them.

"Amir, there has been an accident…"

"Sir...an accident? Where Sir...?" Amir's eyes darted from Andrew to Purat.

Andrew shifted in his seat.

"There was a severe storm in the Indian Ocean...remember our storm?"

The friends nodded and stared.

"Amir...your brother Gulab...tried to save a boy as the ship tilted and the boy was being dashed about on the deck. He nearly fell into the sea. Gulab grabbed him and returned him to the door of the dining hall."

Andrew just plunged ahead.

"Gulab saw the boy alone on the deck in the severe storm. The ship was heaving and tilting. Gulab climbed the iron gate from the steerage side to the other side. He grabbed the boy and banged on the dining hall doors. When it opened he thrust the boy inside. Then...I am ashamed to say, Amir...I am ashamed...the door was closed behind the boy... whichever crewman opened the door to the boy...closed it once the boy was inside."

"Sir...the boy...the dining hall door...Sir...a white boy? Sir...Gulab...Gulab is injured?" Amir's voice trembled with confusion.

"Yes, it was a white boy, twelve years old, an officer's son. I don't know why he had ventured out in the storm. Gulab saw him and climbed the gate and saved him. But when he climbed back on to the gate to come to the steerage side, the ship heaved and flung him into the sea."

Amir wailed and Purat shouted.

"Into the sea? Mr. Landers...is Gulab all right? Where is he?"

Andrew held his head in his hands, closed his eyes shaking his head and Purat continued.

"Sir where is he...where is he?"

"He is gone. There were Indian labourers who had come on deck. They saw him being flung. But by the time they went down to the bottom level and banged on the storage-hold doors...no-one answered right away...it was too late by the time staff answered the door. The ship had moved on."

Amir wailed, put his head in his hands and shook backward and forward.

"Amir I am so sorry. He was a hero…your brother was a hero…the captain said as much. And the officer wants to meet with you and thank you for what your brother did for his son."

Amir did not lift his head. Purat just stared, stunned.

"Please wait here. I will be right back." Andrew walked briskly away and Purat turned around and saw him go up the stairs.

A short while later he returned accompanied by a young family, a British officer in uniform, his wife in a long pale green dress with her arms around the shoulders of a boy dressed in short knee-length khaki pants and white, starched button-down long-sleeved shirt.

"Mr. Pearson, Mrs. Pearson, this is Amir Sing, Gulab Sing's brother."

Amir stared mutely, his eyes red, his face clouded and streaked with tears.

"Yes…yes…quite! So you are that brave man's brother…what? Yes, very brave… your brother. He saved my boy. Michael!! Step forward, Michael!"

The boy stepped forward and stood next to his father.

"Say thank you to this man…heaven knows what business you had to be on deck in that infernal storm. Lost your tongue, boy?"

The boy, visibly afraid, looked at Amir and Purat who had stood up.

"That one!! That one boy!" His father bellowed, pointing at Amir. The boy's mother stepped forward and whispered in her son's ear.

"Sorry…mister…I am sorry," the boy stammered.

Amir looked at the boy with kind eyes. He had seen officers' children back in India and even here on both plantations. He looked for a few minutes then he extended his shaking right hand, with fingers spread, close to but not touching the boy's head almost like he was placing his hand on the boy's head and said,

"*Beta*…Son…are you all right?" He had spoken in Hindi and Andrew quickly translated for Mr. Pearson and his wife.

"Yes…yes…he is fine…strong boy what?" Pearson bellowed and broke into a small laugh before catching himself and clearing his throat.

"Will that be all, Mr. Pearson?" Andrew addressed his peer, his need to curtail this meeting obvious.

"What? Yes, yes…Mrs. Pearson, you know, wanted the boy to thank the family."

Andrew just looked the man in the eyes and stood silent.

The Pearson family strode off and Andrew turned to Purat.

"Purat, Amir is in shock. Stay close to him on your way home."

"Yes Sir." Purat couldn't say too much more.

The two friends walked silently out of the building and started the long walk back to the station but part way there Amir collapsed on a stone bench under a tree and wailed.

"Purat, my brother…my brother…*kala pani*, dark waters took my brother. Purat, you are now my only brother."

As the wails turned to quiet sobs, Purat continued to hold Amir in his brotherly embrace and sat silent and supportive. When Amir rose, they quietly resumed their walk to the station. Overwhelmed by grief, nothing held their interest. The train ride back was long and silent. At the Avoca train station Purat gestured to a friend to go and get a bullock cart. The driver immediately noticed that something was wrong as Purat helped Amir on to the cart. The cart pulled away and the railroad friend ran to Adam's shop to apprise Adam. The driver heard the quiet conversation among the friends as he drove his cart along the dirt road towards the pulp factory and he realized what had happened. He refused to take money from Purat for the fare and just helped Amir down and patted his back.

Purat sat Amir down at the edge of the stream and Amir mutely stared at the gently running stream. It was early evening and Ajit was back in the barracks. Purat briefed Ajit and sent him up the short distance to tell Amir's family. Then he helped Amir up the hill. As they approached, Bhagirathi came running out and abandoning all wifely restraint she flung her arms around Amir and guided him inside into the front room where he collapsed on to the small low bed, where guests usually sat. She clung on to Amir whose unrestrainable tears once again flowed.

"*Pathni*…wife…Gulab…my baby brother…my baby brother."

She said nothing just caressed his back as Purat sat on the other side doing the same. Sibani had started making tea when Ajit had brought the news, and now she brought two tin cups full of steaming, sugary tea, brimming with frothy milk, the aroma of cardamom wafting ahead of her. She quietly held a cup to Amir.

"*Bhayah* Amir…try to drink this."

"*Behn*…" Looking up at Sibani, the tears started anew and this time they all broke down and cried together, Sibani clinging on to Bhagirathi.

Ashok, pulling the babies in his cart came to the door of the front room, looked in, stood quietly for a while, then took the babies out into the yard, playing and keeping them busy. Then voices in the yard were followed by a trickle of men arriving led by Adam, Suleiman, Rajiv and Bhodraj. They were followed by the bullock cart driver, men from the train station, the pulp factory and others who had heard that something was wrong and soon learned of Gulab's death.

Once again the family home had become a house of mourning. As the evening turned to night, many more men arrived and women from the stream-barracks arrived to help Sibani serve tea. The food that was prepared for the merriment of Gulab's arrival was now offered to people who had rushed over, taking no time to go home to their families and suppers. After offering condolences to Amir, they sat around Amir and Purat's family fires. Rajiv talked with Sibani about getting provisions ready for the prayer ceremony that he was hoping to hold on the coming Sunday. Again another ceremony of mourning, within months of that for Amir's parents. Rajiv walked softly to and from Amir's side, tending to Amir, sitting next to him, reciting scripture and moving among the people who had gathered for the condolence visit. Amir was comforted by the presence of this extended family.

Then late at night as people began leaving, Amir heard Mr. Landers' voice in the yard and stood up. Purat, holding a kerosene lantern, met Andrew at the door.

"Amir, Mr. Donaldson is here as well," Andrew said as he gestured to the other estate manager to enter.

Amir, unaware of his action, bowed to them and Andrew straightened him and took him back to the seat. Mr. Donaldson, setting his own lantern down, murmured his condolences and then said, "Amir, this is Basudev, he was Gulab's ship mate." He gestured to the man to enter. The women left the room and the turbaned young man, around eighteen, gingerly walked toward Amir with his hand extended.

"*Bhayah* Amir, Gulab *Bhayah* was my friend. We met at the Calcutta

depot. There are two others who came here with me to this estate…
there was supposed to be a group of four of us…now only three. Gulab
was strong and so helpful to all of us. On the ship he took leadership
and we became like a group of brothers. That night of the *kala pani*
storm, I arrived on the deck just as Gulab jumped to the other side of
the iron gate to save the boy. The boy was frightened and screaming.
He was being tossed about on deck in the fierce storm. I saw Gulab
grab the boy and take him to the ship's door. The door opened half way
and men grabbed hold of the boy and took him inside but then the door
closed."

Basudev fell silent and then resumed.

"*Bhayah*, our friends and I tried to steady Gulab as he tried to climb
back. But the gate is so high…he got to the top…and then the ship tilted completely in the whipping wind and rain. We were thrown to the
floor and watched helplessly as Gulab was thrown into the sea. Why
couldn't he have been thrown on to the deck? Why, *Bhayah*…why?" and
Basudev, breaking into tears, held his head. Amir put his arm around
Basudev and muttered, "God's will, *Bhayah*…God's will."

Mr. Landers and Mr. Donaldson led Basudev away after a while,
Andrew consoling him.

"Basudev, you and your friends can talk to Amir over the next few
days. It is after midnight, you need to rest, no need to start in the field
tomorrow, take tomorrow off."

Amir stayed home the next day. The other *sirdar* came to see him
early in the morning. *Sirdar* Nabraj was a gentle yet firm man and Amir
liked him. They often sat together after work, after the day's conflicts
among workers were resolved and chatted companionably about work,
about families back home and friends here. When they could manage
to join others at the Sunday gatherings they mingled together with
friends and families late into the dusk around *bowlas*, tin drums, filled
with coal fires.

"Amir *Bhayah*, I am so sorry." The men chatted quietly and Nabraj
promised to look after Amir's side of the estate for the day. Amir would
be back at work the following day, a Friday, which was always a long
busy day.

The Sunday prayer day dawned unusually still. The winds had quietened and the early morning sunrise emerged orange and bright above

Amir's agapanthus and poker hill in the east. Rajiv, Sajiv, Adam, their families, Bhagirathi's parents and brother Prabhu, along with Bhodraj, Himal, Bhimnad and their families busied themselves with preparations for the memorial ceremony and for the visitors who were expected. Because Amir's home was a house of mourning, no cooking had been done there since Wednesday when they received the news of Gulab's death. Sibani's cooking fires burned all afternoon and evening with the women preparing batches of *dhal* and rice to serve the continuous flow of people who came to express their condolences.

Like the mourning ceremony for his parents just a few months earlier, Amir performed the rituals, gently led by Rajiv and Sajiv. He now had no birth family in India and no reason to look back. His family was now here, among his ship-brothers, his wife and children, and his in-laws. He had thought long and hard over the past four days and he had steeled his resolve to be successful in this his adopted country, the country of his children. He maintained a tall posture, a friendly demeanor as he greeted the flow of people all afternoon, a man of strength, pride and drive.

Chapter 13

Freedom

Over the next two years, Amir's flowers turned both hills into colourful palettes of flaming red roses on one hill and warm orangey-red pokers all year round crowned at the top of the hill with the cool blue of agapanthus in the summers. The flowers were now completely well established and even without constant fertilizer, they flourished in the rich African soil.

His clientele had grown and as Purat predicted, the flower stall at the Central Railway Station brought in excellent profits for the Harrison Estate. His Saturdays were now divided between sending buckets of flowers by train to town very early in the morning and in the afternoon, he still rented a bullock cart to serve the *memsahibs* on Red Hill. The hard part was loading the buckets of flowers with just a small amount of water at the bottom of each bucket on to the train. He, Ajit and one of his staff brought the ten to twelve buckets by bullock cart to Avoca station.

In the very short stop-over, they had to scurry to load the buckets on to a long wooden pallet that they had fashioned from strips of wood. Ajit and the co-worker lifted the palette into the third class car and went together to town.

Amir returned first to the cane fields to ensure that workers were accounted for, and then he rushed back to the flower plantation to load his next round of deliveries on the bullock cart and head south on the North Coast Road. In addition to the Red Hill *memsahibs*, several stores along the way were now customers, placing bunches of flowers at the entrances of their shops for impulse purchases by women hurrying from shop to shop for daily and weekly shopping.

Amir's third daughter, Chanderkali, meaning moon-rays, arrived at Christmas in the year 1887 and Purat's family also grew, this time with a son, Avanindra, which meant King of the Earth, born in February of 1888.

Purat was now serving in a supervisory capacity at the railways, though no such title was bestowed on him. He was still indentured to the Harrison Estate. Ashok, now nine years old, accompanied his father to the railway offices and even on conflict-resolution visits to the Magazine Barracks and the shipyards.

Ashok was learning the delicate skills of dispute resolution and was quick to work out moneys owed, taxes to be paid, adding up earnings for workers and even confidently scribbling on paper how much money they should be putting into bank accounts, a concept foreign to many labourers. His father encouraged his gifted son and praised him for his respectful approach to men from all walks.

It was nearly five years since their arrival as indentured labourers and Purat and Amir often had long chats about what their freedom from indenture would mean for them. Although Purat still had family back home he had decided that he too, like Amir, would not spend the money on the fare back to Muzzafarnagar. Rather, he and Amir wanted to take advantage of the piece of land that their recruiter in India had promised would be theirs at the end of their indenture. They were looking forward to building their lives in their new adopted country with their wives and children.

It was on a warm morning in April that Mr. Landers asked Amir, Purat and Nabraj to come into his office after their morning rounds. At eleven, after the first wave of work was done and workers were sitting down in the cane fields with their tin cups of tea, the three friends walked back to Andrew's office. Andrew asked them to sit on the wooden chairs against the entrance wall and explained.

"Men, I wanted you to be the first of the indentured labourers to know that this Harrison Estate is being sold to the Natal Sugar Estate."

The men looked stunned but said nothing.

"Amir and Purat, your indenture will be completed in June, that's only two months away and you will need to decide if you want to go back to India or you want to extend your indenture for another five years. Nabraj, you have eight months to go. So you will work for Natal

Estates until completion of your indenture, then you too will need to decide."

Amir and Purat spoke simultaneously.

"Sir, we want to stay...and take the fifteen acres..."

"Fifteen acres?"

Andrew looked confused, his eyebrows and forehead knitted questioningly. Amir and Purat, now also confused, just looked at him wide-eyed.

"Sir, our recruiter told us that at the end of our contract we would be offered fifteen acres of land if we chose not to go back to India."

"Oh! Your recruiter said that? Who was your recruiter?"

Neither Amir nor Purat could remember the name, just that he was Eurasian, well-dressed in western clothes.

"Well, I am sorry. But your recruiter was wrong. At the end of five years, you are allowed to go back to India at your own expense, you are freed from your contract. If, however, you want to renew your indenture for another five years...then yes...at the end of ten years you are entitled to a free trip home or a land grant."

"Ten years?" Both Amir and Purat blurted out their indignation together and then realizing their tone, they softened.

"Sorry, Sir...but we thought..."

"I understand and I am sorry for the confusion. Your recruiter should not have promised you land. He had no authority to do that. But there is a law that allows you to negotiate with your employer."

"Negotiate, Sir...what meaning negotiate, Sir? *Girmit*?"

Purat cut in, "*Nayh Bhayah. Girmit* is the contract we signed after our health check in the Calcutta depot to come here, our contract to work here, *Bhayah*. Negotiate means that we can talk to Mr. Landers and work out something."

"Yes. Especially since the Harrisons are selling their estate and going back to England. You are not entitled to land, but I can let you keep the piece of land on which your shacks are built."

"But Sir...the flowers...all the flowers..." Amir seemed stricken.

"The Natal Estate is not interested in the flower plantations. They don't want it. We will have to sell the flower plantations. Maybe another estate might be interested."

Purat, with his business-honed mind jumped in.

"Sir, how much per acre would you sell the flower plantation?"

"Land is being sold for two pounds per acre…"

"But, Sir, the rose hill is full of rocks and shale. Remember Mr. Harrison could not cultivate it," Amir had now found his voice and was not going to allow his roses to perish.

"Yes, that is true. Why do you ask? Are you able to buy land?"

"Yes!" Both Amir and Purat spoke together, but Purat quickly followed up, "But, Sir, since it is not suitable land we will give the Harrison Estate one pound per acre."

Andrew thought on this quietly. The silence was agonizing for the two friends. Andrew knew that the men were correct. The land could not be cultivated by other Englishmen. Finally, he conceded.

"Well, you do understand the meaning of negotiate," he smiled. "All right. One pound per acre. That side, the rose hill as you call it, is about thirty acres, so thirty pounds…all right?"

"Yes Sir. I will buy fifteen and my brother Amir here will buy the other fifteen."

"But before you sign the deal I need to tell you that I will not be staying. Mr. Donaldson and I have bought the Greenwood Park Hotel on the main North Coast Road, close to here, in Greenwood Park, so there will be new managers here."

"But Sir, can we not complete our transactions with you before you leave?"

"Yes of course. But I did want you to know, especially Nabraj as you will need to adjust to the new owners."

Nabraj had not spoken till now.

"Sir, you will be opening a hotel? With food service?"

"Yes…why do you ask?"

"Sir, I was a cook before I arrived here. Will I be able to go with you?"

"Nabraj, I will be happy to take you with me, but as a courtesy to the new owners you will need to train the new *sirdar* and help with the transition. The workers will be looking to you as the only familiar face left."

"Then can I come to you, Sir…after my eight months?"

"Yes, definitely. You are an excellent worker and my wife, an experienced hospitality expert, can use your skills, not only as a cook but you have a way with the workers which will help us to establish a happy clientele."

Nabraj swayed his head, pleased with his arrangement.

So it was that Amir saved his beloved rose hill, rocks, shale and all, the whole hillside, from the top, past his home under the fig tree, right down to the stream-barracks. Purat chose the other half thus making it a family hill. Andrew was happy to give over that hill as The Natal Sugar Estate had no interest in it since sugarcane could not be grown there.

In the weeks that followed, Bhimnad and Himal also negotiated with Andrew regarding the land they were already cultivating, the silt-rich small strip along the river and the land directly across the road at the foot of the Avoca Road hill. Andrew conceded that the small one-acre silt-strip was no good to anyone else and granted them that piece. But the two friends together with another close indentured friend, Jaga, had to buy land across the road for two pounds per acre. Bhimnad, Himal and Jaga among them, bought six acres. They would have liked the piece right at the corner of the foot of Avoca Road and Umghlangane Road but that corner piece had already been occupied by another family. So they bought the next six acres above. Jaga's piece fronted right on to Avoca Road and Bhimnad and Himal were happy to have theirs set back from the road to continue to cultivate their experimental crops. Each friend built their simple wood and iron home on that land and continued their close friendship as ship-brothers.

Well into the following month, Amir and Bhagirathi talked earnestly many a night about Amir's pokers and agapanthus plantation, lovingly tilled, nurtured, coaxed into producing such a healthy blanket of nature's bounty. They had spent fifteen pounds of their savings on the rose hill, but did they have enough saved to buy that other hill? Finally, at the end of the three weeks of sporadic nightly discussions Bhagirathi shyly pulled out of her wooden bedroom cupboard a neatly folded paper. She always kept meticulous accounts, but in the past few weeks she had gone over the paper and had laboured over it, checking and double checking against their bank book and Amir's little chinks in the wall where he still kept money folded into little rolls. She showed her paper to Amir and he peered at her neat writing.

Amir stared at the piece of paper. He used his finger to go across each row and down each line muttering and calculating. Finally, he looked up at his wife in wonder.

"*Pathniji* we have one hundred and nineteen pounds?"

"More *Pathiji*. A little more. Forgive me, but I took down your little bundles from the walls, there were more chinks than I knew about, and you managed to save a little more than I calculated. The fifteen pounds you gave to Mr. Landers came from one of your wall savings. I could not see it coming out of your bank book. So yes the money we have now is one hundred and nineteen pounds, but I too have some sewing money, grocery savings and gifts from *Mathaji*, *Pithaji* and Prabhu tucked away in my own little holes in the wall," she laughed, unusually fresh and scintillating after so much of sorrow for so long. Amir too broke into a toothy grin and then laughed out loud. The children were asleep and he took his wife into his arms.

***

In early June, Amir went to see Mr. Landers privately, clutching Bhagirathi's account in his hand, which had now been adjusted to one hundred and twenty pounds, reflecting some of the extra money that he and she had tucked away, but not all of it.

"Sir, how many acres in the poker-agapanthus hill?"

"Amir, there are about seventy acres there. The hill was signed over to the Harrison Estate by the Crown Corporation in June 1885." He walked over to the wooden cabinets behind his desk and rummaged through files.

"Ahh…here it is…yes, seventy acres."

"Sir, have you been able to find a buyer?"

Andrew cleared his throat and remained silent looking at Amir. For the past four months, even before he had chatted to Amir and Purat, he and Mr. Donaldson had been trying to find an estate to buy the flower hills. There were no takers. Estates were not interested in either hill as they saw no mass market for flowers. Mr. Harrison was fortunate that Amir and Purat bought the rose hill. The rocks and shale made it unworthy for sale. Now that he and Mr. Donaldson were busy renovating their hotel they were eager to sell off the remaining flower plantation and get on with their own futures. Young Mr. Harrison was already booked to leave for England in September.

"Eh…no, Amir no buyer yet. Are you worried that the new owners may not let you continue?"

"Sir, I want to buy that hill."

Visibly stunned, Andrew just stared at Amir. In the uncomfortable silence, Amir opened his hand and placed Bhagirathi's paper on Andrew's desk. Andrew slid the paper closer and ran his finger down the rows and lines. Finally, regaining composure, Andrew lifted his eyes and looked at Amir, resuming a businesslike manner.

"Amir, this one hundred and twenty pounds will buy you sixty of the seventy acres."

Unusual for the ever-polite Amir, he cut in. "But Sir, there is a large mango grove on the hill close to the pulp factory and also Sir, the river at the foot of the hill, near the barracks, has large strips of wild reeds and bulrushes that make cultivation impossible close to the bottom of the hill. I should not have to pay two pounds an acre for those pieces."

Andrew promised to discuss it with Mr. Donaldson and Mr. Harrison and get back to Amir. He knew what the answer would be. A buyer at last! An unexpected buyer but serendipitously a buyer. However, Mr. Landers remained silent for two weeks. Amir and Bhagirathi fluctuated between losing hope to being hopeful. Perhaps the delay was that Mr. Harrison was busy closing the deal with the Natal Sugar Estate or perhaps tying up the loose ends around the nearly completed bridge for which the Harrison Estate needed payment for conceded land. Amir and Bhagirathi waited anxiously, worried about losing the hill but also scraping together new savings on which to survive once their moneys were depleted from buying the hill. Bhagirathi's sewing orders were robust now and she and Sibani raised their prices for the first time in four years. The white women did not seem to mind, the handwork was impeccable and the children's smocking and clothing were each one-of-a-kind.

Finally, at the end of June 1888, Mr. Landers delivered his decision. Amir handed over one hundred and twenty pounds for seventy acres of land. The beloved flower hills were now owned by Amir and Bhagirathi – *Pulwa Gaon* indeed! Avoca's reputation as the flower village was established and they were the reason this had happened. Their ship brothers were elated and called on the family using the phrase *Pulwa Gaon* routinely as they praised Amir for buying the land and turning their Avoca into a colourful village of flowers.

Chapter 14

Trouble Brewing

Mohandas Karamchand Gandhi arrived in South Africa in 1893 invited by Muslim merchants to serve as their lawyer. By this time Indians worked in many jobs in Natal from barmen and servers to railway workers, stevedores, potters, cowherds, shoe-makers, snake catchers, construction workers, interpreters and machinists in sugar estates. The educated Indians worked as teachers or in clerical positions in back offices of government, railroads, shipyards and some mercantile businesses. Many labourers who had completed their indentures and were able to buy small boats, lived on the tiny Salisbury Island near the harbour, where they established a robust fishing community and were making a decent living.

All non-indentured Indians were now subjected to a three-pound tax and the government, threatened by the success and drive of Indians, made it more and more difficult for Indians to own land and property. Gandhi fought against this disempowerment of Indians and in 1894 he founded the Natal Indian Congress (NIC) to protest unfair treatment of Indians. Gandhi's premise was that Indians were British subjects and deserved the same rights as whites. To show his loyalty and exemplify his status as a British subject, Gandhi started an ambulance corps to lift injured British soldiers on stretchers from the front lines when the South African Boer War broke out in 1899.

Amir, Purat and their close knit ship-brothers and families had by now firmly established themselves as land-owners, business people, railway workers, barbers, shoe-makers, gardeners, teachers and accountants. Many of them now commuted daily into town. The village of Avoca became a bustling suburb of the larger metropolis of Durban.

Many young men from Avoca and Phoenix had joined Gandhi's protests. Now an adult, Ashok and his friends had long discussions about the colonial powers of the British Raj. He attended meetings in the Phoenix rooms of the NIC, but did not want to worry his family and so did not mention it. He was now twenty years old, a tall handsome young man employed as an accountant in the Natal Railways. Because of his fair skin and light eyes, he was allowed by the white staff to regularly act as front office problem-solver when issues arose, especially with merchants transporting their wares and imports. His father was proud of his professional success. Purat himself continued as railway line supervisor and both father and son were paid a decent wage. Amir and Purat were happy and their thoughts turned to helping the community.

On a warm December Sunday, Amir, Purat, Bhagirathi and Sibani visited Bhimnad, Himal and Jaga. All three men, like Amir and Purat and most of their shipmates were now in their late thirties and successful in their work lives. After Gulab's death, Amir had vowed that he would set aside money to expedite the building of a temple in Avoca. He continued the regular donation to Rajiv's temple fund but kept aside a little more as his business grew over the years. Today Rajiv, Bhodraj, their families and other close friends like Basudev, who had been with Gulab on the ship, and their families all gathered at Himal, Jaga and Bhimnad's homes situated just above the foot of Avoca Road.

Amir had many discussions with friends about building a temple on Amir's land. But the temple needed to be near a river and Amir admitted that his land, close to his beloved stream was marshy and not suitable to build a sturdy temple. Besides, its location was a hike for worshippers whose dwellings were closer to the railway station, the Avoca Road hill and the banks of the large Umghlangane River along which Himal and Bhimnad grew their nursery plants. Today's discussion was initiated by Bhimnad, Jaga and Himal who wanted to donate a piece of their modest property in front of their homes to build a temple close to the river at the foot of Avoca Road.

"*Areh Bhayah* Amir, Purat, *kaisa hain*…how are you. *Aiyeh…aiyeh…* come come…Rajiv, Sajiv, Bhodraj, Basu and so many are already here. Come, come."

Himal standing on the wide verandah of his home held out his arms and hugged his brothers in their usual way. Bhimnad, loud as ever, welcomed them heartily, laughing, eyes twinkling and wrestling with thirteen-year-old Avanindra, Purat's pride and joy, just as Ashok continued to be. Jaga, the quiet one, held his hands together in greeting and welcomed them all. The women went through the central hall of the airy tin house to the backyard where several fire pits bore large bubbling pots of vegetarian foods, the heady aromas filling the air.

Being Sunday prayer day, no meats were cooked. Bhagirathi, pregnant and slower, watched as Sibani ran toward her friend Parvati who hugged Sibani and together they gathered Bhagirathi in their arms. Parvati's son, Yatindra was twenty-eight years old, married with two children and was himself a pundit helping his father run the Phoenix temple. Parvati's daughter Minati, now twenty-two, was married in Phoenix and already a mother. All the shipmates and families attended those weddings and all the other milestones in their close-knit group. Bhimnad, Himal and Jaga's wives, like Bhagirathi, were born on the local estates and had raised their children, nearly teenagers now, in these three homes with their shared backyards.

The group ate their lunch on homemade *gudras*, quilts spread out in the flower-rich backyard. Men, women and children sat together, which was a departure from customs back home where men and women ate separately at gatherings. After lunch, the men gathered on Bhimnad's front verandah to talk about the proposed temple. A recently freed labourer, Narainswamy, from the Natal Sugar Estates had been invited. The man was in his mid-twenties, and though fully covered in pale yellow *dhoti* and a thin, white cotton tunic, he bore signs of the lashings he had suffered on the Natal Estates. They had heard from *Sirdar* Nabraj about the cruelty of the new managers and the new Indian *sirdars*.

Narainswamy had arrived on the same ship on which Gulab had died and he, Basudev and their one other shipmate, Munian, often gathered with these friends on Saturday evenings under the tamarind tree near Adam's home and spoke about the abuse. Their indenture had ended in October 1891 and unable to afford to buy land, they had instead banded together and started a small building trade. Another recently freed Natal Estates labourer, Ismail Khan, joined them as well. At first they mostly helped families build extensions to their homes. But word of their workmanship soon spread. When he was indentured from Madras, Narainswamy was already a fine temple builder, having served on many crews that built state-of-the-art temples in and around Madras all the way south to Pondicherry. Narainswamy and Munian spoke mostly Tamil when they first arrived on the estate, but their bond with Basudev, Ismail, Amir, Purat, Nabraj and other friends soon had them fluent in Hindi and the ever-necessary English language. Narainswamy was speaking as Bhimnad was passing out betel nuts wrapped in betel leaves to the gathered men seated on the few chairs, upturned wooden boxes and on the floor.

"This land," he pointed to the lush piece several yards in front of the houses on the gently rising hill of Avoca Road, "is a wonderful spot. The half-acre is enough for a small temple with a large covered verandah and an ample backyard for cooking."

Sajiv, a little older than the other men, interrupted saying, "Yes Narainswamy… also the closeness of this river," pointing to his left, "is an important advantage too. Jaga, Bhimnad, Himal, many blessings to you for giving this land."

"*Nayh…nayh…*" Bhimnad and Himal spoke together gesturing toward Jaga. "Jaga *Bhayah* the blessing is yours. That piece is your land."

Jaga quietly shook his head saying the blessing was to be able to give the land.

Narainswamy continued, "But the savings that you have, though quite a lot, is not enough to build the kind of brick and stone structures like we had back home. We would have to use wood and corrugated iron…"

"Our temple in Phoenix is mostly wood and iron and it has held up very well," Sajiv interjected. "The Campbell Estate held back a shilling each month for a few months from the labourers to pay for the concrete foundations and two concrete walls but the rest is tin, wood and iron and it's beautiful."

Amir had been listening quietly twisting his long moustache between his fingers. He asked, "How much will be needed for a concrete foundation, floor and maybe concrete walls half way up?"

As the earnest discussion continued into the afternoon, plans were drawn, sketches roughly made and lots of tea was consumed. Amir and Purat, both offered extra money from their savings toward a concrete foundation, floor and concrete half-walls which could then be built up with wood frames and corrugated iron walls. By the time all the families departed close to dusk, the Avoca Road Temple was contracted to Narainswamy's company and the community was filled with excitement as the word spread along the roads that everyone traversed on their way home.

***

Amir and Purat's families were growing and with several of their children now teenagers the houses by the fig tree were becoming too small for everyone. Amir's flower business had flourished into a profitable one. Purat and Ashok's salaries were good, so the time had come for Purat and Amir to think about building bigger homes. They were thirty-nine years old, healthy strong, robust men who were making a mark on their community.

"*Bhayah* Amir, where do you think would be best to build our new houses?"

It was almost the end of February in the year 1900, two months after Purat and Amir had committed some of their savings to the temple. Purat, Amir and their wives were seated in Amir's front room after their Saturday dinner. The men had come back from the usual gathering under the tamarind tree but the women stayed home.

Bhagirathi was expected to deliver her baby in March, just a few weeks away and she was heavy with child and moving ever more slowly. Sibani kept telling her that this baby would be a boy since her belly was so much bigger. Sibani's Nina and Bhagirathi's Jaldhara, Sookdhay and Chanderkali were busy cleaning up in the back kitchen and chatting away. Amir and Purat had both built extensions to the back of their tin homes, each adding an indoor kitchen with coal stoves. Their daughters grew up as sisters and went to Bhodraj's school until they were ten. But now at fourteen, thirteen, and twelve, the girls had taken over the cooking, vegetable growing and running of the households. This was in preparation for their marriages, which would begin in a few years for Nina and Jaldhara, who were both fourteen.

Like Bhagirathi, the girls also helped on Amir's flower plantation and with Bhagirathi and Sibani's sewing as both businesses were flourishing. Ashok, busy as he was in his job, came home late in the evenings and left early in the mornings with his father.

"*Bhayah* Purat…what do you think about the very top of this rose hill?" Amir said pointing to his right at the apex of his bloom-rich hill.

"*Aachah!* The top of the hill right on Avoca Road!! *Aachah…aachah.* Our two houses next to each other again," he smiled broadly. "*Areh…* there are electric poles now with power lines going all the way up Avoca Road to reach the Natal Sugar Estate offices and the brickyard on Mill Road. Those lines will go right past our new houses!" They all laughed loudly at the madness of the thought of electricity in their homes. This notion was such a new one no Indian had electricity. Whites only acquired electricity in their homes just two years prior.

"*Areh Pathniji…* wife…don't laugh with your *Bhayah* Purat!" Amir teased Bhagirathi. "Your *Pathi*, husband, might just be the first to give you electricity!" at which both women laughed out loud.

As the women left to see to the girls, Ashok joined his father and Amir *Kaaka.*

"*Aiyeh…aiyeh Beta…*come, come son," Amir patted the spot next to him on the low string coil bed that they used as a couch in the front room and Ashok sat between his father and Amir.

"Did you eat?" Both men asked together.

"Yes Papa…yes *Kaaka*… I ate with our group at Gandhiji's meeting place in Phoenix."

"Where is Gandhiji's meeting place?"

"Close to Prabhu *Maama's* shop on the main road near the station." Having grown up with his father and Amir bonded so closely as brothers, and his mother and Bhagirathi as sisters, Ashok respectfully addressed Bhagirathi's brother as *Maama*, or mother's brother.

"It is just a small room, a shack really. Prabhu *Maama* and many of the free men and estate labourers come. We eat together on Saturday nights."

"Is Gandhiji always there?"

"No only sometimes. He travels all over… to Maritzburg and even as far away as Transvaal. Once he even went to the diamond mines in Kimberley where some Indians also work. A few men from the Transvaal come to Phoenix a few times a year to join us as well."

Ashok was clearly not telling his father and uncle everything and they knew from his quickly flowing words and his fidgeting.

"*Kyaa baath hai Beta…*what is the matter, Son?" Purat leaned over and put his arm on Ashok's shoulder.

Ashok continued to fidget and finally blurted out, "*Papaji, Kaakaji,* you know that there is fighting in the interior?"

"Fighting? Yes, but that is between white men and white men, British and Boer. I hear all about it at work and you know that the railways have been impacted. But *Beta*, what is troubling you about this fighting?"

"*Papaji*, the fighting has reached the interior of Natal too…Dundee, Ladysmith. Coal miners and other Indians are being hit by bullets and shells as they are working, cutting grass on British properties, just doing their jobs. Some are even being used as look-outs on tree-tops and are being hit by enemy fire. The white-on-white fighting is about the possession of gold and diamond mines in the interior, but now the fighting is here in Natal, so close to us for the possession of Natal."

"But *Beta*, have you been asked to fight? Have any of the young men meeting in Phoenix been asked to fight?"

"No, *Kaakaji*, but we are being asked to help as stretcher-bearers to carry wounded whites to hospital tents."

"*Areh nayh…nayh…Beta*, you are here in Durban, you have a job here, why? Why do you have to go up-country to Ladysmith and Dundee?"

"Gandhiji has started an Indian Ambulance Corps to help the British because he says we are all British subjects."

Amir and Purat sat stunned. Sibani and Bhagirathi appeared at the door to the front room with the girls gathered behind them.

"*Papaji*, the first group of Indians already went to Ladysmith and Dundee back in October. Gandhiji went with them. Another group went in December. They did return and are fine, only some injuries…" Ashok's voice trailed seeing the pained looks on his family's faces.

"So now we are being asked to go and help the wounded whites in the field hospitals there. Natal is secure for the British, no more fighting in Natal…" Realizing that he himself was confused about whether or not there was still active fighting in Natal, Ashok plunged ahead. "They are now concentrating their fighting in the Transvaal. The British want to secure that region for Britain. So no more British and Boer fighting in Natal, just many wounded British soldiers in hospital tents, needing help."

None of what he was struggling to explain was sinking in. All that his parents, uncle, aunt and siblings could hear was war, Indians wounded and that their Ashok would have to go and serve.

The men talked late into the night. Bhagirathi walked with Sibani back to her home and with Nina helped a weeping Sibani into bed. She kept wailing, "My boy, my son…" and muttering words that neither Bhagirathi nor Nina understood.

***

Ashok left by train for Ladysmith early the next day with a small group of young men. They carried with them a few clothes, some cooked food and dry groceries like lentils and rice in small bundles. As the train pulled into the Avoca station from Phoenix, Ashok boarded and was welcomed by the five others in the group. The train pulled out of Avoca and continued to the central station in town where the young men transferred on to another train.

Climbing on toward Maritzburg, the lush wattle plantations came into view and the young men's chatter quietened as they tried to get some shut eye. Seven hours later, they pulled into the Ladysmith train station. British officers in uniform stood guard on the platforms inside the station and as the group walked out of the station on to the road the soldiers demanded to know who they were and where they were headed. The leader of the group, a bespeckled young *bunya*, produced papers with Gandhi's signature and they were directed toward an army cart pulled by two horses.

A short ride along dirt roads found them at an army barracks. No permanent structures were visible, only a wide stretch of brown tents, some shorter than others, all grouped for different functions. As they alighted the officer seated in the front with the horse-cart driver, blew on a whistle barking, "Attention!!"

"You are being assigned to Officer Dunne. He will be here shortly!"

He then turned on his heels and walked briskly toward a tent several yards away. The Indian men stood silently at attention. A young officer, in khaki uniform, came out of the nearest tent, bending low to exit from the slit that served as an entrance.

"I am Officer Dunne. Follow me."

The group of six walked stiffly behind Dunne, through the narrow dirt pathway between rows of tents, arriving at the furthest tent, a long, white, canvas structure, with a pointed mid-section held up by poles. It had a small slit for a door. Inside the tent they saw rows of patients lying on cots along both walls. At a glance, Ashok estimated that there were over fifty patients in various degrees of pain. Some had legs strung up on ropes slung from metal poles, others with crude intravenous bags, and still others were bent over buckets held by Indian men as they vomited. The smell was a pungent mixture of disinfectant sheep-dip, medicine and human odour. But the two Indian men were steadfastly running from one patient to another helping wherever needed.

Officer Dunne stressed, "The doctors are in the next two tents, operating in one and resting in the other. You are not to enter those. Your work is in here. The chamber-pots are under the beds, the latrines and washing areas are over on that side," pointing behind the tent. "Get on with it!"

The men looked confused and stood speechless as Dunne strode off and out of the tent. One of the Indian helpers put down his rags and buckets and walked over to Ashok and his mates.

"I am Jawak Singh. Come I will show you."

"*Bhayah*," Ashok spoke as they followed the man. "Where do we put our things?"

Jawak snorted but said nothing. He led them out the other side of the long tent to a spot under a huge tree.

"Here, put your things next to mine. You sleep here."

Shocked, the young men stared. Under the tree, there were blankets rolled up, and cloth bags of possessions stacked neatly into small piles. A small fire-pit with a crude grill held two pots washed and overturned to dry and beside the pit a few spoons, metal plates and cups were neatly stacked. An Indian man, curled up in a fetal position slept, head against the tree, wrapped in a dirty, khaki coloured hospital blanket with blood stains around the leg area.

"There are only three of us left here now. No more fighting, no more stretchers so we are not lifting soldiers. Other groups left after two weeks each. I am here now for my second week."

"*Bhayah*, you sleep here?"

"*Jihaanh*…yes…this is our place to sleep when we can." He saw the look on the faces of the group and continued.

"You are here for two weeks only. You do whatever needs to be done, mostly wash the patients with clean cloths and water, clean their beds, help them do their ablutions and take the chamber pots to the lavatories over there." He pointed a short distance from the tree to several small wooden structures.

"You can wash the chamber pots, there is a pump nearby. The buckets and rags are for you to clean the beds. The nurses will give you clean towels and basins for washing the patients. But the floors are scrubbed by a few Africans and they wash the patients' sheets and clothes."

Ashok and his friends were visibly angry. They were all educated young men who had joined the movement to make a difference, not clean feces. Carrying stretchers to hospital tents was understandable. But being used in this way was not. The man on the ground awoke and started to moan in pain. Ashok composed himself and pointing to the man on the ground he asked, "What is the matter with him?"

Just as he spoke the man struggled to sit up and pulled the blanket away from his legs. Ashok gasped and stared at the bloody rags wrapped around his left ankle. Kneeling next to him, Ashok gently unwrapped the rags and looked in disbelief at the large gaping hole on the outside of the ankle, putrefying, pus-filled and smelling strongly of rotting flesh.

"What happened?"

Jawak looked miserably at the wounded man and then at the new group. "This is Aadit. He caught a bullet as he and another bearer were running from the fighting with a wounded soldier on a stretcher. They brought the stretcher to this hospital, but they were not able to get any help for his wound. He has been here since before I came."

Ashok was visibly livid. He and his young Phoenix friends were dressed in western clothes and wore shoes, but this man would have been carrying stretchers barefoot.

"Did no one apply any medicine?"

"We had some turmeric and made a poultice..."

"But this is a hospital," Ashok spluttered as he ran inside the hospital tent. There was a nurse attending one of the soldiers and he approached her.

"Madam, madam, we have a wounded man under the tree..."

"What man?" she looked alarmed. "A soldier?"

"No, no, Miss, an Indian stretcher bearer."

"We don't attend to Indians in here, they are here to work, they are not patients!"

"But he was severely injured by a bullet as he was carrying a soldier to this tent. He needs proper medical attention!" The nurse shrugged her shoulder and walked out of the tent using the exit at the far end. Ashok fumed, picked up the clean towels and bandages and a clean basin of water that she had left next to the patient and rushed out. The patient looked at him but said nothing.

Ashok cleaned Aadit's wound and wrapped it using clean hospital bandages. He propped up the man to sit against the tree and digging into his things he removed a small package and handed it to the grateful Aadit. It was a small tin with a paste that his *Kaaki*, Aunty Bhagirathi, made for him to reduce fever. It smelled of ginger and cinnamon pounded together with honey. The man gratefully licked the paste.

The first week was grueling, anger tempered by obedience, as officers watched them closely. There were several doctors working shifts two at a time.

The white women who were nurses worked in groups of four in each shift. Ashok and his peers said nothing, simply continued doing what needed to be done stoically. But Ashok's mind was on Aadit. He needed medicine, even if Ashok had to steal it.

The soldier who had heard Ashok's exchange with the nurse on the first day watched Ashok with kind eyes as he cleaned the bed.

"Can you help me. I need the chamber-pot."

Without a word, Ashok pulled out the enamel chamber-pot from under the bed and placed in under the wooden chair with part of the seat cut out. He then pulled back the blanket and was startled to see that the soldier had heavy bandages around a stump where his right foot should have been. Noticing Ashok's reaction, the young man made a sound like clearing his throat.

"Ah yes...the foot...shot to bits...boot and all...but that was over a month ago...don't worry I am not offended...it is a shock at first."

The man was a few years older than Ashok, maybe twenty-six. He clung to Ashok as he was gently eased off his bed and placed on the seat-less wooden chair. Ashok gathered his hospital gown and pulled it back over the backrest. He had no underwear so the soldier was able to pee comfortably into the pot. Returning to his bed, the soldier held Ashok's sleeve just as Ashok made to leave with the chamber-pot.

"Wait." The soldier turned with some difficulty to the small metal table beside his bed. On it was a metal basin containing gauze, bandages and two small tins.

"Here take this for your friend." He handed Ashok two small square pieces of gauze with some sort of paste between the neat folds, a rolled up clean bandage and one of the small tins.

"The gauze is antiseptic and the tin has some antiseptic powder." When Ashok looked around and with a worried look started to shake his hand, the soldier added, "No nurses around. Keep these under your shirt…don't be seen with them."

Ashok said a quiet thank you and left with the handful of medical supplies tucked under his loose tunic in the waistband of his khaki pants, which had a small inside pocket for holding money. He carried the chamber pot to the nearest lavatory, emptied it and washed it at the pump. Setting it down next to Aadit, he applied the antiseptic powder and wrapped the dressing firmly around the wound. He saved the other gauze and some of the bandage together with the tin and tucked it back into the inside pocket of his pants. He returned the pot to under the bed of the soldier who had now dozed off.

In the second week, Ashok saw Officer Dunne on the grounds and approached him with confidence. Ashok was used to dealing with whites at his railway job and walked up to Dunne.

"Sir?"

Dunne spun around. "Yes?" He looked annoyed to see that the voice belonged to an Indian. "What is it? Why aren't you in the tent working?"

"Sir, we have a severely wounded man…" and he hurriedly explained how and where Aadit had been wounded, the state of the wound and the unhygienic and wet conditions under the tree.

"Well, we do not have facilities for coolies…I mean for you people."

"Sir, I know that, but can I be given leave to take him back to the British farm where he works here in Ladysmith? He was a coal miner in Dundee, but he moved here before the war."

"How will you do that?"

"Sir, I can rent an ox cart."

"Very well, just for the afternoon. I need you back in the tent tonight."

Ashok and his peers loaded Aadit on to the cart and Ashok tucked several more antiseptic bandages and another tin of powder into Aadit's small cloth bag. He also showed Aadit a small tin of aloe paste that Bhagirathi had given him.

"*Bhayah*, your wound is healing. I have put more of the medicine and bandages into your bag. Ask if your barracks manager will let you see the doctor. This paste will help the skin heal once the wound closes properly."

Aadit, who was a little younger than Ashok, looked better than he had a week ago. He held Ashok's hand and thanked him.

"May God bless you, *Bhayah*. I don't know how I would have managed. Only two others remained and they were too busy."

"*Nayh…nayh…Bhayah…*just think that you will be with your family now."

Ashok patted his hand and settling next to Aadit in the flat bed of the cart gave the signal to the ox-cart driver to proceed. Ashok placed Aadit's wounded ankle on his own leg and held it in his hand to keep it steady through the journey of several miles to his farm barracks. His family and the other men in the barracks were overjoyed to see Aadit and carried him into his shack. They had no idea where Aadit had ended up. He had left as a stretcher bearer nearly four weeks prior and when he failed to return after the expected two weeks, no one could give his family any explanation of his whereabouts. After hurried greetings and hugs of gratitude, Ashok left and was back at the field hospital by sunset. He had a quick meal of *dhal* and rice that was cooking at the fire pit under the tree and then he rushed back to his duties.

Around midnight, Ashok sat on the floor at the entrance of the tent. He was exhausted, but he was on night duty which meant no sleep. All was quiet. A few soldiers were moaning, but most of them were sleeping soundly. He heard a quiet voice say, "Excuse me…excuse me…can you please come here."

The respectful voice he knew belonged to the soldier who had twice given him medication for Aadit. Most of the soldiers were gruff with the Indian and African helpers, but there were a few who were obviously grateful and this young man was one of those. Lighting the small kerosene latern that sat on the floor next to him Ashok cautiously hurried over.

"Are you all right, Sir?" he whispered.

"Yes I am okay…just wanted to chat."

"But Sir, they are sleeping…"

"We will talk softly." The man smiled showing his hazel eyes and pale features under his carrot topped head of hair. "What is your name? Where are you from?"

"I am Ashok and I live in a place called Avoca many miles from here, in Durban. We are here because a man named Gandhi, a lawyer from India, exhorted us to help British soldiers."

"Ah yes, I too live in Durban. I landed there as a boy with my parents on the Umvoti many years ago. My name is Michael…Michael Pearson."

Ashok was only a boy in 1886, only seven, but the name Umvoti had stuck in his mind.

"Sir, when did you arrive on the Umvoti?"

"Well I can never forget that voyage. It was in October of 1886 and I was twelve years old."

Ashok stood stunned. He had heard the story of how Gulab *Kaaka* had died on the Umvoti – heard it over and over again from his parents, from Amir *Kaaka* and Bhagirathi *Kaaki*, from Gulab's ship-mate and now family friend Basudev – indeed the story was repeated by many in the close-knit Avoca community. But now here was the story lying in front of him on a hospital cot!

"Sir, may I sit?"

As Ashok made to drop to the floor, Michael stuck out his arm to touch him and said, "No not on the floor, sit here on this chair, next to me." Ashok hesitated, but urged on, he sank on to the chair.

"Sir, you were twelve years old? Why do you remember that voyage so well?"

Michael's face contorted as if in pain. He stayed silent and then taking a deep breath he started. "I was a curious boy. I wish I wasn't…I have wished a hundred times that I wasn't…but…"

Both stayed silent and then Michael continued. "There was a storm. My parents had been arguing in the state-room and I just needed to get away. I went up to the library but the storm looked so beautiful…I mean so interesting. Rain pelted the window and far-off I could see the waves rising and crashing…not a sight often seen. I went to the dining hall door and opened it slightly…no-one was around…I ventured out intending to just look. But the ship tilted and I was thrown on the deck floor. I was terrified. I could not get up…the wind and rain…and the ship rocking back and forth…I knew I was going to die. I should have died."

"Sir…you didn't die…Sir…I…I… know the story."

Startled Michael stared at Ashok.

"You were saved…"

"Yes, just as I thought I would slide on to the railings and into the ocean I felt strong arms grab me and drag me to the door which had slammed shut. The Indian man banged on the door but held me strongly in his other arm. The door opened and he shoved me inside. But… but…oh my God…" Michael heaved a dry cry and slowly continued. "The staff did not let the man come inside. I shouted…I can still see it all…I screamed and shouted and flailed for them to let him in but they dragged me into the lounge where many passengers had come running."

Both men stayed silent. The other soldiers slept. No nurses came in which was usual at this time of night as they had scheduled rounds every hour. After several minutes, Michael turned his eyes pleadingly to Ashok.

"You said you know the story…why…why…how do you know the story?"

"Sir, that man who saved you was my Uncle Gulab."

"Yes, his name was Gulab. Oh God…yes his name was Gulab… Ashok, I am so sorry."

Ashok said nothing. Here was this man who had shown kindness by sharing his medicine with Aadit. And here was the boy who had caused Gulab *Kaaka*'s death. The silence and darkness enveloped them. Michael held out his hand and searched for Ashok's. Ashok held back at first but then let his hand be held.

"At the harbour building an officer introduced us to Gulab's brother and another man. I still remember their names, Amir and Purat. And what I remember so clearly is that the man, Amir, placed his hand on my head asking me if I was all right. I was afraid that he would be angry at me…but…he was so kind. My mother noticed it too and that night as she tucked me into bed and consoled me, she reminded me that I was blessed that the man was so kind even in his sorrow."

"Yes, my father Purat was there with his ship-brother Amir. Gulab was Uncle Amir's brother."

"Ship-brother?"

"Yes, when indentured Indians are brought here from India they suffer interminable difficulties in the cramped lower holds of ships. They develop life-long bonds, suffering together on the ships and then suffering as they are abused on sugar plantations. I have seen those congested holds…my father helps stevedores with their problems as part of his job. I have also seen the distress on sugar plantations…I was born on a plantation in a place called Phoenix next to Avoca."

The young men, stilled by the shock of the revelations, sat quietly, speaking intermittently. Michael talked about how strict his father had been, how afraid his mother was of him and he showed a rare smile as he remembered his mother who had died several years earlier, after which his father returned to England leaving Michael to pursue his career as an officer.

"But there is no career for me anymore as an officer…"

They were interrupted by two nurses entering the tent. Ashok stood quickly and straightened Michael Pearson's sheet, tucking it carefully around the stump.

There were three more days until their tour of duty would end. Ashok's was the last group of "stretcher-bearers" as intended by Gandhi. The Boer war had ended in Natal and all that remained now was for people like Michael and Aadit to pick up their broken lives.

Ashok and Michael did not have a chance to talk again until the final night. Ashok had offered to take the night shift so his peers could rest, pack and clean up their under-tree home.

"Ashok, I want to come and see your Uncle Amir."

"Sir…I…"

"Ashok, call me Michael…we are around the same age…"

"No, no Sir…"

"I insist. Ashok I am being transferred out of here to a home nearby that cares for convalescing soldiers. I don't know how long I will be there. But when I return to Durban I will resign from the regiment. My father has left me money and I want to study law. But once I am settled in a flat in Durban I want to come and see your family."

"Sir…I mean Mr. Michael…how will you? Our house is on a little hill…no road…only a narrow footpath up from the stream."

Michael smiled. "I will need to learn a lot of things and climb a lot of hills." Both men laughed softly knowing the double meaning.

Ashok had no idea how he would explain this to his father and Amir *Kaaka* and didn't know if they would be accepting of this visit. Many years had passed since their indenture and the family knew a few good white men, like Mr. Landers who visited from time to time. He brought treats like hard-boiled eggs, sweets and biscuits from his hotel for the little children in Amir's barracks. The barracks now had both Indian and African families and a small team of staff that Amir needed for his flourishing business. Mrs. Landers was still an enthusiastic client of Sibani and Bhagirathi's sewing business. Annie's girls were now teenagers, getting ready to wed, and needed modern dresses. But Ashok was still not sure how Michael would be received by his family. Maybe, hopefully, Michael would not visit for a few more years.

***

As he climbed the little hill up to his house, Ashok took stock of the beauty of nature all around him. He had hopped over the stream, stepping on the stones to keep his shoes dry, his cloth bag slung over his back. He was greeted by the children and their mothers at the stream barracks. The children clung to his legs until he gave them each small sweets that he always bought from Adam's shop at the railway station. Adam, Fatima and the now twenty-five-year-old Asif had been overjoyed to see him. Asif's wife, pregnant and glowing, came out shyly too and greeted her "brother" Ashok. Ashok asked about Ayesha, now twenty-two, married into a family on Grey Street and a mother of two. Asif, who now ran the shop with his father, walked part way with Ashok and caught up on the news of the tour of duty. But Ashok's parents did not know that he was coming home that evening.

Sibani's private pains in her thigh were troublesome recently. The burn had never really healed and, all these years later it still flared up from time to time. She bound her thigh almost all the time and had learned to live with the pain. This morning, after her bath she bound the still deep gash and continued her work, angry at the weakness it caused her. But her positive nature always emerged strong. The children from the stream barracks often came up to her yard and their laughter and pranks were music to her as she went about her daily chores. Like her own children growing up, these little ones enjoyed climbing the two large mango trees in her yard. She gave them salt and chilli powder wrapped in a piece of paper and they happily sat on branches eating green mangoes dipped in the spicy mixture and chattering away. She made sure they left and went home to their parents before sunset. This evening Sibani, sitting on the front step with a tin cup of after-supper tea, was mending Purat's socks by the light of her small lantern. She and Bhagirathi had discovered that if they put a palm-sized, smooth, round rock inside the sock they could deftly darn the holes in their families' socks. Setting her sewing down, Sibani started to pick up her teacup and looked up. To her surprise, there he was—Ashok, her beloved ever-little boy, handsome in the fading sunlight, smiling his cheerful smile. He dropped his sack and ran to his mother, lifting her off the ground into his arms. She cried and held on to him, thanking *Ganeshji* and *Hanumanji* and *Shivaji* and *Durga Maathaji* and more and more godly avatars, on and on, not letting go of him.

"Ma...*Mathaji*...shhh...shhh... I am fine, *Ma*...I am fine," and he kissed her up and down all over her face. Purat ran to them and enveloped both of them in his strong embrace. Soon his whole family had gathered. Amir *Kaaka* and Bhagirathi *Kaaki*, wobbling in her pregnancy, hugged and kissed him over and over until he led her to the wooden stumps that served as chairs around the fire-pit in the front yard. The girls and Ashok's younger brother Avanindra sat on the grass mesmerized by their brother Ashok's every word. Sibani rushed into her back kitchen and fired up her coal stove to cook fresh vegetables from her garden. As Ashok ate in the front yard, she kneaded dough and cooked fluffy *parathas* over the open fire-pit for him as she sat with all the family members listening to his stories.

After his supper, when the girls and thirteen-year-old Avanindra had gone to bed and darkness had enveloped their yard they moved into Purat's front room and settled into the low cot-couches. Sibani rushed to place pillows behind Bhagirathi's back.

Ashok then related Michael Pearson's account to the adults. There was no rancour, just quiet reflection as the adults listened.

"*Beta*, if this boy...this young man...wants to come, he can come. He was a child, younger than Avanindra even. He did not know that tragedy would happen. *Nayh*...nayh...it's all right, *Beta*...God is bringing him back in our lives, for a purpose I am sure. It's all right, *Beta.*"

As Amir spoke these words, Bhagirathi put her hand on his shoulder and neck and massaged gently. His blinding headaches did return from time to time, though not as often as in his indentured days and Bhagirathi, in addition to her soothing head massages, had developed many different pastes and mixtures to rub on his temples or poultices to place over his eyes and forehead. One of Amir's friends, a gardener on the hill of white houses where he sold flowers, had asked him one day why he was holding on to his forehead. When Amir explained his headaches, the gardener had told him about his boss, a gentle, old, white doctor who was kind enough to see a few Indian patients at his back door, in a little shed. But the powder that the doctor had given him for a few shillings had a sedative effect and Amir did not like taking it. He took it two or three times mainly at night and while it stopped his headache, he woke with difficulty feeling tired for most of his busy morning.

Purat asked, "How will Michael Pearson know where to come?"

"*Papaji*, I gave him my address at the Central Railway Station. He will write to me once he is back and settled in Durban."

"*Aachah*. Good then it is settled. My Gulab *Bhayah* saved him. Gulab will be watching over him," Amir said.

Part 3
1900's - Home and Hearth

Chapter 15

A New Era

Amir and Bhagirathi's first son, Dalip, was born in late March 1900. Although both Purat and Amir wanted to build larger houses for their growing families they had to wait. It was no more a matter of knocking together walls and roof. Now the municipality required proper building permits and well-drawn plans. Building inspectors were meticulous in checking these legalities. So Amir and Purat continued to add extensions to their tin homes, which remained comfortable. Like many other Indian families, they built chicken-runs in their backyards and kept a few hens and roosters, for eggs mostly and occasionally for meat.

Ashok and many of his friends had become disillusioned by their experiences with Gandhi's protest movement. Other Indians, however, took up the reins and emerged as leaders in the Indian Congress. A few weeks after the end of the Boer War, Ashok had watched from his tiny railway office as the celebratory, cheering throng of British men and women gathered on the city hall grounds across from the Central Railway Station. He watched dispassionately at the self-congratulatory crowds who cheered as awards were given out. Since Indian stretcher-bearers and helpers were ignored, the Indian merchants and Congress a few months later held their own celebration on Grey Street. They invited white dignitaries to make speeches. Ashok refused to attend. He immersed himself in his work and as he was becoming ever more popular with his bosses, he steadily earned more money. Dressed in smart western clothes, he became their go-to person and was indispensable in the front office where complaining, dissatisfied customers almost always found solutions through this young man.

Michael Pearson's note arrived two years later in September of

1902. He said he was back in Durban after spending a year in and out of hospitals and convalescent homes in Ladysmith. He wrote that he had been fitted with a wooden foot. Ashok was reading the letter sitting on a non-white bench on the street outside the city hall gardens. Many of the construction labourers sat on the few benches or on the cement sidewalks eating their midday meals. Ashok read with curiosity that Michael's prosthetic foot had steel springs at the back which allowed it some little movement as he walked. Michael wanted to meet. Friendships between white and non-white did not occur. Even if some whites were kind, the relationship was always that of master and servant. But Amir *Kaaka* had expressed a positive attitude toward Michael Pearson so Ashok wrote back that they could meet at the railway station.

A few weeks later, red-haired Michael leaning on a wooden crutch and green-eyed Ashok sat talking on a non-white bench on the Central Railway Station platform. Busy commuters looked twice but paid no heed as they hurried on or off their trains.

"Thank you for agreeing to see me."

"No…it's good to see you walking. How does this work?" Ashok pointed at the foot and Michael laughed. He stood quite easily on his feet and turned the prosthesis right and left. With a boot over the prosthesis, it was not visible and looked like a regular foot.

"Ashok, I know that things were not fair at the base hospital…" Ashok waved away his comments, but Michael continued. "The regiment spent thousands of pounds on my prosthesis and my eighteen months of care. I know that Indian stretcher bearers received nothing. It galls me and maybe someday, hobbling or not, I can make amends."

Ashok looked at Michael, took a deep breath as if to respond but chose to say nothing. Michel continued,

"I have submitted my resignation papers to the regiment and I am now working in a law office training to become a lawyer."

"Oh, I thought you had to go to England to study to be a lawyer?"

"Yes, you are right. My boss Mr. William Burnett did study in London and now he trains others who are then certified through the new University of South Africa in a place called Cape Town."

This was new information for Ashok who was not aware that there was a university in the country. Michael continued.

"He works with another more senior lawyer, Mr. Wynette. When my father went back to England four years ago, I was with the regiment but my father needed to transfer his assets here to me. He knew Mr. Wynette but it was Mr. Burnett who handled the transfer."

Michael saw the resigned look on Ashok's face and recognized his own voice of privilege.

"Ashok, there is an Indian lawyer training in the same office too."

Ashok's eyes showed his interest.

"Yes, it was Mr. Burnett who brought him in. His name is Nithendra. When I saw him do that I knew that I wanted to train with Mr. Burnett."

"Where is your office?"

"Several miles north of here, near the ocean. It is near a place called Red Hill."

Ashok's face now lit up.

"My uncle delivers flowers there...my Uncle Amir...Gulab's brother..." and his voice trailed off at the significance.

"Yes Nithendra told me that we are near Avoca...just about seven or eight miles away. Ashok, may I come and see your Uncle Amir?"

"Yes, I did explain to him when I returned from Ladysmith and he welcomes your visit."

The men parted when Ashok's lunch break was over, agreeing that Michael would visit Avoca soon. Ashok's heart lurched as he watched Michael limp on his crutches toward the main entrance where his horse and buggy stood. The Indian driver helped him in and as the crutch was placed beside him Michael waved to Ashok standing at the entrance.

The young men had two more train station visits and chats on the platform bench. They arranged for Michael to visit two months later on a Sunday afternoon. Ashok met him near Adam's shop and hopped in beside Michael on his horse and buggy. As they rode toward the pulp factory and the stream, Ashok pointed out the school, Adam's and Suleiman's shops, the field where several ox and horse carts awaited rentals and the homes of friends like Rajiv and Bhodraj. Ashok regaled Michael with a snake story as they approached the pulp factory.

"Uncle Amir owns all this land on the hills beside the pulp factory. He grows those beautiful blue and red flowers. See that mango grove amid the flowers? Well one day a few years ago Uncle's assistant Ajit came screaming down the hill, 'Snake, snake!' and behind him a man was being carried on the shoulders of two other workers. My uncle was working on plants close to the factory when Ajit found him and gasped out the words, 'Snake bit worker!' Uncle knew about poisonous snakes especially near the mango groves and sent Ajit to the pulp factory to ask for someone to come. He sucked out and spat the poison from the man's leg but he had nothing to apply on the wound. He also had no transportation at that time. His customers from the factory loaded the man on to their horse buggy and took him to a white doctor in Red Hill. Since then Uncle has realized the importance of having his own transport and also carries little packets of herbal salves that he buys from local shopkeepers who get them from India."

The buggy stopped at the stream. Ashok helped Michael off and handed him his crutch. The little children from the stream barracks gathered around admiring the horse and the shiny buggy. Ashok asked one of the teenage boys to provide clean water for the horse and watch over him while the driver and Ashok supported Michael on the walk up the hill to Amir's house.

"*Aiyeh Beta…aiyeh…come…son…come.*" Amir had walked part-way down the hill and offered his assistance. Michael, moved by this welcome, tried to shake his hand but wobbled and was guided back on his crutch by Ashok and the driver.

Bhagirathi had prepared an Indian lunch with rice, chicken, vegetables and sweets which both families and the driver ate together spread out on Amir's front yard. However, a special table was set in the front room for Michael, Ashok, Amir and Purat. Bhagirathi provided a spoon for Michael knowing that the Indian style of eating with his fingers would be strange for him. The conversation among the men focused mainly on Michael's injury, his recovery and his training so close to Amir's flower delivery route. After the meal, hands were washed outside in the front yard with water poured by Bhagirathi. The men returned to the front room and Michael broached the subject that was uppermost on his mind.

"Sir…Mr. Sing… as you see I am grown up now but not a day passes over these sixteen years that I don't think about your brother Gulab."

Amir waved his hand indicating to Michael that it was all right. Amir and Purat both forty-one now, had started to grey and signs of hard work in the open sun had started to leave their mark on their faces and roughened hands.

"No...no Sir...I want you to know how sorry I am..."

"But *Beta*...Son...you were a child...a boy...twelve years old..."

"I know Sir, but I should not have gone out on the deck. I screamed and shouted for the men to open the door to the dining hall, to let your brother in..." Michael put his face into his hands and shook his head.

"*Beta*...*Beta*...Ashok told us. Do not cry...shhh shhh..." Amir stood up from his chair and walked around to Michael. Ashok gave his *Kaaka* his chair next to Michael and Amir sat down and put his arm around Michael's shoulder.

"*Beta*, my brother Gulab would not want you to cry...it was his fate... it was his fate. He would want you to live your life...he saved you and you have come into our lives."

Amir changed the subject to Michael's law training and tried to establish where the office was on his flower route. The men chatted a while longer and when the driver came inside Michael stood up, found his crutches and started to take his leave. As the family gathered around him in the yard he said, "I am not a lawyer yet...four more years to go but if ever you need anything, any advice, any legal paperwork I will help. My boss Mr. Burnett is a good man and a young man Nithendra is training with me. We will be privileged to serve you."

"Nithendra?"

Ashok explained about the firm's commitment to train Indian lawyers.

"Ahhh...*aachah*...all right...that is good," smiled Amir, rolling his head.

Ashok accompanied Michael back as far as Adam's shop. He knew they could not be friends, but he also knew that something happened between his family and Michael that day, a quiet impossible seeming respect between this white man and Ashok's Indian family. No it was more than respect – this man actually felt that he owed a debt to Amir *Kaaka*.

***

By 1903, Sibani's efforts to find just the right bride for Ashok materialized. Sibani often visited her friend Parvati at the Phoenix temple. The women had time together since Sajiv had trained Yatindra to take over many of the temple functions and his young wife looked after the temple chores that Parvati had done over many years. Sibani also had good friends among other women both from her old barracks and in the neighbouring barracks. So whenever she and Bhagirathi visited with their husbands and families there was a great deal of merriment between Bhagirathi's parents, Prabhu's young family, Parvati's extended family and lots of friends. So it was that a young girl named Sanjana came to Sibani's attention.

The girl was the daughter of a free market gardener in Mount Edgecombe, a village close to Phoenix, one train stop to the north. She was a second cousin of Prabhu's wife, Roopmani, whose mother mentioned her to Prabhu's mother and she to her daughter Bhagirathi, who in turn spoke to Sibani and Purat. At eighteen years of age, Sanjana was six years younger than Ashok. She was an only child, and well-educated, having continued at school four years after most girls stopped. Hence, she had completed high school at the local Christian school and was attending a small local institution run by nuns to train as a teacher. She helped at the small Indian school in Mt. Edgecombe while completing her teacher's training.

Just as Amir had gone those many years ago to ask for Bhagirathi's hand in marriage, so too Ashok, Purat, Amir, Sajiv and Rajiv went to Mt. Edgecombe to ask Sanjana's parents for her hand in marriage. Seated in their front room, they chatted formally with her father until the mother approached with a tray of tea followed by Sanjana with a tray of homemade *mitai*, Indian sweets.

Ashok stared at her, obviously smitten by her beauty. Thin and slight, she was dressed in a long bright blue skirt embroidered with gold and silver threads, a short pale blue *choli* blouse and her head was draped in a see-through long blue scarf. He saw her for just minutes and she was gone, hustled out by her mother.

Their wedding was held in September of the same year, before the start of the windy season, at the Mt. Edgecombe community temple. Built before the Phoenix temple, this one had a larger front foyer with shiny white marbled statues of over a dozen different religious Hindu avatars. The groom's procession had arrived by train to Phoenix from where Ashok and Prabhu's friends had arranged a horse-drawn carriage to transport the groom and his few friends. The rest of the family continued by train to the Mt. Edgecombe station which was only a short way away. The temple's huge grounds were bordered by well-tended flower gardens and had a tent supported by wooden poles. After the ceremony inside the temple, the bride, groom and their families walked outside to join the guests. Two hundred Indian villagers had been invited by word of mouth.

Ashok had chosen a typical Indian bridegroom's suit, beige, heavy, knee-length, hand-embroidered tunic, matching tight leggings and bead-encrusted yellow *pugri* turban on his head. Sanjana wore a red, silk, gold-embroidered sari with its *aanchal* draped over her head and covering the top part of her face. Everyone enjoyed *thubla* drum music and singing while eating steaming rice and vegetables on banana leaf plates followed by ample servings of sweet *mitai*. After the feast, as was customary, the bride returned to her parents' home and the guests dispersed.

It was evening and daylight was fading by the time the groom's party returned to Avoca. Amir and Purat's family did not come straight home. They accompanied Rajiv, Bhodraj, Himal, Jaga and Bhimnad's family to the Avoca temple. Still a small basic structure, it nevertheless stood quietly majestic in front of Bhimnad, Jaga and Himal's houses. Ashok and the men entered the inner sanctuary to receive spiritual blessings from Rajiv while the women with their babies and children sat in the small covered verandah. After the ceremony Purat and Amir's family returned home on foot. The bride would be brought home the following weekend amid merriment and a feast at Purat's home.

At home, Ashok retired to his new quarters, a large extension built toward the front right side of Purat's house, away from the rest of the family. He, Purat and Amir had added a large bedroom, furnished with a big, new bed and a shiny wooden wardrobe from Suleiman's shop. They had attached a smaller room with a low couch and table for the young couple to relax and have some private time.

Ashok returned to work the next day as did his father and Amir *Kaaka*, but Sibani, now herself pregnant, together with Bhagirathi and several women friends were busy preparing for the feast the following Saturday when Ashok's bride would be brought home. Trays and trays of rice and *dhal* lentils had to be picked over to remove tiny stones, garden vegetables had to be checked and a list of vegetables not in the garden had to be prepared for purchase from Adam's store. Banana trees had to be checked to make sure there were enough leaves to be used as serving plates. Drums of water had to be filled and stored. Sites for cutting the flowers for prayer and for decorating doorways were identified so cutting them on that Saturday morning would be easy. Bamboo from the two clumps on the property had to be checked to make sure that there were enough tall stems for the flag poles required in the prayer ceremony. In the evenings of that week the men dug the holes in the yard to build temporary structures for the tent.

The Saturday morning was bright and sunny. Children and adults in the family were filled with excitement and a festive spirit. Ashok bathed and dressed in white western pants, a light green shirt and the beige tie that one of his stretcher-bearer friends had given him. Amir and Purat wore traditional *dhotis* and tunics. The two families together with the ship-brothers and their families boarded the train to Mt. Edgecombe arriving at Sanjana's parents' home by noon. Amir and Purat were reminded of the laughter at their own door-blocking ceremonies. Friends of the bride, bedecked in their finery, stood at the door and refused Ashok entry until he had distributed over five pounds in coins.

As Ashok entered the front chamber and saw his bride his heart skipped a beat. She was seated with her mother. Her head was covered in a light green see-through veil, the same colour as Ashok's eyes. Her light green long skirt and *choli* blouse were studded with small silver sequins. Sibani had given Sanjana a new *haar* that she had ordered from their Phoenix jeweller. She had taken an old coin from her own wedding *haar* together with a new coin and had it made into a new gold necklace which Sanjana was wearing. Ashok knelt in front of his bride and with his fingers, gently lifted her face to him. She averted her face shyly, but he gently insisted. The bride and groom locked their gaze on each other and it was only the giggling of her girlfriends that brought them back out of their mesmerizing moment. Two hours of laughter, food, sweets and music ended with preparations for the bride to leave with her new family. Like Bhagirathi's mother had done so many years ago, Sanjana's mother clung to her daughter, her only child, and sobbed uncontrollably, until Bhagirathi gently took her in her own embrace assuring her that Sanjana would always be a daughter to her and Sibani.

At their home, Ashok's bride sat in the family's front room with her veil over her face as the mothers and their friends prepared to serve the food cooked earlier in the day in large pots on open fires in the yard. Sanjana was flanked on either side by Nina, Jaldhara, Sookdhay, Chanderkali and their girlfriends dressed in striking saris and *shalwar kameez*. Every adult woman guest who arrived brought a small gift of a few coins or sweets or costume jewelry and as each handed it to Sanjana she lifted her veil to thank them. This ceremony was called *Mooh Dikhia* or face-showing by the bride. Earlier, as Sanjana entered her groom's home for the first time, both Sibani and Bhagirathi had placed on her wrist the exquisite gold bangles that they had the jeweller make just for their new daughter-in-law.

Festivities ended when darkness enveloped the yard. Lanterns were lit and the departing guests were given a gracious send-off. The adults went to sit in Bhagirathi's front room. Clean-up was left for the next day, which was a Sunday, now usually a lazy day of rest. Amir, Bhagirathi, Purat and Sibani sat cross-legged on the couches in the front room and all the girls decided to sleep at this house tonight, giggling in the two back bedrooms. Fifteen-year-old Avanindra came with his parents and now lay in one of the bedrooms sound asleep. Ashok and his bride had Purat's home to themselves on this their first night as husband and wife.

***

Over the next decade, Amir and Purat's families grew as Bhagirathi, Sibani and Sanjana delivered new sons and daughters amid much happiness. The teenaged girls in the family were being married to grooms carefully selected by Amir, Purat, Sibani and Bhagirathi. Sibani and Purat's Nina was married to the son of a shop owner from Tongaat on the north coast. Jaldhara married a plantation owner's son in Verulum. Sookdhay married a municipal worker in the mining town of Dundee. Chanderkali followed with a marriage to a shop owner's son in nearby Greenwood Park, close to Mr. Landers' hotel. But as the girls left, the two family homes continued to be filled with children born through the decade. Amir and Bhagirathi had a further five children over the decade and Purat and Sibani had a further three. Ashok and Sanjana too welcomed three children over ten years. Avanindra, firmly established as one of a team of managers in a large Grey Street shop, married Leela, a relative of Bhodraj's wife, in 1910, at the age of twenty-two, and the house was extended once again to accommodate his babies which arrived soon after.

But the country was going through turmoil, and more and more the Indian communities were targeted for oppression by the white regime. Ashok's friends in Phoenix had started a weekly newspaper called Indian Opinion written in English, Hindi and Gujerati. It carried details of Gandhi's struggles against the fierce General Smuts to repeal draconian laws demanding high taxes from Indians, blocking Indians from owning land and requiring Indians to register and carry identity passbooks. Ashok was torn between his memory of the disdain of the whites toward stretcher-bearers, his subsequent disillusionment with Gandhi's efforts and now with these renewed efforts to fight for freedom and equality as British subjects. Added to his worry was young Dalip's interest in the movement.

Sanjana, in between pregnancies, helped Bhodraj at his school where Dalip and his two little brothers, Debi and Ranjith attended classes. The boys were thirteen, eleven and nine years old and were clever students. She knew that the boys, together with many others at the school, read the Indian Opinion and were influenced by the articles about Gandhi and the Congress struggles. Visits by leaders and politicians from India like the famous Gokhale in 1912 did nothing to convince Smuts to repeal the punitive laws. Gandhi had been arrested and jailed several times and Congress leaders were invited by Indian teachers across Natal to speak to students and educate them about the repressive laws. So it was in 1913 that Gandhi started his *Satyagraha* movement in Durban. He exhorted Indians to march against the unfair colonial laws in a show of passive resistance against the government. Thirteen-year-old Dalip decided to join the march.

Ashok could not let him go alone and accompanied him on foot on the march from Phoenix to Grey Street in central Durban. According to the Indian Opinion marches were occurring throughout Natal and included Indians from the coal mines of Dundee to the railway and city workers of Maritzburg, to farming estates and even to indentured labourers on sugar estates along the coast. Gandhi was once again arrested and jailed for the illegal act of inciting indentured labourers against their British colonial masters. In November of 1913, the indentured labourers on the Natal Sugar Estate in Avoca, previously the Harrison

Estate, where Amir had worked, went on strike. The chaos and rioting by hundreds of Indians and the retaliation of armed police caused families to keep their children from school and away from public places.

In Phoenix and Mount Edgecombe, estate owners called in the police and the militia to protect their properties. Armed with rifles, white policemen came on horseback even to the Avoca estate, attempting to arrest strikers. Local residents lived in fear. The new groups of indentured labourers were equally fierce and threatened unarmed African policemen with their *pangas* forcing them to release the strikers. When Gandhi was released from prison in December, he rallied in speech after speech against the use of force by strikers. Eventually, support for Gandhi's demands came from an unlikely source.

Mr. Campbell, the old gentleman who owned the estate where Amir was first indentured in Phoenix, supported Gandhi's Relief Bill that would end the taxes on Indians. Shrewd Mr. Campbell recommended the bill on condition that Indian immigration be stemmed. His support coincided with the movement in India to stop indenture. Many labourers who returned to India from Natal, Fiji and the West Indies, reported harsh conditions, abuse and death suffered by labourers at the hands of cruel colonial masters. The one thing that Gokhale did achieve was to petition and convince the Indian government to end indenture and that process had already begun in India in July 1911. Africans were being used by some estates in Natal to make up the labour shortfall and when Africans threatened to join the strikes, this further helped the resistance movement. The strikes spread to railway workers, brickworks, quarry workers and the wattle plantations. Profits were impacted throughout Natal. Smuts had no alternative but to facilitate the passage of the Relief Bill in 1914, according minimal rights to Indians as British subjects. Gandhi left Natal for India in July of the same year.

***

Amir, Purat, their ship brothers and their respective families resumed a quieter life in Avoca and the children returned to school. Several government-aided Indian high schools had opened in the larger cities like Durban, Maritzburg, Tongaat and Stanger attended mostly by boys. Amir's two younger sons, Debi and Ranjith and Purat's two young sons attended high school in town having to leave on an early train each morning. Amir's Dalip at the age of fourteen, together with their old faithful manager Ajit continued to help Amir run his now flourishing flower business and supervise a growing staff of Indian and African flower gardeners.

But with both houses now cramped and scarce flat land around their homes Amir and Purat renewed their commitment to build new homes at the apex of Avoca Road, crowning Amir's rose covered hill and Purat's adjoining land. Though both their finances were adequate to support their families, their house-building plans over the decade had to be put on hold with the wedding expenses of their sons and daughters.

They had, many years earlier, applied for building permits, and the building company of Narainsamy, Basudev, Munian and Ismail, that had built the temple, had been working periodically on securing architect drawings for them. On a hot December night in 1914, Amir and Purat, both now fifty-three years old, sat with these men in Amir's front room.

"*Areh*...we are not getting any younger..." Amir laughed. "We need to start building our houses. Narain, Basu do you have the plans?"

"*Aachah*...yes, here..." and the men spread out the plans on the low table in front of them.

After quietly looking over the plans, spreading the rolled up charts and moving around the table to see better, Amir and Purat smiled at each other and the builders sighed their relief.

"*Bohoth aachah*...very nice. So let us look at Purat's first and tell us about it."

"Purat's house will be to the left of yours facing out to the street, Amir *Bhai*. Purat you wanted it big, with six large rooms here, an indoor kitchen attached at the back, a small room beside the kitchen for *Behnji's* sewing, a room for eating and a room just inside the front door for sitting with guests. This long passageway from the front door to the kitchen will have the sleeping rooms on either side like this. Your bathroom and lavatory is here behind your house. There will also be another small tin building for your horse and cart. This pathway from the road will lead along the side of your house right to the horse and cart shed."

Purat rolled his head in appreciation and agreement saying, "*Bhayah*... the roof will need to be sloped..."

"*Haanh, haanh*…yes, yes…roofs will be sloped to allow rain to slide down."

"Amir *Bhayah*, yours is slightly different. It will face the street also and will have a tall pointed roof. Yours and *Behnji's* bedroom, you said you wanted it at the front of the house with a large window facing the sugar plantation where you were *sirdar*…*aachah*…right?"

"*Haanh Bhayah*, I sat under those trees to rest many days…" Amir stopped and reflected. "I love streams and rivers but up there, there are no streams, so those trees will serve nicely to shade my house." He smiled.

"*Aachah*, so your two front rooms will be that bedroom on one side and on the other side the big room like Purat *Bhai's* for sitting and chatting with visitors. There will be a long passageway from the front door down the middle of the house with your other five bedrooms on either side…*aachah?*"

"*Haanh, haanh, aachah Bhayah*…" and Amir gestured to Narain to continue.

"Your kitchen at the back of your house will be a little lower than the rest of your house but still covered by your roof. But there will be a few steps leading down a little as the hill starts to slope. Your kitchen will be very large since you wanted a large table for family and guests to eat together in the kitchen. On one side of the kitchen will be this small, narrow room to store your dry goods, and on the other side there is a door leading into the backyard to a stone washing area for *Behnji's* pots and pans. You asked for a concrete tank to be built to store rain water…a very good idea, *Bhayah*. That will go outside beside the storage room."

Amir rolled his head in agreement and Narain continued.

"Your lavatory and bathroom will be set back behind the house, the bathroom closer to your stone washing station and the lavatory a little behind that."

Narain and his company had also been asked the previous year to build a small barracks for Amir on his land across from the pulp factory to house his ox-cart which he had purchased many years prior. It was stationed there with one little hut for the African man who took care of it. Bur Amir needed to add two more rooms there so he could hire more men and add a horse and cart for transporting his flowers.

He and his manager Ajit together with Dalip were now taking flowers to town three times a week and more transportation was needed. They had cornered the market for flowers and supplied the large Central Railway Station flower stall as well as many other florists across the city.

"Narain *Bhayah*, you have nearly completed the barracks for my horse and ox carts, but I think I should add a shed like Purat's beside this new house too. I will buy another horse and cart for the family. Can a tin shed be added on the side of the house?"

"*Haanh...haanh...jihaanh*… yes …yes...definitely yes!" exclaimed Basudev and Ismail together.

The builders continued with the description of the verandah that Amir and Bhagirathi had requested to wrap around the front and one side of the house with an additional door leading into the visitors' room from the verandah.

Then came the question of costs. Each house would cost just over five hundred pounds to build. Both families had continued to be meticulous about saving money and despite the weddings and other expenses the cost of the houses would not be unmanageable burdens. The houses would not be expensive brick buildings but rather, like the temple, these would be wood, iron and tin structures.

The builders left after tea and a handshake sealed the agreement.

Three months into 1915, the weather cooled a little, and the foundations were dug, prayers were read by Rajiv and concrete was poured. As the weeks progressed, the four parents together with Ashok, Dalip and Avanindra spent early evenings at the building site for a little while after work and then walked back down to eat supper. It was one evening as they were seated at supper that a messenger arrived accompanied by Asif, Adam's son. Asif explained that the messenger arrived at the Avoca train station from Phoenix looking for Bhagirathi and the station manager had sent him to Adam's shop. The news was not good.

Bhagirathi's father, who had been experiencing severe colds, coughs and fever for the past several months, had passed away that afternoon and Prabhu had sent the shop assistant as messenger to tell Bhagirathi. The messenger and Asif were offered tea which they politely declined, then Bhagirathi together with Amir, Dalip, Purat and Sibani left with them while Ashok, Sanjana, Avanindra and his wife Leela took over both households to look after all the children.

Stoically, Bhagirathi walked to the train station between husband and son, dabbing silent tears. Asif's father, Adam, joined the quiet group and Asif returned to the shop to watch over their family. Together they boarded the next train to Phoenix. They were met at the station by old barracks friends and hurried to Ranjith's home still nestled among the vegetable plantation he so loved.

At the house, dozens of friends had gathered and even in their sorrow Bhagirathi, Amir and their group greeted them respectfully as they walked into the house. Ranjith's body, having been bathed by Prabhu and Sajiv, lay on a canvas stretcher on the floor of the front room wrapped in white cotton cloth surrounded by family and friends. In this new land there was no separation of genders as in India. The widow, together with her son Prabhu and Pundit Sajiv sat cross-legged beside the body quietly reciting prayers. Bhagirathi sat between her mother and brother who embraced her. She touched her father's face and then the tears came flooding. Her sobs brought tears from others in the room. Amir, Dalip, Purat and Adam sat on the floor behind the other mourners and joined in the quiet prayers.

In India Hindus were cremated, but here in Durban those rites were not yet allowed and in some, not all, indentured settlements, the estate owners had portioned off small areas to be used as Indian cemeteries. Here in Phoenix, that piece of land was behind the walls of the small Christian church's own cemetery. It was accessible through a laneway between the walled boundary of the church property and the farm next to it. But since it was approaching darkness the burial would need to be done the next morning. After the prayers were read, Sajiv asked people to wait outside so the coffin bearers could bring the coffin from their cart on the street on to the front verandah. Sajiv, Prabhu and Amir completed the covering of Ranjith Singh with the white cloth and gently lifted his body into the coffin. The bearers closed the lid and covered it with another white cloth. The bearers then left to complete preparations at the cemetery while some dusk still remained.

The night vigil began with family sitting on the verandah and friends in the yard. Most friends left as darkness fell but a few stayed, squatting in the yard talking quietly, some smoking hand-rolled cigarettes. Late at night, on the last train, Ashok and Sanjana arrived and joined family on the verandah. After all their children were asleep in their home, their friend Ajit had offered to stay with Avanindra and his wife and all the children while his wife took care of their own children in their home, still at the stream-barracks. Prabhu's wife Roopmani, Parvati and Sibani were not on the verandah as they were tending to the children inside and Sanjana joined them. Since this was a home where a funeral was taking place there was no cooking but friends kept bringing steaming pots of tea throughout the night which Sanjana, Parvati and Sibani served.

Early in the morning before sunrise, Amir, Purat, Adam, Prabhu, Ashok and Dalip took turns bathing in the family's bathroom behind the house and dressed in clean white *dhoti*s and tunics. The women did the same and wore clean white saris, although, by Hindu custom, they would not accompany the funeral procession to the cemetery. They all sat on the verandah as the villagers returned to pay their last respects. They were surprised to see Rajiv, Bhodraj, Bhimnad and Himal arrive on the early morning train.

Soon after sunrise the funeral cart arrived drawn by two horses. The men on the verandah picked up the coffin and carried it slowly to the cart. Bhagirathi and her mother were overcome with grief. Sibani, Parvati, Sanjana and Roopmani held on to them consoling, but weeping as well. Other women friends from the barracks and the neighbourhood sat around the grief-stricken family, some wailing, some sobbing quietly. The cart moved away slowly with the fifty or so men walking behind. The ceremony at the cemetery was performed by both Sajiv and Rajiv, and Ranjith Singh was laid to rest.

Chapter 16

Family Roots Entrenched

There was another occurrence in the eventful new century that would continue to shape Amir's family. With Gokhale's edict in India ending indenture, the last indenture ship leaving Calcutta had arrived in Durban in June 1911. On it was a three-and-half-year-old girl Jaso, a name which meant helper, and her mother Bachni, which meant promise. Amir first met them when the little girl was seven years old and was busy helping a gardener in one of the white *memsahib's* homes where he delivered flowers. His clientele had grown from the original Red Hill where he started so many years ago and had spread over several little hills of exquisite homes right to the busy new Beachfront Road by the sea. His bullock cart was not fast enough so he had started renting horse carts to bring flowers to the *memsahibs* and for Dalip and Ajit to take flowers into town. His intention was to buy both carts as soon as his new home was built.

On a sunny late September morning in 1915, he stopped at the house to deliver his usual large order of pokers, roses and ferns and a few scarce early agapanthus flowers. As the gardener came to the gate, the little girl clung to him walking to the gate beside him.

"*Namasthe Bhayah…yeh choti bacchi kon hai?* Good morning brother…who is this little girl?"

"*Namasthe Bhayah…yeh meri beti hai…*this is my daughter."

Amir looked confused as he had not seen the little girl before and he had been delivering to this house for over a year. The gardener whom his friends called Maharaj by caste, was known to the indentured as a man who had to hide his caste in order to enlist as an indentured labourer since the British did not indenture high castes for fear that they would not work in fields. However, Maharaj worked the cane fields of Tongaat and afterward found employment as a domestic gardener.

"*Bhayah*, I married her mother two years ago and we have another baby, a baby boy. *Aiyeh...andhar aiyeh...* come, come inside," he gestured to Amir to come in as he opened the metal gate.

"Come, there is no one else here. Master and *Memsahib* went up country and will not be back for another week. *Aiyeh...*"

Amir and Maharaj settled on the lush lawn, and crossing their legs yoga-style resumed their chat. The little girl sat on her father's knee.

"*Beti...*daughter...*Namasthe bolo...*say *Namasthe* to uncle...say?" But the little girl hid her face on his shoulder.

"Her name is Jaso. She is seven years old, nearly eight." Amir touched her long braided plaits and said hello.

Maharaj gently untwined his daughter's arms and told her to go inside and ask her mother to make tea. As the girl ran up the soft grassy slope to the house he continued his story.

"Her mother Bachni was married and lived with her in-laws in Meerut. But her mother-in-law was cruel and often hit her and threw boiling water at her. Bachni's husband died when the little girl was two and the abuse became worse. Bachni was beaten and burned on her skin and the child was starved. Bachni had friends in the village and two of the women were contracted by the British to come as indentured domestics. On the day that those two friends started their journey to Calcutta, Bachni's mother-in-law threw boiling water at her, close to the cooking pit where Bachni was picking out stones from *dhal* lentils with her child clinging to her. The boiling water just missed the child but burned the side of Bachni's face. She grabbed her child and ran to the home of her friend just as the young woman was taking leave of her brothers to get on to an ox-cart for her journey to Calcutta and the ship. The woman and her brothers spirited Bachni and Jaso on to the cart. The other friend was picked up from her home and together they tended to Bachni's burn and comforted the child."

Amir flinched at the story. He remembered his and Purat's journey thirty-two years ago. That journey may have improved over the years but for three women and a child it must have been very difficult.

"When they arrived at the Calcutta depot an Indian nurse took pity on Bachni and the child and somehow managed to get an Anglo-Indian agent to stamp Bachni as an indentured domestic and got her on the ship, Umkuzi. When the women arrived at Port Natal they were distributed close to one another as they told the officers that they were all from one extended family. The other two are domestics close by here."

Amir was riveted by the story. He knew that although many women continued to arrive as plantation workers many more women had come over as domestics over the past decade. As the white population grew, more and more help was needed in the *memsahibs'* homes. Bachni was indentured to this family as cook, cleaner, babysitter and housekeeper and lived in a small but comfortable brick room in the backyard next to the one that the gardener occupied. They were officially registered and married two years after her arrival. There was no wedding ceremony just a few friends and a priest gathered on the nearby beach to read the Hindu wedding ceremony.

"*Chalo...chai...*let's go and have tea," Maharaj gestured to Amir as the men rose and walked toward the sprawling house. The large windows on the front and side of the house revealed exquisite furniture, sturdy, shiny wooden cabinets, cushioned chairs and sofas and a winding staircase leading up to the second floor. There were electric lights hanging from the ceiling which fascinated Amir when Maharaj explained what they were. Past the house, past the outdoor scullery and garden tool shed were two rooms close together. Maharaj's family used one as bedroom and the other as eating room which is where Amir was led. The room was meticulous, shiny red cement floor, wooden table and chairs, the cloth-covered table laden with tea and fresh made *chappatis* and sweets. Bachni, with Jaso clinging to her sari, and a baby on her hip, put her hands together in greeting and gestured for the men to sit. She hovered and served.

That evening the conversation between Amir and Bhagirathi took a curious turn.

"I know she is just a child, but in another seven years her parents will be looking for a match, *nayh?*"

In the privacy of their bedroom, Bhagirathi made a facial expression close to suggesting that her husband had gone mad.

"*Pathiji*, what are you saying? When your daughters were seven would you have been promising them to a boy in marriage?"

"No, no, I am not saying we do that. I am just saying that once you meet this family you will be thinking the same thing."

They laughed together and no more was said. But over the months that followed the two families did become friends. While Bachni and her family were not free to entertain in their servant's quarters, Bhagirathi and Sibani often entertained them in their homes on Sundays. So it was that a tacit agreement was quietly reached that when Jaso turned fifteen she and Dalip would be married.

The other milestone for fifty-four-year-old Amir and Purat was more somber. As their new homes were being built over the six-month period, their thoughts turned to their age. They were both successful with a thriving business and employment, strapping sons doing well and daughters married into good families. But Amir and Purat wanted one more thing. For this Amir turned to Michael Pearson.

After his mid-week deliveries to *memsahibs'* homes were completed, he parked his horse cart on a small side road outside a two-storied brick building. Motorized cars were appearing more and more on the paved main streets and Amir had to be careful to park his horse-buggy on a side road away from that traffic. He walked around to the front of the building where he recognized a Benz and a Ford car parked in front, open aired, with shiny dark green seats and protruding metal steering wheels. The large rubber rimmed tires sat poised on the black tar of the jacaranda-lined street. Amir admired the cars but did not go near them as there was a uniformed African standing guard a few feet away. The front of the building bore a stone sign that read Burnett and Burnett Law Firm.

As he opened the heavy front door, he entered a reception area with a heavy wooden desk behind which sat a young white woman typing away on a black typewriter. She looked up smiling at first, but changed her expression when she saw Amir.

"Yes?"

"Madam, I would like to speak with Mr. Pearson. Mr. Michael Pearson."

"Do you have an appointment?"

"Madam?"

"Does he know you are coming?"

"Yes...No...Madam...he said to come anytime...but no...no appointment today."

"Wait here," and she left him standing as she disappeared to Amir's left side of the reception area. There was a wooden plate above the large door that read "Whites." On the right side of the reception area was another door with the sign "Non-Whites" leading to a small room. Amir remained standing, slumped at first but then straightening up and standing tall. The Non-White room must be for clients too, business is business.

The woman returned and told Amir to wait in the Non-White room. He entered and sat on one of the four wooden chairs around a sturdy wooden table. At the far end of the room was another door leading to a small office out of which entered a tall young Indian man, in his early thirties, well dressed in a beige western suit and tie. His face was bright. He sported a thin moustache and smiled cheerfully.

"Hello, hello, Sir. My name is Nithendra." He offered his hand and gestured to Amir not to stand up.

"How can I help you today?"

"*Namasthe Beta*...Hello Son. Michael Pearson told me to come any time so I came."

"Yes...yes the reception lady told me. I handle Indian clients...what can I help you with?"

"Nithendra... yes I am sorry. I did not mean any disrespect..."

"Don't worry, Sir. I can help you."

"*Beta*, as you know we Hindus do not have the facilities here to cremate..." Amir shifted in the chair uncomfortable about plunging into his issue. But Nithendra's style was friendly and elicited trust and ease, so Amir continued.

"It's all right. I am not here to ask for cremation facilities. I understand this is a white country. But, *Beta*..." and there was the hesitation again.

"The Indian cemetery is a distance from Avoca...well not too far... but it is beyond the main North Coast Road, on the other side, beyond the hill."

"Yes Sir, I know it, it's beyond Red Hill."

Amir became quiet for a few minutes and Nithendra just let him think uninterrupted. When Amir and Purat's new homes were completed just a month earlier they had sat together in their tree-rich backyard looking across to Amir's other hill of flowers. The blue agapanthus and red-hot-pokers bloomed, painting that hill in fresh blue and red hues. At the apex of that hill, beside Amir's property border on the right side, were several wild apple and pear trees standing majestically on vacant crown land, overgrown with brush and weeds. Amir often sat under those trees to rest on the grass in the quiet peace of the shade.

"I want Mr. Pearson's help…sorry…your help to buy a small piece of crown land for me and my family to…for me and my family…to bury… to make a cemetery."

Nithendra looked surprised. This was the first such request. Amir plunged ahead explaining that the little church in Avoca by the train station did have a cemetery behind it that was used for the few white families associated with the sugar plantations but the Indian cemetery was the only one for all plantations and free Indians in a large area. He explained about other places like Phoenix, Mount Edgecombe and Tongaat having more cemeteries and as he tangled himself in nervous explanations, the door thankfully opened and Michael Pearson entered on crutches.

"Hello, Mr. Sing."

Amir and Nithendra stood and Amir instinctively put his arm under Michael's to help him in.

"No, it is okay. This wooden foot is a great friend," and Michael laughed with genuine humour. "Come follow me." He led them out of the room, past the surprised receptionist and into the corridor on the "Whites" side. He walked steadily on his crutches past the mahogany lined walls, past large offices with shiny wooden desks and cushioned chairs and out on to a white-painted verandah with large cement pillars. As they stepped out Amir noticed the Beachfront Road which ran behind Michael's office and just beyond that the shiny aquamarine sea with sunlight shimmering on the surface. They were only a few hundred yards from the road and beyond that the beach on which many white families could be seen playing. Carefree children ran after balls and plunged happily into the strong waves.

"Come sit down. Alfred! Alfred!"

A young African man appeared, neatly dressed in dark blue pants and a starched shirt with a white half apron.

"Alfred, bring tea."

Amir started to decline but knowing that Michael had once accepted his own hospitality he thought it might be rude for him to refuse.

"Sir…Mr. Pearson…my horse carriage is on a side street. I must go soon…"

"No it's okay. Alfred, ask the guard to check on Mr. Sing's horse, some water for the horse."

Alfred quietly nodded and walked back into the corridor.

Amir sat and looked out at the sea. He no longer called it *kala pani*, even though it had claimed his brother. Seated on his horse cart, he trotted by two or three times a week and became used to seeing the sea and admired its deceptive beauty. The waves were strong and he knotted his brows as he looked at the spontaneous way in which the children plunged in.

Amir and Nithendra explained the purpose of Amir's visit to Michael and he promised to start the paperwork at the firm as soon as possible. Amir thanked him and asked about the fee.

"Mr. Sing, I owe you, I mean I owe your brother my life." As Nithendra looked from one to the other knitting his brow, Amir held up his hand.

"No Sir. God saved your life. And Sir, business is business…I insist on paying the fee and I hope the cost of the crown land is reasonable. I trust you and I know my sons and maybe even my grandsons will remain your clients."

"Oh I think we can get it for you at a reasonable price."

It took several months and in July of 1916 the extra piece of land at the apex of Amir's plantation became his. He toiled alongside his staff to clear the overgrowth, careful not to disturb the apple and pear trees which he personally trimmed. They carried buckets of water from the stream and bags of cement all the way up the hill. The workers mixed the cement while Amir shaped and built two cement benches under the shade of the trees. It took two months but once complete the two-acre patch was transformed into a peaceful little retreat where the workers could rest and eat their midday meals.

Chapter 17

Cycles: Happiness and Sorrow

The First World War raged in Europe from 1914 to 1918. Hundreds of Indians serving the British joined the war effort to fight in South West Africa and many were shipped to Europe. Indian families in South Africa suffered many losses. Amir and his immediate brotherhood of friends were not impacted but many of their indentured friends from the Phoenix area and other parts of Natal said tearful goodbyes to their young sons. The Indian community supported friends who lost loved ones and silently vowed "never again." Their lives remained hard despite their contributions to the regimes that exploited their skills and labour. Together with Blacks they were denied rights and freedoms so amply available to whites both British and Boer.

But Indians laboured on, succeeded and flourished as a community. With iron will and an unequalled Indian work ethic, the Indian farmers, gardeners, merchants, small business people, hospitality workers, railway and municipal workers flourished all around the country. Amir's second son, Debi, joined the Congress that had been started by Gandhi, so determined was he, like other young Indians, to fight for the rights of Indians and Blacks. His oldest son, Dalip, took over the running of the flower plantations while his youngest son, Ranjith, continued in school.

Bhagirathi's mother passed away in her sleep two years after her father's death. Her mother had never bounced back after her husband's death and had spiraled deeper and deeper into depression. Her heart had been frail even before her husband's death, but like many Indian women she was stoic and did not frequent the one or two doctors' offices in the area. Bhagirathi and Prabhu took her death in stride and rationalized that she was at peace with her husband whom she had loved so dearly. Prabhu and his wife and children continued to live in the family home and the market garden around them flourished as did their shop.

Dalip's wedding to Jaso took place in Amir's big house in late 1922. Dalip was twenty-two and Jaso was fifteen. Their first baby, a girl, was born in 1923 when Jaso was sixteen. They named the child Soorsuthi, a variation of Sursut, which meant river, in honour of Amir's love of rivers. Names were important to Indians but their white masters and *memsahibs* still made Amir and Dalip flinch when they were called "flower sammies" by white clients. Many Indian names had the ending "samy" and the whites found it insultingly easy just to call all Indian men "sammies." What galled the family too was that Jaso's mother, and countless Indian maids were named "coolie Mary" by their white employers.

Life took on a routine for Amir and Purat's families with hard work and family togetherness continuing to be the centre of their world. Jaso had learned many important lessons from her gardener father and housekeeping mother. She and Bhagirathi transformed the huge garden in front and around their house into a botanical wonder. Inside the house, they made sure that vases of flowers were placed on tables in the front reception room where visitors usually sat and chatted. Jaso learned sewing skills from Bhagirathi and the embroidery on bed linen and table cloths gave the house its welcoming character. But Bhagirathi was beginning to tire more easily than she had for all the years before and Jaso made sure that her mother-in-law did not undertake any work that would cause the increased heart thumping that she heard her quietly talk to Amir about. Bhagirathi was fifty-six, eight years younger than Amir. She had never complained of illness and was not going to start now. Jaso, understanding this pride did not say a word about it. She simply did not let her mother-in-law do any work that she herself could do. The family now had an African servant who helped in the home and garden. The man's son Freddie had become a part of the household. Similar in age to Dalip, the young Freddie and his father had been given rooms in the barracks behind the house and Jaso worked alongside Freddie in the garden and cleaning inside the house.

On a cold June evening in 1925, Amir and Purat's families were sit-

ting in Amir's large kitchen after their meal. Parvati and Sajiv had been
invited and with all of them, except Bhagirathi, now in their mid-six-
ties they were comfortably allowing Dalip's wife Jaso to cook and serve
with her little daughters playing in the kitchen. Sibani's cough had become worse and the cold and fever that she had been experiencing over
the past several weeks had not subsided. She had finally agreed to allow
Purat to take her to see a doctor in town that day and he had given her
two types of medication to drink. She now took her leave to go home
and Parvati and Bhagirathi, picking up one of the two lanterns on the
table, accompanied her. She was obviously sick, but she also appeared
sad as the three of them walked quietly next door. They helped her into
bed and as Parvati and Bhagirathi prepared to leave, Sibani held on to
their hands and exhorted them to stay.

"I need to tell you…tell you something…"

"*Bolo Behnji*, tell us sister …is something hurting…we can massage
you…"

"*Nayh*…just sit by me."

After a quiet pause, Sibani looked at Parvati, searching her face.
"*Behnji*…I know…I think I know…who killed Gobind…remember
Gobind the cruel *sirdar* at our Phoenix barracks?" Parvati, shocked, just
stared not knowing what to make of this. "Remember that night forty-
two years ago? Remember when I left my little Ashok with you and
went to my shack?"

Parvati knitted her brow. She remembered that night clearly as the
most shocking night of her life. But she said nothing, just held on to
Sibani's hand. Bhagirathi adjusted Sibani's pillow and sat quietly.

"When I went to my shack there were two women from the neighbouring estate barracks waiting for me."

Sibani looked into the eyes of her two best friends, looking for clues
that they might know what she was about to say. But they just stared
bewildered. So she plunged ahead.

"When my first husband had burned me and disappeared, those two
women, Kusum and Padmini came to see me. I was being nursed by
women in our own barracks but these two women came on a Sunday
to pay their respects. They gave me a dagger to protect myself and my
baby. I protested but they said that the manager with the green eyes had
raped them too…"

Sibani buried her head in the pillow and started to weep. Her friends leaned over and held her to them.

"I took the dagger and dug a hole at the back corner of my shack and covered it up. I never needed to use it as that manager had stopped coming after my baby was born. But that night when little Devi had been snatched by Gobind in the sugar fields these women came and asked for the dagger back. I asked them what they were going to do and they simply shook their heads and said that there were many little girls in their barracks and Gobind had to be stopped. I dug up the dagger and gave it to them."

"But *Behnji*...the managers always checked our shacks regularly... did they not know about that dagger?'

"No, no one suspected that it was buried in my shack." The women became quiet and Sibani continued. "After Gobind was found dead I thought that maybe Kusum and Padmini had done it but they were just women...he could have over-powered them and killed them."

"Yes that is what I am thinking *Behn*...I know how big and powerful that *shaitan*...devil...was!" Parvati was agitated. "Why do you think it was them?"

"I don't know that it was them. Many weeks later, when things had calmed down I met them by the shops and I asked them but they remained tight-lipped only saying that they took the dagger for protecting their daughters and they did not know who killed Gobind."

Parvati pressed on, "But could that green-eyed manager Harper not have killed Gobind? Remember the two managers went down to Gobind's little office that night. Remember? They questioned all of us about the commotion. They came to our shacks, marked off our names into their log books and then they walked down to his office."

"Yes it might be...but *Behnji* that Harper was with the other manager who was good to us..."

"Yes that is true. But why are you remembering all this today?"

"When I went to the station today on my way to the doctor I met a friend who heard that Kusum died earlier this week. Both she and Padmini were working in a factory after their indenture, close to here and I often met them at the Sunday gatherings by the tamarind tree. Padmini died two years ago but Kusum kept in touch."

"Didn't you ever ask her again about who killed Gobind?"

"I did twice again over these years but she always said she did not know. Her daughter and Padmini's daughter grew up into pretty girls and married into good families and I did not want to keep asking."

"No you are right not to ask. I am sorry that you have felt this burden over so many years. But *Behnji* you cannot be sure that they knew..."

"Yes you are quite right, but her death brought it up again."

Parvati continued, "*Behnji*...you and I, my son, my husband...we are all temple people. We don't know what happened to Gobind and we cannot take that burden on our shoulders."

Bhagirathi had remained quiet through this conversation. She was not part of the barracks and at the time she had heard the conversations among the elders but did not know much. She shuddered at the thought of little girls being snatched by the *sirdar* for the white manager.

Sibani recovered somewhat after a few weeks but her cough, fever, muscle and bone pains returned often. She did not complain nor share her condition with anyone except occasionally with Parvati and Bhagirathi, but even to them she did not talk about her most private injury on her thigh. That she bound every day and when it flared up and the pus started to ooze she treated with herbs and salves and hid the pain from everyone.

Life in Avoca took on a welcome rhythm and routine. The five years that followed were uneventful except for births, marriages, deaths and other milestones for the close-knit Avoca community. One highlight for Amir and Purat's families was that in 1927 they had electric lights installed in their front rooms. It was several years behind white families, but the brothers had to be sure that they could afford the rates.

The light poles ran in front of their homes to carry electricity to Mill Road, the white managers' homes and most importantly to the sugar estate. So the government workers easily led the single line from the nearest street pole to each of their homes. Though the families were excited, there was no need to rush into lights for the whole house. Their lanterns would suffice and the women liked cooking on their coal stoves.

Bhagirathi deflected any concern that Amir expressed about her heart condition and instead she and her daughter-in-law pounded different herbs from the garden for poultices to relieve Amir's blinding headaches that had continued even though he had reduced his work-load by half. When Amir was well and not having headaches, he and Bhagirathi would go and visit Prabhu's family and Sajiv and Parvati, all now with settled routine lives. Bhagirathi, Sibani, Parvati, Namita and their other women friends, all in their sixties now, would often gather together from time to time, sometimes at Bhagirathi's and often in Adam and Fatima's warm kitchen where they would sit and chat for hours. A distinct pleasure for all of them was to sit back and be served by their daughters-in-law.

As 1930 approached, Amir now sixty-nine years old and Bhagirathi sixty-one, settled into a routine of their own. They spent more and more time at the Avoca Temple, the two of them walking slowly down Avoca Road greeting neighbours along the way. Bhagirathi, graying now, with a neat hair-bun nestling low on the nape of her neck, al-ways looked distinguished. She liked saris in light pale colours of pinks, blues, greens and yellows in the modern fabrics that Adam and Ebra-him imported.

She often wore embroidered Indian shawls on her shoulders es-pecially in the cold June and July months. Amir, dressed in his signa-ture white *pugri*, long cotton tunic over cotton western pants, himself looked distinguished especially since his long moustache was turning silver. They wore *chappals* on their feet in summer but in June and July Bhagirathi insisted that Amir wear warm, closed shoes, though she herself always wore her sandals summer or winter, jokingly claiming to be younger and steadier. Amir's hand always rested on her shoulder as they gingerly walked downhill on the steep part of Avoca Road ap-proaching the temple.

Bhagirathi helped Jaga's wife to clean and polish the temple icons once a week and decorate with fresh flowers from Amir's flower estate. The congregation grew and now in addition to the Saturday afternoon gatherings at the tamarind tree, worshippers gathered at the temple on Sunday mornings for prayer and a communal lunch cooked in the temple's backyard. Life took on a pleasant hum, newborns were named there, weddings were held and the community bonded. Bhagirathi and Sibani especially appreciated the company of a woman who lived in a small tin shack across from their own homes. They often went to her for ideas about poultices and herbal healing. Even though the woman was much younger than Bhagirathi and Sibani, the children running around, playing in the dust of Avoca Road called her *"Boorya"* meaning old lady. Her cheeks were lined with hard work and poverty but her pride and resilient spirit were so evident to Bhagirathi and Sibani. *"Boorya"* was widowed at an early age and eked out a living for her and her two sons from her vegetable garden and from the healing potions that people bought from her. Now her sons had grown, obtained good jobs and extended the tin house to make it more comfortable like Amir and Purat's old house by the fig tree.

This happy rhythm of life was abruptly jolted several months into 1930. Amir and Bhagirathi awoke early as usual in their large front room and Bhagirathi as always insisted on heating his bath water herself as she had done for the forty-six years of their marriage. What was unusual this particular morning was that while Amir bathed she went back and lay down on her freshly made bed with her hand-stitched embroidery on the white pillow cases and her vase of fresh flowers beside her bed. She was breathing heavily and these days, the tasks that she had routinely done all those years made her very tired. But as soon as she heard Amir walking back along the hallway, she got up from the bed and started pulling out his fresh clothes from the cupboards and pretended that everything was fine. She laid out his clothes and went down the hall to the little bathroom beside the kitchen and took her bath.

Together she and Amir took their *lotas*, small brass urns of water, into the small east-facing shrine in their sprawling side garden and facing the rising sun silently said their morning prayers and reverently poured the water on the many flowering plants around the central *tulsi* tree in the shrine. She took Amir's *lota* and, walking slowly through her verdantly blooming garden, past her grandchildren's swing on the sling-berry tree, she returned to the kitchen while Amir took off on his usual morning walk in his flower estate. He loved visiting his red roses the best. Sometimes he walked further and went down to the river barracks and even up the agapanthus hill. Bhagirathi took the *lotas* back to the kitchen, but unusual for her, she did not stay in the kitchen that morning to prepare vegetables with Jaso, who was still busy with her many children in her part of the house. Bhagirathi instead went back to her bedroom and lay on the bed.

Amir wandered quietly in his close-by rose plantation, inhaling the fresh morning fragrances of the flowers. He ventured a little way further down to the fig tree house to greet Ajit's family who now occupied it but decided not to go any further. He walked back up among the roses, picked one stem with a plump red bloom for his Bhagirathi and climbed back up to the house. He looked in the kitchen but it was empty. He walked slowly along the long hall, entered their bedroom and was surprised to see that Bhagirathi had lain down which was unusual for her. He stood still for a moment and just looked in awe at the serene beauty of his wife, her face as smooth and beautiful as the day he married her. The intricately handcrafted wooden wardrobe beside him at the entrance, the glass paned door beside it leading out to the front verandah, their high wooden drawer cabinet, the vase of flowers on the little bedside table, the light filtering in through the delicate white lace curtains on the large front windows, all normal and serene. He hesitated, not wanting to disturb her peaceful rest but went to sit beside her. Her stillness, her hands folded on her stomach and her not waking up immediately when she sensed his presence - that was unusual. He set the rose beside her, touched his wife's face and froze.

Amir's single, long, anguished scream brought Jaso and Dalip scrambling into the room followed closely by Sibani and Purat from next door. One look and Purat knew. He ran outside and instructed one of Dalip's daughters to go and get "*Boorya*," who was there in minutes. She looked at her friend's still body and beautiful serene face and walked calmly into the kitchen. She came back with a cup of water and teaspoon and as the family gave way to let her approach, she cradled Bhagirathi in her arms and spooned a little water into her mouth. She set the cup on the table and moved away, allowing Amir to continue to hold his wife's body in his arms and wail. Sibani's sobs choked her repeatedly and her writhing sorrow swallowed her as she held Bhagirathi's cold feet and collapsed at the foot of the bed.

Bhagirathi's funeral the next day was attended by hundreds of people. Almost every family in Avoca came as well as friends and family from Phoenix, Mt. Edgecombe, central town and Red Hill. Michael Pearson, in his late fifties now, stood quietly and respectfully, leaning on his walking stick, behind other mourners, at the outer edge of Bhagirathi's beloved front garden. Like her father's funeral, her body had been washed by Sibani and Jaso, wrapped in white sheets and lay in the front lounge on the floor amid family and other mourners until the undertakers came with the coffin. She was then laid in the coffin. The drawn, tired and tear-stained face of Amir drew wails from mourners as he laid his hands on the coffin while the undertakers closed the lid. The horse drawn carriage, followed by male mourners on foot, drove down the Avoca Road hill, past the temple, along Umghlangane Road and back toward the pulp factory where it stopped. The coffin was then carried by Amir, Prabhu and Purat, together with her sons Dalip, Ranjith and Debi, as well as in turn by Ashok, Ajit, Rajiv, Sajiv, Bhodraj, Bhimnad and Himal, up the agapanthus hill to the burial site so lovingly prepared under the wild pear trees by Amir.

His cries and wails grew in intensity as he repeatedly muttered, "*Pathniji*, you should not be the first one laid here, it should be me." His friends, elderly men now, cried openly. The grave dug at the foot of the pear tree received Bhagirathi's coffin and as Rajiv and Sajiv read prayers, Amir, his sons and his ship brothers pulled the soil over and did not stop until a mound had formed. Amir's workers had brought freshly unearthed agapanthus and poker plants and began planting. But Amir took the single hardy rose bush, with its wide spreading roots that they had brought and he planted that at the head of the grave. Hours later, the afternoon sun filtered through the pear trees and shone on Amir's back as he lay on the mound weeping inconsolably. Purat had been last to leave but Amir would not budge, so he left his friend to mourn in privacy.

But sadly, only a few months later, it was Purat lying inconsolably on another mound of earth covering his beloved Sibani. Sibani was Purat's age, seventy and grey-haired, but unlike Purat she had weakened considerably. She had never fully recovered from her regularly recurring fevers; and her coughing spasms and high temperatures did not respond to the many medications that her doctor prescribed. In addition, the severe burns that she had suffered decades ago, especially the deepest, most personal ones on her thigh and close to her crotch, never properly healed. These gouges caused her countless infections and fevers which she hid from everyone, even her closest friends Parvati and Bhagirathi. She had never sought medical attention for that very private, very personal area of her body, since her doctor was male; and.

even though Purat saw the pain and the limp in her nerve-damaged left leg, all he could do was support her on her intermittent days of quiet agony.

Over the decades, these intimate wounds, would flare up and ulcerate into abscesses. She tried to keep the wounds dry but with bathing and washing that was not always easy. A crust had originally formed in the year after the burn but working on the sugarcane field, heavy lifting and rubbing of the legs together during manual labour, did not allow the crust to heal. The wound kept opening from time to time and Sibani continued to apply salves and her own concoctions, bandaged the site daily and continued to suffer her private distress. Even her recurrent coughs and fever were not properly diagnosed over the years. Her doctor never gave the condition a name; consumption, malaria, and tuberculosis were diseases that the Indian community had heard about and dreaded, but when those were not named regarding their own family's health, they breathed a sigh of relief and continued home treatments for their illnesses. As did Sibani.

Ashok was broken-hearted. He and his mother had a private history, an intense bond that was no-one's but theirs. He knew that his eyes had not come from the only loving father he had known. At age five he was overjoyed when his mother married Purat, and he accepted the joy and blessing of his new life as any child would. Growing up he never questioned his bloodline, never asked questions, to do so would hurt the only parents he knew. As a mature adult who had seen his share of colonial abuse by the British and Boers, he knew in his heart that his mother had suffered abuse. She had loved him fiercely and protectively and had chosen a father for him who loved him unconditionally and that was her gift to Ashok. His job now was to console his father and bury his own anguish.

Chapter 18

A Life Lived

Amir and Purat, both seventy years old, no longer worked after their wives' passed away. Sorrow drew its harsh dark curtains over them, their whole beings transformed into old men, older than their age. Purat, already quite westernized in his clothing and mannerisms, a symptom of the fast-paced work he did for his railway bosses, wore western shirts and trousers, which were much simpler now, loose fitting and flapped around his thinning frame. He had remained clean-shaven and his hair was completely grey but he was not balding as much as Amir under his *pugri*. Amir too had given up his *dhoti*s and wore cotton shirts and pants, but his white beard, bushy white eye brows and weather-worn complexion added years to his stooped frame.

For the first year they walked every day to the burial site and sat on the concrete bench, heads bowed in prayer and sometimes just bowed. It was like their backs took on a new shape, mighty tree-trunks forever bent by a severe storm. The strong, strapping, hard-working men were no more. After long, quiet, distressed hours they walked back through the breathtaking, fiery beauty of the red hot poker flowers and in the summer the cool, blue, dancing heads of agapanthus flowers. Jaso and Ashok's wife, Sanjana made sure that their fathers-in-law ate, even if they pushed away their plates, the women pressed on. They helped the old men into their beds each afternoon to sleep, a new and completely strange habit for both men.

Ashok was able to draw his father out asking for help at his workplace, for odds and ends around the yard and horse stable, advice about dispute resolution or any excuse to get Purat up and about. In the New Year, Ashok took Purat to Michael's office, seeking his advice and counsel on a business project that Ashok was intent on starting. The concept of large grocery stores that stocked both Indian and British goods was new and Ashok had seen the patterns of shoppers in the city. They went from Indian grocery stores to Indian clothing stores, to dry goods stores and sometimes to white stores for products that were not specifically Indian.

It was early 1932 and Ashok was now fifty-three years old. He felt that he needed to plan his later years. Sanjana no longer needed to teach since Ashok's comfortable salary from the railways paid for all they wanted. But his entrepreneurial spirit wanted something different. So he went to see Michael to inquire about the sorts of financial possibilities available for him to open a large shop on the main North Coast Road that stocked Indian, British and African goods. He knew it would take time but there was no hurry. Purat, once again became excited. He embraced his son's idea and did his own research by going into town, looking at stocks carried by various shops, talking with customers at the Victoria Street fresh vegetable market and following their paths to various stores. He talked with African workers at their various work sites like roadworks and railway lines. As a grey, old Indian man who effused politeness, Purat was respected by Africans. He even went regularly to their *kraals*, clusters of mud-huts, brightly decorated with painted walls and thatched roofs. He sat with them, shared their *pootu*, mealie meal staple diet, and chatted for hours. Purat had returned a little closer to his healthy self. The memory of Sibani still throbbed in his heart. He missed their quiet times together, their conversations, their unspoken communications, her touch, her voice, her humming tunes when busy sewing. He missed all of it. But his children and grandchildren were now his focus. And his brother Amir needed him.

"*Bhayah*, let us go and see Adam *Bhai* today," Purat searched Amir's lined face as he spoke.

The two had just stood up and stretched their limbs after their usual daily meditation at the gravesite. They had been doing this for nearly two years. Purat recently was leaving before Amir, going on his errands for Ashok's research. Amir sometimes lingered alone on the bench and on occasion a worker would see that he needed help and would come by. Amir's piercing headaches came more often than before. The headaches elicited uncontrollable tears as he remembered Bhagirathi's tender hands rubbing her potions on his temples. The sobs brought workers quietly to him and they walked him back home. There was no headache today just an acute sadness as thoughts and memories ran in waves and spasms through his mind. Today Purat lingered with Amir. His *Bhayah's* sadness was overwhelming to see and left a constant lump in Purat's throat.

"*Nayh…nayh…Bhayah*. I am not good company for anyone," Amir objected holding up his hand but he was persuaded to go with Purat. The two brothers walked through the little pathways among the waning end-of-season agapanthus, through the bright, dancing heads of the red-hot-pokers, past the mango grove and down toward the pulp factory. But instead of following the road which would be a direct route to Adam's place, Amir gestured to Purat to walk further down to the stream. They crossed over to the stream-barracks side and Purat followed Amir as he walked along the stream leading toward the big Umghlangane River. In several places there were large rocks smooth and shiny as adults and children alike used them as seating places. Amir sat on one of them.

"Look Purat…the stream turns into a river just about here," and Purat followed Amir's pointing hand where the stream picked up strength round a gentle bend.

"You sit here often, don't you *Bhayah*," Purat looked at Amir kindly.

"*Haanh…jihaanh…*yes I do. Sometimes *Pathniji* and I used to come here on our walks. Look, look at those frogs," and Amir's face lit up for a split second.

"You love rivers and streams, Amir *Bhai*."

Amir said nothing, just held on to his thoughts and the two sat quietly watching the water and occasionally looking up at local residents crossing the small pedestrian bridge just up ahead. Amir had allowed a long, soft, white beard to grow on this chin, a result of intense sorrow that caused him not to care about shaving, even though he was meticulous about his daily morning baths. After half hour, they proceeded over the bridge and took the road toward Adam's shop.

Bhodraj was standing outside the little school house talking to some students and parents at dismissal time. He came over excitedly and embraced his ship brothers.

"*Areh Bhayah* Amir, *Bhayah* Purat…so nice to see you. The half day children are just leaving to go home. Where are you going?"

"We are going to visit Adam *Bhai*. Can you come with us?"

"Yes...yes...it is my lunch time too. Wait I will just tell the caretaker and other teacher who is looking after the full day children."

Bhodraj, now in his late sixties and still with a slight limp, showed no signs of slowing down. He hurriedly disappeared into the school house. Purat reached up and plucked two tamarind pods from the huge tree and the two friends chewed on them, enjoying the tart, sour taste.

The three of them crossed over the railway lines and knocked on Adam's back gate. Fatima opened and was surprised to see her ship brothers whom she had not often seen since Sibani's funeral. She ran ahead of them calling for Adam as the men closed and secured the gate.

Over a lunch of curries and *roti* at Adam's kitchen table, the discussion turned to their ship days.

"Amir, Purat...you know Himal and I owe you so much for removing the stigma from us about our caste..."

"*Areh*...Bhodraj...*Areh*...what are you talking about? No...no...it has been fifty years ago...a whole lifetime ago...*nayh nayh*...you are our brother..." Amir's voice took on the familiar vigour so cherished by his extended family of ship brothers and sisters.

Purat and Adam also chimed in and soon the brothers were chatting animatedly about their bonding on the ship.

"You know *Bhayah* that ship's hold was awfully uncomfortable but that is where we became brothers," Purat mused as he put his arms around Adam and Bhodraj sitting closest to him.

"Yes and the *kala pani*..." Amir paused as he remembered that the ocean had claimed his brother. But he continued, pushing the cloud away from his mind, "Yes the *kala pani* was responsible for much distress, but you know I have made peace with the ocean. I think it happened as I passed it regularly on my flower delivery routes to the *memsahibs* and visiting Michael's office."

"*Haanh...aachah*...Michael," Bhodraj started and then became quiet.

"He is a good boy...good man..." Amir smiled. He did a lot for us. "My *Pathniji* and Purat's lie in peace close to us because of Michael."

Sensing that the mood might turn, Adam quickly started talking about Asif's children and Bhodraj piped in about how well they did at school and were flourishing as young accountants in town.

Bhodraj took his leave after an hour and by mid-afternoon Purat and Amir left as well. Their daughters-in-law would be concerned if they did not show up at home.

***

Amir did not always take his walks among his flowers. He sometimes walked down Avoca Road to the temple and if he found Bhimnad, Himal and Jaga along the way they sat at the temple and enjoyed the comfort of conversation. But there were many walks that Amir took alone. One such walk took him once or twice a week to his old workplace at the sugarcane barracks on Mill Road near the brickyard. The barracks no longer housed Indian men like they did when he was *sirdar*.

The Natal Sugar Estates now employed African men. The barracks looked a little different now, not only did it house African men, but they were allowed to have their families live with them. So women cooked outside while children played. Amir greeted them respectfully as he walked past.

Cutting through the tall sugarcane stalks and maneuvering through the meandering paths brought back memories both good and bad. He did not miss the stress of the *sirdar* work but he did often think about the men who worked there and wondered about their lives.

Past the managers' offices and close to the brickyard, Amir crossed the road to the river bank. He walked along the rushing water a short distance to the new bridge spanning the river and sat under the bridge on concrete blocks left lying at the edge of the water. It was a peaceful place, water washing over his feet, frogs and wild birds at the water's edge and the silence only disturbed occasionally by the sound of a train overhead or the sirens from the brickyard or barracks. This day, still early, saw Amir sitting quietly with the rising sun on his back. His western khaki pants and shirt were neatly pressed and his *pugri* and soft white beard remained his signature features. He also now wore a long beige overcoat, his slender work-worn frame easily chilled on cooler days.

This morning as he walked through the cane stalks he felt the headache slowly claiming its place on the side of his head. He defiantly kept going, angry at the demon pain.

Once seated under the bridge he wet his handkerchief and the cold compress over his eyes and forehead felt good.

A tap on his shoulder made him swing around. A young African man with kind eyes asked in Zulu, "Are you all right, old man?"

Amir, smiled, took the man's hand in his and assured him in Zulu that he was all right, just a headache. They chatted briefly in Zulu and English and then the man continued hurriedly on his way past the bridge toward the low factory buildings in the distance. Several more men, mostly Africans hurried by, some in rowdy groups, others quiet and focused. Amir looked on, smiling at the progress that had been made over his half century in this corner of the country that he now called home. When the quiet returned after the morning rush, Amir sat looking at the water for several hours. At nearly midday he finally rose and started the slow, uphill walk through the cane fields back to his home on the Avoca Road hilltop.

The coolness of October with its whipping winds and rain curtailed Amir's long walks, but only for a month. The friends walked regularly even on the hot December days but they did not go far, the heat was too oppressive even to climb up to the gravesites. But as the cooler months returned, the friends welcomed their walking routine and resumed their walks with lighter hearts and steps. Ashok and Purat often took advantage of long, cooler evenings to hold outdoor week-end gatherings for their friends and families. Pots of food were cooked on outdoor fires, laughing young women gathered together, children played, groups sang and young men smoked in groups and told raucous stories. Amir and Purat enjoyed these evenings and the ship bonds, so strong and unbreakable, grew even stronger. These ship brothers' families were their family and Ashok, Dalip and their wives were touched to see their *Bapujis*, respected fathers, laughing, eating, gossiping and being carefree.

Ashok's shop on the main north coast road opened in June of 1933. Purat took charge since Ashok still kept his job, a good strategy when opening a fledgling business. Imported goods from India and England were handled by Ashok as he was already an expert with his experience at his job in the Central Railway Station. Despite the gathering storms of war in Europe, he was still able to import wool suits, coats, trousers, tools, boots, shoes, as well as English food staples not easily available in Natal such as syrups, tobacco, specialty teas and coffee. Purat handled the acquisition of African goods since he had the network of contacts and could access African blankets, house paints, different kinds of African beverages, and a range of African arts, crafts and carpets popular with the *memsahibs*. Ashok and Purat were careful not to stock the kinds of everyday goods sold by Adam and the large furniture-type goods sold by Suleiman. Integrity was important to father and son and they were not interested in under-cutting family businesses. Instead they sold bulk items like large sacks of English flour, a range of fancy rice preferred by the British, the kinds of pots and pans that the more modern women desired and very significant stocks of English clothing, stoves, electric lamps mostly for whites who could now afford electricity. Also tires for automobiles that were becoming more and more popular with the whites.

At first customers were few. Most Indians were still choosing to take the train ride to Grey Street and Victoria Street to buy all they needed. Whites chose to continue shopping on West Street in the European shops as they routinely did. Michael had negotiated a lower interest rate from the bank for Ashok but he had to dig into his savings and salary to pay the bond each month. But as word spread over the ensuing months, business picked up, surprisingly mostly among whites and Africans.

Most local Indians continued shopping at smaller grocery stores like Adam's and, not being affluent, they continued to find the modest furnishings they needed at shops like Suleiman's. Ashok was fine with that, grateful even, that he was not putting his extended families out of business.

Amir continued his walks and walked alone on most days. His gravesite visits were now not every day. He spent time with Rajiv at the temple or with Bhimnad, Himal and Jaga and sometimes with Bhodraj when he was finished teaching. He waited for Purat to return from work and the two spent quiet after-dinner hours together, watching the stars at outdoor fire pits or sitting in their comfortable front rooms. But his solitary walks were his favourite. He cherished sitting along the stream at the bottom of his land, under the *jamun* tree or in the quieter spots of the mighty Umghlangane close to Bhodraj's school. He also regularly cut through the cane fields, down to the bridge by his old workplace on Mill Road. This was his preferred haunt. He figured out that early morning was the noisy time when men walked past the bridge to get to work so he went there two or three times a week after his midday meal. He found his comfortable cement block under the bridge and sat quietly, contemplatively, with frogs, birds and the occasional snake for company. His headaches occurred more often now, at home, at the gravesite and at his water-side meditation places. At home he allowed Jaso to apply the salves and poultices learned from Bhagirathi. But when the headaches came on his walks he simply sat by the water's edge, took off his *pugri* and pressed his temple, closing his eyes and massaging his head until the pain eased.

When the fierce October winds came Amir could not go on long walks so he stayed close to home venturing just to the rose bushes or sitting under his avocado trees or in Bhagirathi's beautiful garden with her lemon trees now bearing huge bright yellow fruit. But the weather soon improved, the winds stopped and the warm breaths of gentle November breezes signaled the arrival of the hot summer. Purat's regular weekend gatherings with food, families and chatter started up again and Amir resumed his daily walks.

On a Monday in late November, the twenty-seventh to be exact, after a Sunday night gathering at Purat's house, Jaso went over to help Sanjana with the cleaning up.

"How is *Bapuji* Amir today?" Sanjana asked as she emptied pots into containers of left-overs.

"*Bapuji* is okay. He still gets his headaches which seem to be worse than before. But you know the doctor's medicines are not helping much and he does not like taking them. They make him drowsy which is all right at night but he wakes up feeling drowsy."

"*Areh* that is not good. He likes to get up and go for his walks among his flowers. I have seen him often from my backyard. And sometimes even from my front yard, he waves as he goes down the sugarcane hill toward Mill Road."

"Yes, his walks take him everywhere. It's good, he gets to see old friends."

"*Jihaanh*, yes, he really misses *Mathaji* doesn't he, Jaso *Behn?*"

"Yes very much."

The women worked quietly thinking about their mothers-in-law and how much Bhagirathi and Sibani would have enjoyed Purat and

Ashok's Sunday gatherings with so many families, friends and especially the children.

Jaso returned home after three o'clock and found her daughters happily cleaning up their lunch dishes and they already had rice and *dhal* boiling away on the coal stove for supper. She asked where *Bapuji* was and the girls said he had gone for his walk.

"It's hot this afternoon," Jaso mused but went about her work and told the girls that she and Freddie would be cleaning the weeds in the garden but not for long in the heat.

It was still light at six-thirty. Jaso and Freddie had given up weeding because the heat was oppressive. She had her bath and as she was vigorously towel-drying her hair in the backyard she called out to her daughters, "Where is *Bapuji*? Did you give him something to drink?"

"No, Ma. He is not home yet."

"Oh… maybe he is visiting friends today – too hot to be walking."

But when Amir had not returned by eight o'clock Jaso sent Freddie to the flower fields to find Dalip. Usually at this time most of the workers would have gone but Dalip, old Ajit and a few workers would be hauling cut flowers on to wheel barrows to push up to the house and sort them into bunches for early morning deliveries. Dalip hurried home and instinctively knew that something was not right. His father always came home by six, never wanting to cause worry for his family. He sent one of the workers to Ashok's shop on the main North Coast Road, a half hour-run away. The shop would be closed but Ashok and Purat would be finishing paperwork. Then Dalip and two of his staff ran out into the flower plantation to search. Ajit and the one remaining worker went down to the temple to inquire.

When Purat and Ashok heard, they locked up and ran out of the shop, hitching their horse buggy and speeding off with the worker accompanying them. Purat knew Amir's sitting places along the stream at the bottom of his fields.

"Ashok, send the buggy back home with this man. Let's get off here," Purat instructed as they neared the schoolhouse. "I know where Amir *Kaaka* goes to sit on his walks."

They first went to the large Umghlangane river bank close behind the school house near the Avoca train station and searched under the railway bridge but there was no sign of anyone. Then they took the road toward the pulp factory heading for the stream at the bottom of Amir's plantation. They crossed over the small pedestrian bridge. Purat laid his hand on the large, smooth rock where he and Amir had sat a few months ago. They continued along the stream to the stream-barracks. Dalip was there talking to the African and Indian residents of the barracks.

"*Bapuji* is not in the plantation," Dalip said to Ashok and Purat. He ran his hand through his hair, a usual familiar sign of Dalip's distress.

"*Aachah*. I will run up to the grave-site maybe he is sitting there..." Purat started but Dalip interrupted, "We searched there too."

The barracks friends followed the family back up the hill to Amir's house. They were met by Jaso shaking her head indicating that Amir had not returned. It was now after nine o'clock and the sun had set in the western horizon behind the forest beyond the cane fields of Mill Road. Dozens of friends had gathered, Bhimnad, Himal, Jaga, Adam, Bhodraj and Rajiv among them. Rajiv spoke, "It is getting dark. Please go to your homes and come back with lanterns. We will disperse from here so we know who is looking where. Adam, Bhodraj, Rajiv and I – our houses are furthest off. Jaso *Beti*, do you have enough lanterns in the house for us?"

Jaso, Sanjana and the girls gathered lanterns from both houses and were back swiftly. As the men were preparing the search parties, Sanjana looked for her father-in-law. She found Purat and Ashok huddled together in Bhagirathi's garden talking quietly.

"*Papaji?*"

"*Ji Beti bolo*...yes my daughter say what is on your mind."

"*Papaji*...I see Amir *Kaaka* sometimes walking down toward his old workplace on Mill Road."

"To the sugar estate?'

"Yes, *Papaji*."

"*Aachah*. Ashok let's go and check. Maybe the workers there know where he might be visiting."

The search parties had gathered and formed and were dispersing. Purat and Ashok set out across the road in front of their home and entered the sugarcane plantation. The tall stalks were difficult to traverse especially in the pitch dark. Africa's reputation for quick darkness after sunset was well known to the indentured over the years. But they persevered holding their lanterns high in front of their faces. By the time they reached the barracks most of the residents were asleep, the next morning being an early-rising work day. A few men sat drinking around a small fire but said that they had not seen Amir. Ashok and Purat, frustrated by the darkness and tall stalks continued to look along some of the footpaths familiar to Purat from his days on the estate. But to no avail.

Back home the search parties were returning empty handed. There was nothing that could be done until sunrise. At five the next morning the search parties resumed, combing through areas already covered the night before but which were now better lit.

"*Papaji*, I want to go back to the Natal Estates barracks. Maybe someone there has seen Amir *Kaaka*."

As Purat and Ashok approached the barracks, they saw welcome activity, with women cooking porridge at fire pits, men washing at the pump and even children awake and hanging on to their mothers' skirts.

"*Kunjani* Mama…how are you, madam?" Purat spoke in Zulu, greeting a woman sitting by a small fire tending a pot. He asked if anyone had seen Amir, giving her a description of his distinguished looking, white bearded old brother.

The woman shook her head and they continued asking several other people. Many African workers, getting ready for their early 6 o'clock start, gathered around looking concerned. Sensing from the agitated inquiries that something serious was going on, one of the workers sent his son to the manager's office where one of the two managers had already opened the office door and was getting ready to start his supervisory duties. A young African man, no more that nineteen, stood at the pump washing his face along with several other youth. He looked up as he heard the inquiry. He walked toward Purat and Ashok drying his face.

"You looking for *indoda*…a man…like this?" and he stooped a little indicating old man.

"Yes…yes…old man…white beard…Indian…"

"Yes I saw him a few times sitting under the bridge in the early mornings, but not these days."

"Which bridge?"

"Come I will show you. I talked to him once on my way to work at the factory. Nice man…"

He led them behind the barracks close to the brickyard and pointed to the railway bridge. The other young men followed and one of them said, "You looking for old man – Freddie's boss? I know Freddie…I see his boss sometimes walking by the river. I will go and get Freddie. I know where he lives…I go there with my big brother to visit him often." With that the boy, around seventeen years old, ran up into the fields toward Amir's house.

"You can go this way – cross the road and walk along the river," the young man who had talked with Purat and Ashok at the pump led them and stayed with them together with several other boys.

The river was full, fast moving. They walked along the edge careful not to slip in. Close to the bridge, the rocks were less slippery with the morning sun constantly drying the moss. Sunlight was strong now though not yet as hot as the day would bring.

Purat was the first to see Amir and started to run, calling "*Bhayah… Bhayah!!*"

His calls turned to frantic cries as he neared the bridge. Amir was sprawled forward and slightly to his left, his *pugri* in his hand resting on his lap and his head on a sharp cement block.

"*Bhayah…Bhayah…*," Purat reached Amir and began lifting him.

"*Bolo Bhayah…bolo…bolo nah…bolo…*speak, speak, please speak… won't you speak please."

Blood had congealed on Amir's face and forehead where his head had struck the sharp edge of the cement block. His eyes were closed. His face looked anguished in pain. As Purat held him and wailed, a voice from behind the group said, "Don't move him. We have called for an ambulance."

It was the white estate manager who had been hurriedly summoned by the worker's son. The man came close to where Ashok and Purat held Amir in their arms. The manager's eyes were blank, expressionless and he looked away. He held out his arms and kept the group of young African men away. New voices approached behind them and they parted to allow Dalip, Rajiv, Freddie and others in the search party to come closer. Rajiv touched Amir's face and prayed. He knew that Amir was gone. But Purat did not give up his pleas for Amir to wake up.

The ambulance arrived after nearly an hour. Though motorized, the white, closed vans had to traverse the stone roads from Phoenix to Avoca and were sometimes slower than horse and buggy. This was a non-white ambulance driven by an Indian man accompanied by a middle-aged African man with kind eyes who politely and gently pushed back the growing crowd. They lifted Amir on to a stretcher and carried him into the ambulance.

"We will take him to Holy Trinity in Phoenix," the Indian driver explained as Dalip stepped into the back of the ambulance to accompany his father to the Christian mission hospital. There were two large government hospitals in the centre of Durban town, serving non-whites, but the smaller communities like Avoca and Phoenix had to rely on the compassion of Christian churches that set up small mission hospitals in several non-white communities.

Ashok held his father in his arms as Purat continued to wail. Freddie and other young African men helped Ashok to support Purat back through the cane fields to Amir's home. Once his father was settled, Ashok saddled his horse and buggy and taking Rajiv and Bhimnad with him they rode to the hospital. There was silence in the buggy as Ashok urged the horses to speed along the stony road. As they entered the main road in Phoenix, they turned left down the pathway so familiar to Amir, as he had, so many years ago, walked past the church to the Campbell Estate. The little church had expanded and the small hospital, a long, low, brick building, only a few years old, stood beside it, in what used to be a farmer's field. The non-white cemetery was behind it. The ambulance was parked at the front entrance of the hospital.

They were met in the small entrance area by a nurse behind a counter. When they inquired, she called for a turbaned old Indian man, dressed in khaki pants and shirt, pushing a broom along the floor. He was grey bearded, older than Purat and Amir, slightly bent but walking steadily. He led them down a narrow hall with small rooms on either side. "I knew Amir *Bhai*," the man whispered. "We worked on the same estate near here." He turned his face to them, eyes red with obvious signs of weeping. He continued, "I am Ramsamy. Amir *Bhai* saved my daughter Devi long time ago. I have sent a boy to tell Pundit Sajiv and Prabhu *Bhayah*. Come." Ashok holding his palms together, nodded his thanks and followed the man. He led them to a room with four patients in narrow, clean beds. One bed was curtained. Ramsamy pulled back the curtain and allowed them in.

Dalip, with his head held in his hands, was seated on a stool beside the bed. Amir was covered completely with a white sheet. Dalip looked up at Ashok and shaking his head started to weep. "*Bapuji* is gone, Ashok *Bhai*. There was nothing the doctor could do."

As he choked on his sobs, Ashok held him. Bhimnad and Rajiv, old men now, leaned over both younger men, holding them together and weeping. Rajiv held up the sheet and looked at the pained, still face of his friend and prayed. But Bhimnad was inconsolable.

"Amir *Bhayah…phir milengi Bhayah*…we will meet again, my brother," he sobbed and gently replaced the sheet.

Ramsamy brought Sajiv and Prabhu, white mustached, but upright, tall old men, both agitated and then further shocked to see the white sheet. Composing himself, Sajiv lifted the sheet off Amir's face and recited a prayer. The others held their palms together, eyes closed.

A young white doctor entered and the family stepped aside. With starched white coat, spectacles and a paper board in his hands, the doctor asked, "Who is next of kin?"

Dalip answered, "I am *Bapuji*'s son and these are his brothers and family."

"All right then. I examined Mr. Sing. He suffered trauma to his head as he appears to have fallen forward on to a sharp object which I am told by the ambulance men, was a cement block. That is what caused his death – more than twelve hours ago…perhaps even fourteen hours before he was discovered. There is no blow to the back of his head so he was not likely attacked on his head…he fell forward probably from some kind of health issue?"

"He suffered intense headaches all his life," Ashok cut in. "Sorry, I have known him all my life and I know that when his headaches became intense he needed to lie down and put a poultice over his eyes and forehead."

Dalip concurred and asked, "Could a spasm of pain cause him to drop sideways like that?"

"It is possible. The headaches sound severe. We can examine his head further and try to determine if there was any kind of aneurysm. But we do not have the facilities here to do a proper autopsy. I will have to send him to a government hospital in town."

"Please Sir…no…don't send him away. Your assessment will suffice and then we must take my father home and lay him to rest."

Amir's other family in the room concurred with Dalip. They all knew about Amir's severe headaches and in their hearts they understood that he was blinded with pain at the water's edge and fell on to the cement block. The doctor nodded saying he would return with the paperwork to release the body.

Ramsamy came back into the room with another man. He addressed Dalip.

"*Beta*, this is our local undertaker, Abheet. He has helped our community to bury many of our brothers and families."

Prabhu recognized the middle-aged man and confirmed that he had buried his father Ranjith and also his mother. Sajiv concurred and greeted the undertaker politely.

Two hours later, Abheet and his staff of two others returned and placed Amir on a stretcher into the back of their horse drawn buggy. Followed by Ashok, Rajiv and Bhimnad in their buggy and Sajiv, Parvati and Prabhu in the third buggy, the solemn caravan started along the stony road from Phoenix to Avoca. They stopped at the foot of Avoca Road to rest the horses before the climb up the hill. Himal and Jaga, having returned to their homes to take their families to Amir's house, stood by the buggy and rested their hands on Amir's covered head and sobbed. Rajiv went inside the temple and brought a flower garland which he placed on Amir.

"*Bhayah*, these flowers are from your beloved plantation. The women inside are weaving more for you *Bhayah*…" and he could not continue, breaking down into sobs.

The horse buggies struggled to slowly climb up Avoca Road and arriving at Amir's gate, covered in the climbing vines so lovingly planted by Bhagirathi, they stopped. The men gently gestured to Abheet to allow them to pick up the stretcher. They carried it past the gate and walked along Bhagirathi's long, red polished, cement pathway to the door of Amir's home. Purat walked out slowly to meet the group and wordlessly put his hand on his brother's stretcher and helped to carry it to the front room. The yard was overflowing with mourners. It was nearing midday on a Tuesday, a work day, but men and women from all over Avoca and the opposite hill at the peak of the agapanthus plantation, were there. Once again, at the outer periphery, stood Michael, looking older than his sixty years, leaning on his cane, signs of weeping on his red, blotched face and swollen eyes. Next to him stood Andrew who was now seventy-three years old, silver-haired, slender and distinguished in his light grey suit. He stood respectfully holding his hat at his chest and supported Michael with his other hand.

Amir's body was bathed by Purat, Sajiv, Rajiv and Dalip in the bathroom he had so lovingly constructed especially for Bhagirathi and for his family. He was then wrapped in white cotton fabric and carried on another clean stretcher back to the verandah where he was laid on *gudras*, handmade quilts, three or four piled high lifting him up several inches off the floor. His daughters, sons, grandchildren, family, ship brothers, friends, co-workers and strangers filed through paying their respects in quiet meditation.

At three o'clock Abheet returned with a coffin and Amir was once again readied for his final journey in Avoca. The women from the temple had placed many wreaths and garlands of flowers from his plantation on Amir's white shroud and now as the coffin was closed they added more on top of the lid. The hearse buggy left the gate and proceeded slowly downhill followed by several other buggies but mostly men on foot, a hundred or more, dressed in white *dhotis* and *pugris*, solemnly walking in groups of fours and fives. At the bottom of Avoca Road the buggy took Amir one last time along the road beside the Umghlangane River, turned right at Bhodraj's house and followed the road toward the pulp factory and along the memory-filled stream at the bottom of Amir's plantation.

Like Bhagirathi's coffin, Amir's too was carried from the hearse on foot by Amir's three sons, and Purat, Prabhu, Ashok and alternately by his ship brothers, all old now in their late sixties and early seventies like Amir. They carried him past his red-hot-pokers and waded into his magnificent blue agapanthus flowers in full November bloom. At the top of the hill, under the shade of the wild pear trees, a grave had been prepared by Abheet's men, who had been toiling since mid-morning.

As Amir's coffin was lowered, Purat cried, "*Bhayah* rest now...your *Pathniji* is here. She and my Sibani will welcome you. Wait for me, *Bhayah*...I will come soon..." and choking back tears he started pushing the earth into the grave. The gravesite was overflowing with men, spilling over the side of the hill into the agapanthus plantation. Ship brothers, some grey bearded, others clean shaven but all overwhelmed with grief, had slowly climbed the hill to be with Amir in this last farewell. Surprisingly, Michael, limping on his wooden leg had climbed the hill supported by Andrew. They could have ridden their horse-drawn buggies around the hill and approached the gravesite on their buggies from the main North Coast Road. But they had chosen to come with the other mourners.

Andrew, not as agile as he had been all his life, was now himself discreetly helped by younger Indian men, unknown to him, but who were respectful of his age and because they recognized that it took unusual grace for these two white men to attend the funeral of their own beloved Amir.

Purat took the large red rose bush from the worker who held it to him, its strong earth-covered roots growing outward and he firmly planted it at the head of the grave just as Amir had done before at Bhagirathi's and Sibani's graves, now flourishing with flowers tended by both men.

The mourners stood silently for what seemed like hours and then quietly dispersed leaving Amir's sons, Purat, Ashok and his ship brothers to sit quietly. Even after this extended family departed back to the house, Purat remained lying on top of the mound. Ashok tried to lift him to take him home but gave up and left. Finally, as evening approached Purat whispered, "*Aachah Bhayah...jawoh Bhayah...phir milengi...mera Bhayah...phir milengi*...all right...go brother...we will meet again my brother, we will meet again."

Author's note and acknowledgements

My grandfather Mr. Amir Sing died at the age of seventy-two in Avoca, Durban, South Africa on November 27, 1933, fifteen years before I was born. My father Dalip Sing passed away in 1971 soon after I immigrated to Canada and his siblings soon after that. My oldest sister, who is now ninety-three years old, was ten when our *Aaja* (father's father), died and she remembers him fondly. Her memory of him is about his *pugri*, or turban, his fair-skinned good looks, his unusually tall bearing and his hard work on his beloved flower plantation.

There is no-one else really who can help to fill in the blanks in family history. My cousin Champa Sing wrote a university paper about our grandfather based on the information found in public records such as indenture documents. My sister Uma, always helpful and a great mentor, remembers conversations she had over the years with our late parents. This story is my attempt to piece together *Aaja*'s journey to South Africa and what his ensuing life might have been like. The central and supporting characters in the story are fictional composites. Circumstances described are based on historical realities of the time.

My grandfather procured nearly a hundred acres of land in exactly the location I describe and grew red roses, blue agapanthus and orangey red-hot-pokers and my father Dalip Sing continued working that plantation throughout his life.

Aaja is buried on the land I describe at the apex of his beloved agapanthus and pokers hill. The stream that ran past the barracks through *Aaja*'s property is where we played as children under the *jamun* tree. The first house he built was under the fig tree, the flattened ground still visible, and his larger house that I describe on the top of Avoca Road was where all my siblings and I grew up. My mother Jaso and grand-mother Bhagirathi designed the beautiful garden that surrounded that house. Just as I describe, the land near the foot of Avoca Road was donated by *Aaja*'s friend Jaga and the ship brothers started the first small temple there, which has today flourished into a large modern temple with a wonderful congregation. The little Avoca church and Indian schoolhouse with the tamarind tree in front remained so for generations and it was where I went to primary school. Today it has reverted to a tiny church.

The Adam family's shop was exactly where it is in the book and remnants of the tin structure are there today. When my mother Jaso was three years old, her widowed mother Bachni literally grabbed her in her arms and, escaping physical abuse by her in-laws, made her way to the last indenture ship leaving Calcutta.

Bachni did re-marry a man named Maharaj who was indentured in the same household as she. My mother Jaso was, in fact, promised to my father in marriage when she was eight and they were married when she was fifteen. My sister, who is now ninety-three, was born when my mother was sixteen.

At the end of the book I describe *Aaja*'s death the way his daughters described it to my cousin before they passed away. In addition to books, articles, and internet searches, the most important research to inform my work was done by our late relative Mr. S.S. Singh, a Sastri College teacher in the 1960's to 80's and then an inspector of schools across South Africa in the late twentieth century.

As a renowned educator, Mr. S.S. Singh tirelessly and meticulously researched the lives, struggles and achievements of indentured labourers in Phoenix, Avoca and all across Natal. He shared his work with us as my siblings, nieces and nephews grew up in his enlightened presence. His collection of articles and precious photographs of indentured families from the 1860's till the mid-twentieth century, together with his own writings on the subject, formed a coveted academic cachet.

This meticulous and painstaking work by Mr. S.S. Singh has, for decades, informed South African professors, scholars and students about the history of the Indian settlement that grew from indenture.

I read and admired the novel, The Lotus People by Aziz Hassim that touched on the lives of indentured sugarcane workers and more specifically on the early Indian traders in Durban and their struggles with state oppression. His sister Rashida Mulla, my childhood friend, edited the first draft of my manuscript.

I also read recent books about indentured Indians by Ashwin Desai, Goolam Vahed and Suresh Bhana and perused the pictorial collections of Kogi Singh and Ebrahim Osman. The final edits and summary were done by Cheryl Antao-Xavier and I thank her for her keen eye for structure.

We owe my grandfather so much. He gave us the roots of our lives and in his memory I want to acknowledge his struggles and those of his young wife and family whom he nurtured under such harsh conditions in the cane fields of Durban, South Africa.